Authoritarianism
in the Middle East

Authoritarianism in the Middle East

Regimes and Resistance

edited by
Marsha Pripstein Posusney
Michele Penner Angrist

LYNNE
RIENNER
PUBLISHERS

BOULDER
LONDON

Published in the United States of America in 2005 by
Lynne Rienner Publishers, Inc.
1800 30th Street, Boulder, Colorado 80301
www.rienner.com

and in the United Kingdom by
Lynne Rienner Publishers, Inc.
3 Henrietta Street, Covent Garden, London WC2E 8LU

Library of Congress Cataloging-in-Publication Data
Authoritarianism in the Middle East : regimes and resistance / edited by
  Marsha Pripstein Posusney and Michele Penner Angrist.
    p.   cm.
  Includes bibliographical references and index.
  ISBN 1-58826-317-7 (hardcover : alk. paper)
  ISBN 1-58826-342-8 (pbk. : alk. paper)
  1. Arab countries—Politics and government—21st century.
    2. Authoritarianism—Arab countries. 3. Middle East—Politics and
government—21st century. 4. Authoritarianism—Middle East. I. Posusney,
Marsha Pripstein. II. Angrist, Michele Penner, 1970–
JQ1850.A58A94 2005
909'.0974927083—dc22   2005011302

British Cataloguing in Publication Data
A Cataloguing in Publication record for this book
is available from the British Library.

Printed and bound in the United States of America

The paper used in this publication meets the requirements
of the American National Standard for Permanence of
Paper for Printed Library Materials Z39.48-1992.

5 4 3 2 1

For our sons,
Eric Devin Pripstein and Jordan Isadore Angrist,
and for the children of the Middle East,
in the hopes that they will grow up to experience the freedoms
that our sons enjoy

Contents

Acknowledgments

This book addresses the critical puzzle of why authoritarian regimes in the Middle East have endured for so long while formerly authoritarian governments in many other countries have given way to democracy in the past several decades. The book brings together an accomplished group of Middle East specialists who have been working on this issue for a number of years, and its chapters collectively offer broad coverage of the region. Earlier versions of some of the chapters appeared previously in scholarly journals, but all of the material has been revised and updated. We have also endeavored to make the material accessible to the anticipated audience for the book, which includes students, scholars, policymakers—indeed, anyone with an interest in Middle East affairs.

The book grows out of a special issue of *Comparative Politics,* published in January 2004 (vol. 36, no. 2), devoted to the durability of authoritarianism in the Middle East. We are grateful to *Comparative Politics* for permission to include, in updated and modified form, the chapters by Eva Bellin, Ellen Lust-Okar, Michele Penner Angrist (Chapter 6), and Vickie Langohr. Portions of Chapter 1 by Marsha Pripstein Posusney are also drawn from that journal and are included with permission. The special issue was the product of a series of workshops titled, and with the aim of, "Bringing the Middle East Back in . . . to the Study of Political and Economic Reform." The workshops were held at Brown University and Yale University in the spring and winter of 2001, respectively. We are grateful to the Watson Institute for International Studies at Brown, the Yale Center for Globalization Studies, the Leitner Program in Political Economy, and the Kempf Fund at the Yale Center for International and Area Studies for their generous funding of these events. Barbara Geddes, Lisa Anderson, Nelson Kasfir, Michael Hudson, Robert Kaufman, Bahgat Korany, and Jim Mahoney contributed generously to the discussion at the workshops. For comments on individual presentations at the Yale event, we would also like to thank Augustus Richard Norton, Paul Salem, Steven Heydemann, Greg White, Jim Scott, Meredith Weiss, Pierre Landry, Vickie Murillo, and Jose Cheibub.

Jason Brownlee's chapter draws on an earlier article published in *Studies in Comparative International Development* (vol. 37, no. 3; Fall 2002), and Posusney's empirical chapter (Chapter 5) is updated from an earlier essay in the same journal (vol. 36, no. 4; Winter 2002). We thank Transaction Publishers for permission to include these chapters. We are also grateful to the *Middle East Journal* for allowing us to publish an updated version of Michael Herb's piece, which appeared in the summer 2004 issue of that journal.

Clerical assistance in preparation of the original manuscript was provided by Cleo Lindgren and Greg Tumolo at Bryant University. Fred Fullerton of Brown University and Caline Jarudi helped with the final draft. We are grateful to the Watson Institute for International Studies at Brown, and to Union College's Faculty Research Fund for their financial support for various stages of the preparation of the final manuscript.

Marilyn Grobschmidt, our editor at Lynne Rienner Publishers, provided invaluable assistance at every step of the process and was a real pleasure to work with. We would also like to thank Lynne Rienner for her encouragement of this project.

Authoritarianism
in the Middle East

The Middle East's Democracy Deficit in Comparative Perspective

MARSHA PRIPSTEIN POSUSNEY

This book was in the final stages of preparation as the recently elected Iraqi parliament completed negotiations over the shape of a new government. At the same time, Syria—in the face of a mass outpouring of protest in Lebanon—had agreed to withdraw its troops from that country, and Egyptian president Hosni Mubarak was yielding to popular pressure for contested presidential elections there. The Bush administration was claiming credit for having ushered in a new era of political reforms in the Middle East;[1] some prominent pundits concurred.

The recent democratic stirrings notwithstanding, it is too soon to herald the dawn of a Middle Eastern "democratic spring." The protracted negotiations over the composition of Iraq's new government and the ongoing insurgency there are but two indicators of the challenges of initiating and consolidating democratic reforms in the region. The Middle East is home to some of the world's most tenacious authoritarian rulers, whose very longevity calls into question the potential for rapid transformation in the region.

Back in the 1950s and 1960s, the prevalence of authoritarian government there did not distinguish the region from other developing countries then known as the third world, nor from the Eastern European communist countries. But the Middle East was not swept up in the third wave of democratization that began (among developing countries) in Latin America in the 1970s, spreading to other third world regions and, in the 1990s, to Eastern Europe. Only in Turkey and Lebanon was an authoritarian era followed by contested elections that, despite constraints, resulted in a circulation of elites. Elsewhere in the region, political liberalizations that had begun in a number of countries have stalled, if not suffered reversal; no authoritarian executive has been removed from office through competitive elections.

To be sure, the Middle East is not the only region of the world where authoritarianism persists. China, the most populous authoritarian country, is also among the most long-lived; in the latter regard it is joined in Asia by Vietnam, Laos, and Burma; in sub-Saharan Africa by Somalia; and in Central America by Cuba. There are also numerous nondemocracies of more recent vintage, but seemingly stable, particularly among the new republics formed after the collapse of the Soviet Union. But in these other regions, nondemocratic systems exist alongside countries that have undergone, or are in the process of, democratic transitions. What distinguishes the Middle East is not simply the *phenomenon* of enduring authoritarianism but rather the *density* of it and the absence of a case of successful democratization.[2]

Today, pundits and policymakers offer daily pronouncements about the causes of this deficit and the prospects for its undoing. Yet until very recently, Western political science has had little to offer by way of explanation for this deficit. The political shifts occurring elsewhere in the world spawned a large literature on democratic transitions, but these studies excluded cases of persistent authoritarianism from their purview. Consideration of Middle Eastern countries is almost completely absent from the most important works on political transitions,[3] including those that explicitly focus on the developing world.[4] Correspondingly, prior studies devoted exclusively to the study of economic and political reforms in the Middle East—or the lack thereof—do not appear to have achieved significant recognition outside the community of specialists on the region.[5]

Thus, prior to the U.S. invasion of Iraq, scholarly work on the Middle East had been marginalized within the study of developing countries, and even more so in the broader comparative politics field.[6] The authors in this book are part of an effort to correct this imbalance. We share a belief that the study of politics in authoritarian countries, which today still encompass nearly half of the world's population, should be, sui generis, more valued by comparative scholars. In addition, we know that the development of knowledge is inhibited when studies of economic and political transitions are focused only on successful cases. By selecting on the dependent variable without assuring different outcomes of it, scholars cannot be certain of the explanatory power of the independent variables they investigate (Collier and Mahoney 1996; cf. King, Keohane, and Verba 1994: 128–149). This last point is especially salient to the study of political reform because numerous countries once hailed as democratizers in the transitions literature, such as Peru, Ecuador, and Thailand, are now assigned more equivocal labels, such as "semi-authoritarian," "electoral authoritarian," or "competitive authoritarian."[7]

These efforts to bring the Middle East back in to the study of political reform and democratic transitions bore fruition, significantly, with the January 2004 publication of a special issue of *Comparative Politics,* a leading journal, devoted to the durability of authoritarianism in the Middle East. This book grew out of that special issue.[8] The authors have revised and updated their original essays, and the editors added to them several additional pieces to allow for broader theoretical coverage as well as more country cases.[9] Chapters here include single country case studies, small-n comparisons, and sweeping regional overviews, but all are distinguished by their application of broad comparative theory to Middle Eastern cases. The authors advance theoretical knowledge about what factors encourage democratization and what may explain the resiliency of many authoritarian regimes. Their chapters thus offer rich lessons for those—both within the region and outside of it—who seek to further the cause of democratization in the Middle East and elsewhere.

The Study of Stubborn Authoritarianism

The chapters in this book have been organized according to whether they place their greatest explanatory emphasis on state- or society-centered variables (Parts 1 and 2, respectively). Stateside factors involve the individuals who hold political power in a country and the agencies and institutions of government. Societal variables consider the population that is ruled over: ordinary citizens and the activities they engage in—and any groups or organizations they may participate in—as they interact with the government. The purpose of this introductory chapter is to highlight the book's theoretical contributions to the existing literature on regime change. Toward that end, rather than summarizing each chapter, I draw out different lessons from each, in a variety of contexts.

As noted in numerous recent essays, the major approaches in the democratization literature can generally be divided into two categories: the "prerequisites" school, whose arguments posit economic, cultural, or institutional necessities for transitions from authoritarianism to begin; and the "transitions" paradigm, which sees democratization as a contingent choice of regime and opposition actors that can occur under a variety of socioeconomic and cultural conditions.[10] This dichotomy is a subset of the larger divide in the social sciences between theories that emphasize the constraints on human behavior posed by macrostructural variables and those that privilege human agency.[11] The chapters in this book advance important propositions that fall within both schools of thought. Their collective message and arguably most important contribution, however, is to highlight the importance of various institutional arrangements for choices made by political activists and elites who serve to perpetuate authoritarian rule. Therefore, this book responds to the recent call by some scholars for more integrative approaches to the study of political change (Snyder and Mahoney 1999; Jones-Luong 2002).

Cultural Prerequisites to Democratization?

Much of the literature seeking to explain the democracy deficit in the Middle East has fallen into the prerequisites, or structural, category. Within this, cultural analyses have vied with economically based arguments. The authors here in some cases reject, and in some ways amplify and elaborate on, these prior approaches. They also identify new structural variables, in particular emphasizing heretofore neglected political-institutional factors.

For the Arab societies that predominate in the region, one set of cultural arguments posits a patriarchal and tribal mentality as an impediment to the development of pluralist values (inter alia, Sharabi 1988). The former is said to render Arab citizens prone to accept patrimonial leaders, while the latter impedes the sense of national unity that some (e.g., Rustow 1970: 350–351; Karatnycky 2002; Horowitz 1993) have posited as a prerequisite to successful democratization. Indeed, the ethnic divisions that are complicating the U.S. effort to democratize Iraq have led numerous pundits to view sectarianism as the main barrier to democratization in the region as a whole.

Here, Michael Herb seeks to understand whether Arab constitutional monarchies with weak but elected parliaments might follow the path of earlier European monarchies toward parliamentary democracies with only ceremonial thrones. He finds that ethnic divisions do pose a salient barrier to the development of parliamentarianism in several Arab monarchies. In Jordan, he observes, sectarian divisions in society are reflected in malapportioned electoral districts, which weakens the legitimacy of the legislature itself. One reason for the very limited powers that the Bahraini ruling family grants to that country's parliament is that the royalty is Sunni, whereas the country's majority population is Shiite.

Ethnic divisions thus emerge as a contributing factor to resilient authoritarianism in the region, but Herb does not claim them as either a necessary or sufficient condition. He identifies several other factors impeding democratization in Bahrain, in Jordan, as well as in the other monarchies where such divisions are less pronounced. And, as other scholars have noted, tribalism cannot account for the durability of authoritarianism among the more religiously and linguistically homogeneous Arab republics, such as Egypt and Tunisia.[12]

The broader, and prevailing, cultural theory for authoritarianism in the Middle East links it to the Islamic religion that dominates the region. Often labeled as "orientalist," following the influential work of Edward Said, it posits an intrinsic incompatibility between democratic values and Islam. Early versions of the argument attributed this immiscibility to the conflation of political and spiritual leadership in the early days of the Arab/Islamic empire, purportedly precluding an acceptance by Muslims of secular political authority and subordinating civil society to the state. In what Yahya Sadowski labeled as a contradictory, "neo-orientalist" approach, however, Islam has also been said to foster weak states that can never achieve the concentration of power necessary for its subsequent dispersion to occur.[13] The 1979 Iranian revolution and the subsequent spread of Islamist movements seeking (some by violent means) to capture political power and impose Islamic law (*shari'a*), has leant popular credence to orientalist arguments.

Recent efforts to test the alleged association between Islam and authoritarian government quantitatively have produced contradictory results. A large-n statistical analysis by Steven Fish (2002) showed the correlation to be robust; among a variety of causal variables he investigated, Fish found the best explanation to reside in higher levels of gender discrimination in Muslim-majority countries.[14] However, Alfred Stepan and Graeme Robertson (2003), using similar data, argue that when levels of economic development are taken into consideration, it is only the Arab Muslim countries that show a comparative lag in democracy.

Eva Bellin forthrightly repudiates the orientalist approaches in her pages here, noting that "other world cultures, notably Catholicism and Confucianism, have at different times been accused of incompatibility with democracy." Nevertheless, she observes, "these cultural endowments have not prevented countries in Latin America, southern Europe, or East Asia from democratizing."[15] And, as Jason Brownlee notes in his chapter analyzing regime survival of popular uprisings that occurred at different times in Syria, Tunisia, Iraq, and Libya, Islam in these cases "provided a set of ideas for mobilizing *against* dictatorships." The notion of Islam, as a religion, posing an intrinsic obstacle to democracy is thus not supported here.

The Role of Rents

An alternative prerequisites explanation for stubborn authoritarianism in the region, sometimes posited explicitly as a challenge to the cultural arguments, focuses on the particular nature of Middle Eastern economies. Many countries in the region, particularly those in or adjacent to the Arabian Peninsula, derive a substantial income from hydrocarbon exports; their poorer neighbors are linked to the oil economy through a reliance on labor migration and the resultant remittances, direct aid from the Gulf countries, and/or transit-associated earnings.[16] The "rentier state" theory posits that this access to a nonproductive source of income makes Middle Eastern regimes less reliant on extraction of wealth from their populations in order to finance the state as well as better able to win popular support through the generous provision of social services and government jobs. If opposition to arbitrary taxation was the engine to democratization in the West, then both patronage and the lack of an onerous tax burden on Middle Eastern populations can account for the presumed failure of citizens of these countries to seek greater participation in government.[17]

Rentier arguments originally arose in the 1980s to explain the deviation of the region's wealthiest oil exporters from the correlation—widely accepted since the seminal work of Seymour Lipset (1960)—between countries with high per capita wealth and democracy,[18] but they were not generally tested outside the Middle East. However, the "no representation without taxation" argument has been challenged by John Waterbury, who finds that extraction policies in the region do not differ substantially from those in other developing areas (Waterbury 1997b, 1994).[19]

Bellin rejects the prerequisites approach in general terms. Rather than *absent* cultural or socioeconomic prerequisites for democratic initiatives to begin, she attributes the robustness of authoritarian regimes to the *presence* of institutional and conjunctural factors, in particular those that strengthen the coercive apparatuses of these governments. In this context, though, she does find rentier income to be salient, in that it contributes to the ability of authoritarian incumbents to maintain extensive and effective security agencies. Fiscal health is essential for rewarding those individuals who comprise the state's coercive apparatus, she argues, and the Middle East region is distinguished by the comparatively high proportion of government expenditures devoted to security forces.

Arang Keshavarzian verifies that effect in his chapter on Iran. Noting that some recent variants of the rentier state theory predict political instability when oil revenues fluctuate sharply, he questions the utility of that argument with regard to the Islamic Republic, which, over the past twenty-five years, has survived major price swings and periods of declining per capita oil revenues. However, access to rents has facilitated elite resort to patronage and has financed multiple coercive agencies, both contributing to the elite fragmentation and the management of factionalism by hard-liners to which Keshavarzian attributes the durability of the Iranian regime.

A reduction in access to rents may therefore not be considered a sufficient or even necessary condition for democratization but appears, nevertheless, to be a precursor to some measure of political liberalization. Although prior to the 1980s the region was characterized overwhelmingly by single-party states and party-less monarchies, a number of countries have since the 1980s witnessed a pluralizing trend.[20] Today, contested (albeit to various degrees controlled) legislative elections are held in Iran, Turkey, Bahrain, Kuwait, Yemen, Lebanon, Jordan, Egypt, Algeria, Tunisia, Morocco, and (when permitted by Israel) the Palestinian Authority (PA).[21] This list includes almost all of the region's oil-poor countries,[22] but—with the exception of Kuwait, whose political opening can be linked to unusual international pressures after the first Gulf War—it excludes all of the wealthiest hydrocarbon exporters.[23] This strongly suggests some causal link between declining rentier income and political *pluralization,* even if *democratization* is neither the intended nor ultimate outcome.[24]

The Importance of Institutions

The concept of institutions refers to both formal organizations and informal rules and procedures that structure political conduct. Institutional analysis entails "the whole range of state and societal institutions that shape how political actors define their interests and that structure their relations of power to other groups." Included in this context are "the rules of electoral competition, the structure of party systems, the relations among various branches of government, and the structure and organization of economic actors like trade unions" (Steinmo, Thelen, and Longstreth, 1992: 2). Noneconomic associations such as international and domestically based human rights and environmental groups are also considered under this rubric.

In a recent critique of the transitions paradigm, Thomas Carothers (2002: 8, 16) calls for renewed attention to the role played by institutions in political reforms in authoritarian countries. The chapters herein oblige with arguments focused on a variety of institutional variables. However, whereas Carothers anticipates the identification of institutional arrangements that may be necessary for democratization to occur, thereby posing institutions as prerequisites, the authors here adopt divergent approaches. Some do employ a prerequisites analysis, but others treat institutions as

the backdrop against which the crucial decisions of the actors in the
transitions game are made. Taken together, these two approaches show
how institutions may act as bridges between other variables and the role
of human agency.

Political Parties and Elections

Political party structures and electoral rules capture considerable attention here. Implicitly using a historical-institutionalist approach,[25]
Michele Penner Angrist (Chapter 6) seeks to explain why competitive
party politics appears to have taken firmer root in Turkey than elsewhere in the region, as well as to account for variations in the forms of
authoritarianism that Middle Eastern countries exhibit. Her approach
posits the demise or departure of imperial power as a critical juncture at
which "the nature of nascent indigenous party systems significantly
affected the types of political regimes that eventually emerged." In
countries that had a single, dominant party at the time of independence,
one-party states resulted. Single, preponderant parties did not render
authoritarianism inevitable, she argues, "but enabled nondemocratically
inclined elites to quickly and effectively build authoritarian regimes
because they faced no rival actors and because single parties are effective political tools. Where there were multiple parties, two other aspects
of party systems come into play: the degree of polarization and—in an
important new variable Angrist introduces here—"mobilizational asymmetry." As explained below, Angrist sees these factors as affecting the
strategic calculations of elites vis-à-vis the likely outcome of partisan
electoral competition.

Angrist's party system variables point to the importance of the practices governing electoral competition. This is further underscored in the
contribution by Marsha Pripstein Posusney, which looks at contested legislative elections in six Arab countries from the 1970s through 2000. Not
surprisingly, these elections all returned parliaments favorable to the
incumbent executives. Although ballot box stuffing and outright vote
coercion, in various forms, were obvious operative factors here, Posusney also points to a more subtle means by which incumbent elites manipulated the election outcome: district design and the rules for choosing the
winners themselves. She demonstrates how the rulers of both Egypt and
Jordan changed and how the PA initially designed electoral rules to
ensure loyalist legislatives; in Yemen, use of a different electoral system
might have averted the civil war that broke out shortly after unification.
Posusney's chapter thus shows that electoral systems, whose importance
to outcomes in established democracies is well known (Reynolds and

Reilly 1997; Grofman and Lijphart 1986; Cox 1997) and whose optimal design in new democracies is the subject of current debate (Lijphart and Waisman 1996), can also be important to the unfolding of politics in countries whose rulers are resisting democratization.

Herb's research, too, shows that electoral engineering poses a formidable obstacle to democratization. Among the European constitutional monarchies he studied, only those whose elections were clean saw a successful transition to parliamentarianism; where fraudulent elections were suspected, the resulting legislatures lacked legitimacy and the citizenry refrained from pushing for greater parliamentary powers. Herb finds government tampering with election results to be most serious, among the Arab constitutional monarchies, in Morocco. In Jordan and Bahrain, as mentioned earlier, results are also manipulated through district malapportionment.

In Ellen Lust-Okar's chapter, the relevant electoral rules are not those determining the outcome among contestants but rather those governing which parties or movements may compete. Using a formal model that presupposes that economic crisis will generate opposition activity and that oppositional elites will exploit popular economic discontent to seek political advantage, she examines aspects of the relationship between economic crisis and political reform movements in two of the pluralizing monarchies, Jordan and Morocco.[26] Given crisis-generated political mobilizations, she argues, the durability of such movements will be a function of the structures of contestation created by the incumbent ruler. Mobilization will be more sustained in unified structures—when opposition parties are uniformly either given access to, or denied, opportunities for formal political participation—as opposed to when the opposition is divided between those who are formally recognized versus excluded movements. Lust-Okar sees the divided environment—where some parties are granted limited opportunities to participate in elections while others are excluded—as producing moderation among the included parties, who fear that an alliance with excluded groups could force the regime to punish the moderates by further constricting their avenues for participation.[27]

In different ways, Herb, Keshavarzian, and Vickie Langohr all spotlight the weakness, or absence, of opposition parties, even in countries that have some degree of electoral contestation, as a central explanatory variable. Herb argues that developed parties were necessary for the success of parliamentarianism in Europe, because "only parties could make parliament's preferences durable and give parliament the ability to dictate the composition of the ministry to the monarch." But among today's Arab monarchies, he finds, all except Morocco lack a strong party system.

In the Iranian case, Keshavarzian notes the lack of a party as a factor weakening the reformist camp. Iran is unique in the region in that reformists succeeded (for a period) in capturing the presidency and dominating the legislature, making them part of the governing elite. Hard-liners, however, were able to stymie their efforts through control of other governmental institutions. At this juncture the reformers needed to mobilize their supporters among the citizenry but were handicapped in their ability to do so by the lack of an institutionalized and well-rooted political organization.

Langohr comes to party weakness indirectly, by studying the role of civil society organizations in mobilizing dissent in Tunisia, Egypt, and the PA. Much of the recent literature on transitions, she observes, based on the experience of Latin America, Eastern Europe, and other democratizing regions, has singled out women's, environmental, and other advocacy associations as the most propitious groups to steer democratization forward. Nongovernmental organizations (NGOs) have therefore been able to attract significant funding from foreign donors, in addition to generally facing more permissive organizing environments. In contrast, nonruling parties in the Arab pluralizers have been weak vehicles for opposition because of government repression, severe financial constraints, and a marked tendency for excluded elites to run as independents, where possible, rather than joining parties. Advocacy organizations therefore became the key vehicles of opposition in the countries Langohr studied. But this has negative ramifications for Arab democratization, as NGOs' single-issue focus and dependence on foreign funding render them unable to mobilize and maintain widespread support. Thus, following Carothers (2002: 5–21), she argues that it is time for scholarly and policy analysis of democratization in the region to focus less on the role of NGOs and more on the importance of developing viable political parties.

A lack of democracy within the oppositional associations also contributes to their ineffectiveness, thus posing a challenge to the literature that posits NGOs as training grounds for the tolerance and civility needed to sustain partisan democratic practices in a society. It may be, however, that it was the single-issue focus of these groups (as encouraged by donors) that inhibited this development and that other types of organizations can better play such a role. In Carrie Rosefsky Wickham's (2004) work on Islamists in Egypt, the activities of the Muslim Brotherhood within student organizations and professional syndicates—namely, functional rather than advocacy groups—did contribute to their political learning of greater tolerance for diverse points of view.

Government Agencies

Military and security agencies are part of the state, but countries vary in the way in which these agencies interact with policymakers. Bellin's chapter emphasizes the structure of relations between incumbent rulers and the military, drawing a contrast between an institutionalized military, where entry and promotion standards are rational, and one based on primordial ties to executive authority. In the former situation, which is also associated with the military having a greater sense of national purpose, the prospects for officers rejecting roles in government or as the guarantors of internal security are higher. In most countries in the Middle East, however, patrimonial militaries are the norm.

Brownlee, too, is concerned with the capacity of the security apparatus to repress dissent, particularly in times of political crisis. Whereas Lust-Okar's study specifies mobilizations generated by economic crises, Brownlee casts a broader net by looking at situations where regimes' survival was threatened by popular uprisings, independent of the underlying cause. In Syria (1982), Tunisia (1987), Iraq (1991), and Libya (1993), he finds "moments of political contestation" analogous to crises that elsewhere in the world resulted in the breakdown of authoritarianism; in these Middle East cases, however, the result was regime restabilization. Brownlee attributes this outcome in part to the ability of the incumbent rulers to suppress dissent through each regime's coercive apparatus. His study thus provides concrete case evidence that supports Bellin's emphasis on the importance of security agencies to authoritarian endurance.

In Iran, Keshavarzian finds a multiplicity of security organizations, each able to act independently of the other. This has meant, in particular, the existence of coercive agencies that are able to escape supervision both by the legislature and by international monitoring agencies. The control of these autonomous security forces by opponents of change has enabled them to crack down on reformers both within and outside of the regime.

Finally, while excessive executive powers characterize all of the countries covered here, except contemporary Turkey, it is worth noting that the legal framework for the distribution of powers among the branches of government may differ. Studying the charters of the Arab constitutional monarchies, Herb finds significant variation in the degree to which they grant powers to parliament. Where the legislature's powers are more limited, the monarchs are less likely to resort to electoral manipulation or to suspension of the parliament. It follows that constitutional overhaul will need to accompany other political reforms for the achievement of parliamentarianism in some, but not all, of the Arab monarchies.

The Role of Human Agency

Human agency occupies pride of place in the transitions paradigm that characterizes much of the recent literature on democratization. Inspired by the early article of Dankwart Rustow (1970), contingency approaches stress that democracy will emerge when incumbent authoritarians opposed to change (hard-liners), as well as challengers (soft-liners, or reformists) who may themselves have antidemocratic leanings, come to see the uncertainty associated with free and fair electoral competition as the best option among other alternatives. Thus, the contingency school emphasizes the strategic choices made by political elites, a category understood to include not only incumbent rulers but also opposition activists. This book embellishes the transitions paradigm in a variety of ways.

Keshavarzian argues that fragmentation of the elite in Iran stands in the way of the negotiations necessary to the transitions scenario. On the one hand, the existence of multiple and overlapping government agencies provides outlets for regime elites to influence policy and establish patronage networks even if they have been marginalized from the major centers of power; this reduces the likelihood that they will push for systemic reform. On the other hand, fragmentation within the reformist camp inhibits its ability to coalesce around a platform for change and mobilize mass support behind it. The divisions in both camps also impede the compromises and mutual assurances entailed in pacted transitions. He writes,

> The diverse and institutionally scattered hard-liners and soft-liners are in no position to make credible commitments, for instance, that [one of the security agencies] will not organize a military coup or that reformists will enact sweeping reforms that put the entire system of the Islamic Republic under question. The risk of tolerating each other and the cost of creating a system of mutual security increases as the polity is more fragmented because it is necessary to bargain with a larger, and by definition more heterogeneous, collection of political competitors.

For Angrist, party systems form the backdrop to the choices made by opposition elites and incumbents in those countries that had two or more viable parties at independence. Sharp differences in the platforms of political parties discourage democratization because they increase the

costs to elites of an electoral loss to a rival party. But even with relatively low levels of political polarization, mobilizational asymmetry can
impede the opening or expansion of an electoral arena because elites of
the weaker parties will feel they are not facing a level playing field.
Hence, Angrist argues that despite the presence of partisan contestation
in numerous countries in the region as they emerged from the colonial
era, competitive politics survived (albeit with occasional setbacks) only
in Turkey because it enjoyed a uniquely favorable party system that
facilitated elite willingness to risk losses at the ballot box.

Opposition Actors

The remaining chapters with an agency argument focus on either the
opposition or the incumbent side. Lust-Okar, like Angrist, spotlights
decisions made by party leaders, but while presuming the existence of
multiple parties with an array of ideological platforms, she models party
leaders' choices as more constrained, as the power to expand or constrict partisan competition rests solely with ruling executives not subject
to popular recall. In this environment, as previously noted, Lust-Okar
holds that opposition elites will be more likely to jointly mobilize for
political reform when they are all uniformly either granted or denied
access to limited legislative participation; in a divided contestational
structure, the included parties will forfeit the potential mobilizational
gains of coalitions with excluded groups, fearing the higher cost that
they would be punished by the regime with exclusion themselves.

Posusney explores the options available to legalized opposition
party activists when faced with legislative elections whose results they
expect to be falsified. She argues that participating in such elections
cedes to them a measure of legitimacy, but abstaining denies the opposition one of the few legal avenues available for clarifying their policy
differences with the regime. Election boycotts, when mounted by a unified opposition, are a powerful political critique and can succeed in
winning reforms, as happened in Morocco in the early 1970s. But differences in ideology, size, and mobilizational capacity have generally
impeded efforts to sustain electoral boycotts in the countries she studies; the Islamist/secularist divide is particularly salient here. Finding
that efforts to minimize ballot box stuffing through voting-day monitoring programs are on the rise in the region, she suggests that as elections
become cleaner, opposition parties might benefit from campaigns to
modify those electoral rules that favor incumbent authoritarians.

Langohr also spotlights the strategies of opposition activists, but her
emphasis is on associational groups. She portrays activists as political

entrepreneurs who face a decision whether to concentrate their energies on parties versus NGOs. Although the civil society literature has tended to assign NGOs and parties different roles in the democratization process, assuming that they draw on different reservoirs of support, Langohr proposes that both be seen as part of a larger "topography of opposition" in which opposition activists choose the organizational form that seems to present the best opportunity for effective political expression. In both Tunisia and Egypt, activists turned to NGOs partly as a response to donor initiatives but also because of numerous weaknesses associated with the existing opposition parties. For different reasons, independent Palestinian forces also channeled their talents into civic associations. In all three cases, these decisions contributed to the phenomenon of multiple and competing NGOs while at the same time impeding the internal reforms in opposition parties necessary to transform them into viable contenders for political power.

Ruling Elites

For Brownlee and Bellin, however, the focus should be less on societal actors and more on incumbent elites. Brownlee argues that the comparative work on transitions has concentrated on societal opposition forces and regime soft-liners to the neglect of those in power who resist reform. It is the latter's willingness and ability to turn to brutality in order to avert a breakdown that explains the survival of the four personalistic dictatorships he examines. The Middle East's neopatrimonial rulers have not been unusual in this regard, he suggests, but the explanatory power of this resort to intense repression has been overlooked by theorists eager to find some uniquely Middle Eastern factor to account for authoritarian endurance there.

Bellin likewise observes that the robustness of authoritarianism requires not only the regime's capacity but also its will to repress opposition, and she posits several factors affecting that propensity. Where the ruling regime came to power through a coup (as in Egypt, Syria, Iraq, Algeria, and, at times, Turkey), military institutionalization, as discussed earlier, impacts officers' calculations about the potential risks of a return to the barracks. High levels of institutionalization foster the development of soft-liners who believe that the military's effectiveness and cohesion are compromised by holding the reigns of power. Where patrimonialism reigns (as can characterize monarchies as well as military regimes), however, officers have reason to fear that their positions would be jeopardized by political reforms.

Incumbent leaders and their security elites also make calculations about the potential costs of suppressing dissident movements. Here is where, Bellin posits, a relatively low level of political mobilization in the region comes into play: when there are not large throngs protesting in the streets, the political costs of repressing dissent are lower. It is significant in this regard that the final stages of the Iranian revolution were bloodless, as when millions were marching against the shah, the army refused to fire on them.

International Actors

Whereas transitions theory centers on the choices made by political elites within authoritarian countries, several of the chapters in this book demonstrate that political decisions made by external actors can also play a role in either undergirding or undermining authoritarian rule. Posusney points to a positive role that international agencies can play through election monitoring, which has helped in a limited way to restrict vote coercion and ballot-box stuffing in some countries discussed here. In Langohr's analysis, however, some well-meaning foreign organizations have contributed inadvertently to keeping incumbent elites in power. Convinced by the civil society literature that NGOs are the critical agents of democratization in authoritarian societies, international agencies have channeled funds and political support to local advocacy groups. This, in turn, had the effect of steering opposition activists in the countries she studies toward establishing NGOs rather than struggling to reform political parties.

For Bellin and Brownlee, maintenance of Middle East authoritarianism has been an intentional Western policy. Bellin posits continued diplomatic support for existing regimes as one of the four advantages that Middle East authoritarian rulers enjoy relative to their present and former counterparts elsewhere. Foreign military aid, or what Alan Richards (2002) has labeled a "strategic rent," also contributes to the fiscal health of some countries' security apparatuses. Bellin attributes this support to two key Western strategic concerns: the stability of oil supplies and containing the Islamist threat. Arguably, Western backing for Israel is a third prominent consideration.

Brownlee echoes this point, particularly in the current context of the U.S.-led war on terrorism. In his four cases of regime restabilization, though, it was not international support for the incumbent rulers but rather their lack of reliance on external patrons that enabled their resort to brutality. Thus, it is not international backing per se but rather an absence of international constraints on the rulers' use of force that is the operative factor in his analysis; this absence of constraints can occur either through active Western support for authoritarian regimes or as a result of the latter's independence from the West.

Conclusion

Taken together, as Angrist's concluding chapter underscores, all the chapters here leave little cause for optimism that authoritarian countries in the Middle East will undergo transitions to democracy in the near future. The incumbent executives enjoy a number of advantages relative to their former counterparts elsewhere in the world, including loyal and well-funded security agencies and, for most (including, during the late 1970s and 1980s, Saddam Hussein's Iraq), the benefits of Western acquiescence to their continued rule. At the same time, the institutions serving regime challengers are weak: opposition parties are highly constrained and typically nondemocratic themselves; advocacy groups are fragmented and structurally ill-suited to mount broad campaigns for political reform; and professional associations, even if they serve as incubators for tolerance and pluralist values, are underdeveloped throughout the region. Consequently, strong popular mobilizations against incumbent rulers are infrequent and until now have been readily suppressed. Legislative elections, where they are permitted, are often manipulated and fraudulent, and elected parliaments have only limited powers vis-à-vis the executive branch.

The study of resilient authoritarianism is normatively imperative for a discipline that had largely, before the U.S. invasion of Iraq, turned its back on this region, as on other stubbornly nondemocratic countries outside of it. The chapters in this book demonstrate that this study can be both empirically rich and theoretically fruitful, and thus able to contribute concretely to hastening the downfall of nondemocratic regimes.

Notes

I would like to thanks Lisa Anderson, Michele Penner Angrist, Eva Bellin, Melani Cammett, Vickie Langohr, Jim Mahoney, Ellen Lust-Okar, Rich Snyder, and Carrie Rosefsky Wickham for their helpful comments on earlier drafts of this chapter. The customary caveats apply.

1. The Middle East is generally understood, geographically, to include both northern Africa and southwest Asia. Although some scholarly works, drawing on the old British concept of the "Near East," set the western border at Egypt, it is today more commonly considered to extend from Mauritania in the west to Iran in the east and from Turkey (thereby also incorporating that country's European territory) in the north to Sudan and Yemen in the south.

2. Israel, with a political and economic trajectory unique to the region, never went through an authoritarian era and is the only Middle Eastern country today that can be considered a consolidated democracy, in so far as the institu-

tionalization of competitive elections and the rights and freedoms of its citizens are concerned.

3. The list includes, but is not limited to: O'Donnell and Schmitter (1986); O'Donnell, Schmitter, and Whitehead (1986); Linz and Stepan (1996); Haggard and Kaufman (1995); and Anderson (1999). See also the critique by Ross (2001).

4. For instance, Diamond, Linz, and Lipset (1990); and Chehabi and Linz (1998a). For a related critique of the latter work, see Brownlee (2002b).

5. Especially noteworthy in this regard is the excellent two-volume study by Brynen, Korany, and Noble (1995); and Korany, Brynen, and Noble (1998).

6. For documentary evidence, in terms of faculty positions, see Diamond (2002a); on scholarly publications see Lustick (2000: 192) and Hull (1999).

7. See especially Diamond (2002b); Schedler (2002); Carothers (2002: 5–21); Ottaway (2003); and Levitsky and Way (2002).

8. The special issue was the product of a series of workshops titled, and with the aim of, "Bringing the Middle East Back in . . . to the Study of Political and Economic Reform." See the acknowledgments in this book for more details.

9. Because of space considerations, it was not possible to include all of the original *Comparative Politics* essays here. We encourage readers of this book to also study Wickham (2004).

10. For excellent overviews see, inter alia, Anderson (1999); Carothers (2002); and Burnell (1998).

11. For an elaboration and literature review, see Mahoney and Snyder (1999).

12. See also the critique of Sharabi and others in Anderson (1995a: 77–92). For a large-n study disputing that ethnic diversity is negatively correlated with democracy, see Fish and Brooks (2004).

13. Sadowski (1993: 14–21, 40).

14. Gender relations do not figure prominently in the arguments presented in this book, but see Doumato and Posusney (2003).

15. See also Wickham (2004), which notes the possibility of political Islamic groups moderating their long-term platforms in a direction that embraces certain democratic values, though not necessarily a secular framework based on a separation of religion and state.

16. Tourist revenues, which have been important particularly to Egypt and some of the North African countries, are another form of rent.

17. The seminal work on this is Beblawi and Luciano (1987). See also Anderson (1995a, 1997).

18. Recent work which generally corroborates, while qualifying, this association includes Przeworksi et al. (2000); and Huber, Rueschemeyer, and Stephens (1993).

19. More recently, a large-n study by Michael Ross (2001) does demonstrate cross-regional support for the rentier effect, but his statistical evidence has been challenged by Michael Herb (forthcoming).

20. When referring to the moves toward expanded contestation in these countries, I use the terms "pluralizing" and "pluralization" as intentional substitutes for either "liberalizing"/"liberalization" or "democratizing"/"democratization." To apply democratization to the multiparty experiments described here implies an

endpoint that does not appear to be the intent of their initiators and may not be realized even as an unintentional consequence of these policies. Political liberalization captures the initial easing of repression associated with these openings, but it is noteworthy that multipartyism can coincide with the maintenance of notably illiberal policies toward gender, ethnic, and/or religious freedoms, as is the case, for example, in Iran.

21. Carothers (2002) includes most of these countries in his gray area category of being no longer authoritarian but not yet, and not necessarily in any stage of transition to, democracy. It is the consensus of the authors here that the authoritarian label still applies to them and that developing a useful subclassification scheme remains an important challenge for comparative work on the region. However, we do not necessarily agree on how much significance should be attached to the difference between those that remain as hereditary monarchies (Kuwait, Bahrain, Jordan, and Morocco) and those whose chief executive is subject to some mechanism of popular approval.

22. Syria and Sudan are exceptions.

23. Significantly, Bahrain's turn to contested legislative elections occurred only after the country's oil resources had dried up. Algeria exports large quantities of natural gas, but its export earnings must be spread over a population significantly larger than that of the Arab Gulf countries; it encountered balance of payments difficulties (and implemented structural adjustment policies) during the 1980s. Iran likewise combines oil wealth with one of the region's largest populations; in addition, its oil export capacity, and economy overall, were severely damaged by the eight-year Iran-Iraq war in the 1980s. Contestation—within Islamic parameters—was expanded after the war's end.

24. On the link between economic crisis and pluralization in some of these cases, see also Anderson (1997) and Brumberg (1995).

25. Historical institutionalists emphasize the importance of certain critical junctures that set countries on a path that constrains future options. See Steinmo, Thelen, and Longstreth (1992); and Collier and Collier (1991).

26. Lust-Okar's approach does not invoke the concept of rents when discussing the advent of economic crisis in these countries. Her argument implicitly suggests, though, that where political reform movements are missing elsewhere in the region, this may be attributable to the absence of economic crisis. In this sense it is compatible with the original rentier state theory.

27. The divided environment Lusk-Okar describes can also have a moderating effect on *excluded* groups. In Egypt, for example, the Muslim Brotherhood, though its members have sometimes been permitted to contest elections as independent candidates or in party coalitions, are legally excluded from party formation. Wickham (2004) traces the strategic thinking of the self-named Wasati (or middle-of-the-road) Islamists who split off from the Brotherhood, and sees the opportunities for formal partisan participation as an inducement for them to moderate. Readers should note, however, that the term "moderation" has a different meaning in these two pieces. Wickham uses it to address changes in the ultimate political agendas of the actors she analyzes. For Lust-Okar, moderation refers to the demands that an opposition group is raising in a given tactical situation; the long-term goals of the group are understood to be unchanging.

Part 1
The Reins of Power

2

Coercive Institutions and Coercive Leaders

EVA BELLIN

This chapter explores the following question: Why have the Middle East and North Africa proven exceptionally resistant to democratic transition, in marked contrast to other regions in the world? The answer, it argues, lies not in cultural or socioeconomic factors but rather in the character of the Middle Eastern state and, most important, the exceptional strength and will of its coercive institutions to repress all democratic initiatives. Four factors explain the exceptional coercive capacity and will of the Middle Eastern state: the region's access to rent, the persistent support of international patrons, the patrimonial character of state institutions, and the limited degree of popular mobilization for democratic reform.

Why has the region of the Middle East and North Africa (MENA) remained so singularly resistant to third wave contagion? While the number of electoral democracies around the world has nearly doubled since 1972, the number in the MENA region has registered an absolute decline over the same period.[1] Today only two out of twenty-one MENA countries qualify as electoral democracies, down from the three observed in 1972.[2] Stagnation is also evident in the guarantee of political rights and civil liberties. While the number of countries designated "free" by Freedom House has doubled in the Americas and in the Asia-Pacific region since the early 1970s, increased tenfold in Africa, and risen exponentially in Central and Eastern Europe (CEE), there has been no overall improvement in the MENA region.[3] Aggregate scores in 2002 differ little from 1972. Fifteen MENA countries are designated "not free," five "partly free," and only one "free" (see Table 2.1). Although a

Table 2.1 Freedom House Rankings for MENA Countries, 1972 and 2002

Country	Political Rights/Civil Liberties (composite score)		Freedom Rating[a]	
	1972/3	2001/2	1972/3	2002/3
Algeria	6.0	5.5	Not free	Not free
Egypt	6.0	6.0	Not free	Not free
Iran	5.5	6.0	Not free	Not free
Iraq	7.0	7.0	Not free	Not free
Libya	6.5	7.0	Not free	Not free
Oman	6.5	5.5	Not free	Not free
Palestinian National Authority	—[b]	5.5	—[b]	Not free
Qatar	5.5	6.0	Not free	Not free
Saudi Arabia	6.0	7.0	Not free	Not free
Sudan	6.0	7.0	Not free	Not free
Syria	7.0	7.0	Not free	Not free
Tunisia	5.5	5.5	Not free	Not free
United Arab Emirates	6.0	5.5	Not free	Not free
Yemen (South)	7.0	6.0	Not free	Not free
		(North & South)		
Lebanon	2.0	5.5	Free	Not free
Bahrain	5.5	5.5	Partly free	Partly free
Jordan	6.0	5.0	Not free	Partly free
Kuwait	4.0	4.5	Partly free	Partly free
Morocco	4.5	5.0	Partly free	Partly free
Turkey	3.5	4.5	Partly free	Partly free
Yemen (North)	4.4	—[c]	Partly free	—[c]
Israel	2.5	2.0	Free	Free

Notes: a. An average rating of 1 to 2.5 is generally considered "free," 3 to 5.5 "partly free," and 5.5 to 7 "not free." For Freedom House's methodology, see www.freedomhouse.org.
   b. The PNA was created in 1993.
   c. North and South Yemen united in 1990.

few MENA countries, notably Morocco, Jordan, Bahrain, and Yemen, have registered noteworthy progress toward political liberalization since the mid-1990s, overall, the vast majority of countries in the region have failed to catch the wave of democratization that has swept nearly every other part of the world. Why?

Many analysts have put their minds to this question. Typically the explanations offered suggest a litany of MENA failures.

First, civil society is weak and thus proves to be an ineffective champion of democracy. Labor unions are empty shells; businessmen's associations lack credible autonomy; nongovernmental organizations lack indigenous grounding. The weakness of associational life undermines the development of countervailing power in society that can force the state to be accountable to popular preferences. It also contracts the opportunities for citizens to participate in collective deliberation, stunting the development of a civic culture, that essential underpinning of vibrant democracy (Norton 1995, 1996; Brynen, Korany, and Noble 1995).

Second, the commanding heights of the economy remain largely in state hands. Despite nearly two decades of experimentation with structural adjustment, the public sector continues to account for a major share of employment and gross national product (GNP) generation in most MENA countries (Page 1998; Henry and Springborg 2001: 6).[4] This legacy of statist ideologies and rent-fueled opportunities undermines the capacity to build autonomous, countervailing power to the state in society.

Third, people are poor, literacy rates are low, and inequality is significant. It is not unusual for a fifth of the population in a given country to fall below the poverty line, 32 percent of adults are illiterate, and MENA states rank in the bottom half of the UN's human development index despite the enormous wealth of several MENA countries.[5] These conditions compromise both elite and mass commitment to democratic reform. The masses don't prioritize it and the elite have reason to be frightened by it. The champions for democracy are few and far between.

Fourth, countries in the region are geographically remote from the epicenter of democratization. Few, save Turkey, border directly on successful models of democratic rule. The demonstration effect that has proven so important to fueling the third wave in other regions of the world is diluted in the Middle East and North Africa (DiPalma 1990: 1–26).

Fifth, when all else fails, many analysts fall back on culture. Culture, and specifically MENA's saturation with Islam, really does distinguish the region. Surely that must explain some of the region's exceptionalism, especially given Islam's presumed inhospitality to democracy (Kedourie 1994; Vatikiotis 1987; Kramer 1993).

In short, the Middle East and North Africa lack the prerequisites of democratization. The lack of a strong civil society, a market-driven economy, adequate income and literacy levels, democratic neighbors, and democratic culture explain the region's failure to catch the third wave.

None of these explanations is satisfying. The MENA region is in no way unique for its poor endowment with the requisites of democracy. Other regions similarly deprived have nonetheless managed to make the transition. Civil society is notoriously weak in sub-Saharan Africa, yet twenty-three out of forty-two countries carried out some measure of democratic transition between 1988 and 1994 (Bratton and van de Walle 1997: 1–13, 72; Brattton 1989; Herbst 2001). The commanding heights of the economy were entirely under state control in Eastern Europe prior to the fall of the Berlin wall, and yet the vast majority of countries in this region successfully embraced transition during the 1990s (Banac 1992). Poverty and inequality, not to mention geographic remoteness from the democratic epicenter, have characterized India, Mauritius, and Botswana, and yet these countries have successfully embraced democracy (Kohli 2001; Bratton and van de Walle 1997: 69, 246). And other world cultures, notably Catholicism and Confucianism, have at different times been accused of incompatibility with democracy; yet these cultural endowments have not prevented countries in Latin America, southern Europe, or East Asia from democratizing.[6]

Prerequisites—A Useful Approach?

Cross-regional and cross-temporal comparisons indicate that democratization is so complex an outcome, no single variable will ever prove to be universally necessary or sufficient to compel it (Huntington 1991: 38; Rustow 1970: 343). Any notion of a single prerequisite of democracy should be jettisoned. But must the notion of prerequisites be abandoned altogether? It might be tempting to hold on to the idea. Cumulative failure to realize many of the conditions historically associated with successful democratization is bound to hinder democratic transition today. In the Middle East and North Africa, the failure to realize so many of these conditions simultaneously (e.g., weak civil society, state-dominated economy, low literacy, low per capita income, and remoteness from the democratic epicenter) may explain the region's resistance to transition.

I am not persuaded. Again, the MENA region is not unique in this cumulative failure.

The inability to fulfill these conditions is the reason why democracy is on such shaky ground in so many part of the world, why analysts must resort to "democracy with adjectives" (another term for imperfect democracy) when categorizing so many products of the third wave in Africa, Asia, and Latin America (Collier and Levitsky 1997; Linz and Stepan 1996). Cumulative failure to achieve the prerequisites of democracy clearly undermines the consolidation of democracy. But alone it cannot explain the failure to carry out democratic transition because many countries burdened with "prerequisite failure" have nonetheless made that leap successfully. The transition to democracy accomplished by sub-Saharan African states that typically rank as poorly if not worse than many MENA states on standard socioeconomic indicators, proximity to successful democracy, and the vigor of civil society makes this point clear. The puzzle posed by the MENA experience is not why democracy has failed to consolidate in the region (such failure would be expected) but rather why the vast majority of MENA states have failed to embark upon transition at all. Herein lies the exceptionalism of the region. To explain it, it is necessary to look beyond failure to achieve the prerequisites of democracy, since this failure is not exceptional to the region at all.

Insights from the Literature on Revolution

Why has democratic transition largely eluded MENA countries? It is not as though the region has been deprived of all democratic impulse. The MENA region has indeed seen the fledgling emergence of civil society (human rights groups, professional associations, self-help groups, etc.), only to see the lion's share of them either repressed or corporatized by the state (Norton 1995; Harik 1994; Wiktorowicz 2000; Langhor, Chapter 9, in this book). Etatist regimes have increasingly liberalized their economies (often under pressure from international forces), but any glimmer of autonomous political initiative expressed by their newly emergent private sectors is typically punished by the powers that be (Bellin 2002: 86–121). Progressive interpretations of Islam that endorse democratic norms and ideals have been parsed by Islamic theorists, only to be buried by hostile state elites (Ahmad 1985; Wickham 2004). In each case, a coercive state deeply opposed to democratic reform has quashed initiatives favorable to democracy.

To understand the rarity of democratic transition in the MENA region it is necessary to return to a classic work on revolution written by Theda Skocpol more than twenty-five years ago. The puzzling thing about revolution, Skocpol pointed out, is that although the intuitive prerequisite for revolution—mass disaffection from the regime in power—is a relatively common phenomenon in human experience, successful revolution is a relatively rare event. What explains this divergence between cause and outcome? The answer, Skocpol argued, lies in the strength of the state and, most important, the state's capacity to maintain a monopoly on the means of coercion. If the state's coercive apparatus remains coherent and effective, it can face down popular disaffection and survive significant illegitimacy, "value incoherence," and even a pervasive sense of relative deprivation among its subjects (Skocpol 1979: 32).

In short, the strength, coherence, and effectiveness of the state's coercive apparatus discriminates between cases of successful revolution and cases of revolutionary failure or nonoccurrence (Skocpol 1979: 34). The same might be said of democratic transition. Democratic transition can only be carried out successfully when the state's coercive apparatus lacks the will or capacity to crush it. Where that coercive apparatus remains in tact and willfully opposed to political reform, democratic transition will not occur.

What this suggests is that the solution to the puzzle of MENA exceptionalism lies less in absent prerequisites of democratization and more in present conditions that foster robust authoritarianism, and specifically a robust coercive apparatus in these states (Crystal 1994). In the MENA region it is the stalwart will and capacity of the state's coercive apparatus to suppress any glimmers of democratic initiative that have extinguished the possibility of transition. Here is where the region's true exceptionalism lies.

Some conceptual clarifications are in order. First, will and capacity are two independent qualities that do not covary and ought not be collapsed into one. A regime may have the capacity to repress democratic forces but not the will, as was the case in South Korea under Roh Tae Woo in 1987. Or the reverse may be true, as was the case in Benin under Mathieu Ahmed Kerekou in 1989.

Second, this argument admittedly veers toward conflation of the coercive apparatus and the authoritarian regime it undergirds. The distinction between the two is often difficult to draw even in regimes (for example Egypt, Syria, and Algeria) where the official head of state is a civilian, because the head of state is often closely allied with the coercive apparatus and highly dependent on coercion to maintain power. The mutual controls exercised by the security apparatus and the civilian leader endow each with a measure of veto power over the other and make it difficult to tease out who exercises superior agency in the dyad.

Classic indicators used to tease out relative power (control over appointments, political succession, budgets, and policy) often do not yield a clear-cut picture.[7] Patrimonial linkages between the regime and coercive apparatus further enmesh the two. In the case of Algeria, for example, conflation of the regime and the coercive apparatus is so pronounced that one analyst, paraphrasing Mirabeau's description of Prussia, declared that "every state has an army but in Algeria the army has a state."[8] This problem of conflation between authoritarian civilian regimes and the military is in no way peculiar to the MENA region. Robin Luckham, for example, explores it in the African context (Luckham 1994: 42–50). Nevertheless, the prevalence of patrimonial logic in many MENA regimes makes this a particularly pervasive problem in the Middle East and North Africa.

To restate the argument: authoritarianism has proven exceptionally robust in the MENA region because the coercive apparatus in many

MENA states has proven exceptionally able and willing to crush reform initiatives from below. Comparative analysis is helpful in explaining why. The experience of other regions reveals what is exceptional about the Middle East and North Africa.

Robustness of the Coercive Apparatus

What shapes the robustness of a regime's coercive apparatus? Under what conditions will it lose its capacity and will to hold on to power and permit society to experiment with democratization? Comparative analysis of extraregional cases of such renunciation suggests at least four variables that are crucial to this outcome.

First, the robustness of the coercive apparatus is directly linked to maintenance of fiscal health. The security establishment is most likely to "give up the ghost" when its financial foundation is seriously compromised. When the military can no longer pay the salaries of its recruits and the security forces cannot guarantee supplies of arms and ammunition, the coercive apparatus disintegrates from within. This is the lesson of sub-Saharan Africa, where, as Jeffrey Herbst points out, democratic transition was less the work of strong societies and more the consequence of weak states (Herbst 2001: 372). Prolonged fiscal crisis led to the "hollowing out" of the coercive apparatus in many African countries. Soldiers went unpaid and materiel deteriorated. Democratic transition was possible because decomposition of the military and security establishments opened up the political space in which demands for democracy could be pressed (Luckham 1994: 50–59; Luckham 1995: 52–55). According to Michael Bratton and Nicholas van de Walle (1997: 83, 144–149, 211), the strength and disposition of the military were among the most significant determinants of the fate of transition on the African continent.

Second, the robustness of the coercive apparatus is also shaped by successful maintenance of international support networks. The security establishment is most likely to lose its will and capacity to hold on to power when it loses crucial international support. Coercive regimes especially face this problem if they have grown up in the lap of massive foreign support (and few authoritarian regimes of the twentieth century escaped the benevolence of one great power or another during the years of the Cold War). Withdrawal of international backing triggers both an existential and financial crisis for the regime that often devastates both its will and capacity to carry on. This scenario proved key in Eastern Europe, where the Soviet Union's withdrawal of support for the Brezhnev

Doctrine spelled the end of the coercive backbone of these regimes and their will to hold on (Janos 2000: 342; Thompson 2001). It also proved important in Latin America, where the United States' abrupt shift away from supporting authoritarianism in the post–Cold War era dealt many regimes an important existential blow.[9] And this scenario proved central in sub-Saharan Africa where, as the Cold War waned, foreign patrons, both Eastern and Western, withdrew massive supplies of military aid and where Western donors increasingly made foreign aid conditional on democratic reform (Luckham 1995: 53–56).

Third, the robustness of the coercive apparatus, or perhaps more accurately, the robustness of its will to repress reform initiatives, is inversely related to its level of institutionalization. The more institutionalized the security establishment, the more willing it will be to disengage from power and allow political reform to proceed. The less institutionalized it is, the less amenable it will be to reform.

Institutionalization of the coercive apparatus should not be confused with professionalization in the Huntingtonian sense. Institutionalization does not refer to the depoliticization of the security establishment and its subordination to civilian control (Feaver 1999). Rather, institutionalization invokes the constellation of qualities that Max Weber used to distinguish bureaucracies from patrimonially driven organizations. An institutionalized coercive apparatus is one that is rule governed, predictable, and meritocratic. It has established paths of career advancement and recruitment; promotion is based on performance not politics; there is a clear delineation between the public and private that forbids predatory behavior vis-à-vis society; and discipline is maintained through the inculcation of a service ethic and strict enforcement of a merit-based hierarchy. In contrast, in a coercive apparatus organized along patrimonial lines, staffing decisions are ruled by cronyism; the distinction between public and private mission is blurred, leading to widespread corruption and abuse of power; and discipline is maintained through the exploitation of primordial cleavage, often relying on balanced rivalry between different ethnic/sectarian groups.

Patrimonialism confers a number of distinct advantages on authoritarian regimes that can contribute to their longevity (Brownlee 2002b; Geddes 1999b). These include demobilizing the opposition and building a loyal base through selective favoritism and discretionary patronage. Patrimonialism can also makes authoritarian regimes particularly resistant to democratic reform (Bratton and van de Walle 1997: 82–97; Geddes 1999b). With regard to the coercive apparatus, patrimonial organization will spell less receptivity to political opening. By contrast, institutionalization will spell more tolerance for reform.

The logic is twofold. First, where the coercive apparatus is institutionalized, the security elite have a sense of corporate identity separate from the state. They have a distinct mission and identity and career path. Officers can imagine separation from the state. They believe they will live to see another day, even in the wake of relinquishing power. In short, they do not perceive that they will be "ruined by reform" (Bermeo 1997: 315; Dahl 1971). To the contrary, they are more likely to be ruined by holding on to office too long because over the course of long-term office, political failures are bound to develop and trigger political divisions within the elite. These divisions, in turn, may threaten the institutional integrity of the security apparatus. One of the main factors that drove the military elite to transfer power to civilians in Brazil and Argentina was their concern to save the institutional integrity of their establishments (Stepan 1988). Similar incentives are present whenever the coercive apparatus is strongly institutionalized.

Second, where the coercive apparatus is institutionalized rather than patrimonial it is distinguished by a commitment to some broader national mission that serves the public good, such as national defense and economic development, rather than to personal aggrandizement and enrichment alone. Where the elite has successfully delivered on these missions, they again have good reason to be persuaded that they will not be "ruined by reform." To the contrary, where they have successfully delivered on public goals like national defense or economic development, they might be confident of their ability to ride democratic transition successfully and maintain a hold on power, this time as popularly elected officials. Both Augusto Pinochet in Chile and Roh Tae Woo in South Korea reasoned this way. Whereas Pinochet was overly optimistic (he failed to win the plebiscite that would have elected him Chile's president in 1988), Roh Tae Woo's confidence was well placed. The South Korean general rode his record of achievement to win the highest office of the land. Here again, the institutionalized character of the security apparatus spelled tolerance of democratic reform.

Finally, the coercive apparatus's capacity and will to hold on to power is shaped by a fourth variable, the degree to which it faces a high level of popular mobilization. Mowing down thousands of people, even if it is within the physical capacity of the security forces, is a costly prospect. It may jeopardize the institutional integrity of the security apparatus (will the soldiers shoot?); it may jeopardize international support to the regime (will the patron pay?); it may jeopardize the domestic legitimacy of the security forces (will popular opposition be amplified?). Clearly, the high costs of massive repression will not deter elites who believe they will be ruined by reform (Bermeo 1997: 317). The

slaughter of thousands at Hama by Hafez al-Assad's regime in Syria and
the massacre of hundreds at Tiananmen Square by the Communist regime in China are only two salient examples of the human tragedy
wreaked by coercive elites bent on repression and undeterred by the very
high costs associated with it (Friedman 1989: 76–105; Thompson 2001:
63–83). However, where the elite do not perceive reform to be so dev-
astating, the higher cost of repression posed by high levels of popular
mobilization may serve as a tipping mechanism, pitching the elite onto
the side of reform. In Korea, mass demonstrations on behalf of democratic reform, manned by a broad, cross-class coalition with sizeable
middle-class participation, persuaded Roh Tae Woo to forgo brutal repression of the democracy movement and instead opt for reform (Hamilton
and Kim 1993; Eckert et al. 1990; Hsiao and Koo 1997). Similarly in
Latin America, the presence of a serious labor movement and an active
civil society, both mobilized on the side of democratization, made coercive regimes in Argentina and Peru reconsider repression when other
options seemed possible and safe (Collier and Mahoney 1997).

Two objections might be raised to this fourth variable, popular
mobilization. Some may protest that this variable introduces an element
of circularity to the argument because the level of popular mobilization
in society is, to some degree, shaped by the coercive capacity and will
of the state. For example, in Egypt the state's coercive capacity and will
has led to harsh repression of civil society; consequently many popular
forces have been reluctant to mobilize politically. This reluctance has
lowered the cost of repression for the state and refortified its will to use
coercion.

But here is where the circularity ends: there is no simple correlation
between a state's coercive capacity and will and its demobilization of
society. Some coercive states nurture the development of civil society
through corporatist measures. Others repress inconsistently, demobilizing some groups (for example, leftist unions) but not others (for example, the church). Tolerated pockets of mobilization can come back to
haunt the state, forcing the elite to confront the calculation: is the cost
of repression worth the benefit? This was the case in South Korea in
1987 where the mobilization of tolerated groups such as church and student movements created significant pressure to reform. Consequently,
popular mobilization must be measured on its own, independent of
assessment of the state's coercive capacity and will.

A second objection to the popular mobilization variable may center
on the complaint that this variable actually smuggles in some of the logic
of the social prerequisites approach rejected earlier. After all, the level of
popular mobilization is clearly shaped by such variables as literacy,

urbanization, and socioeconomic inequality. However, one variable cannot be reduced to the other. Popular mobilization is also shaped by ideological factors (is there an alternative vision present in society, say communism or Islamism, that captures the popular imagination?), leadership variables (has a charismatic leader emerged?), and sudden moments of crisis that spur a spontaneous popular response. Measurement of socioeconomic variables will not account for such spurts of mobilization, and that is why popular mobilization must be measured on its own.[10]

Conditions in the MENA Region

No single variable, whether poor fiscal health, declining international support, strong institutionalization, or high levels of popular mobilization, is either a necessary or sufficient condition for retreat from power by the coercive apparatus. But cross-regional comparison suggests that these four variables have proven important to prior cases of retreat. It is interesting, then, to reflect on how countries in the MENA region rate on these variables. Their performance suggests the reasons why authoritarian regimes are exceptionally robust there.

First, with regard to fiscal health, although many states in the Middle East and North Africa face economic difficulties of one sort or another, few, save perhaps the Sudan, face economic collapse of sub-Saharan proportions (Shafik 1998; UNDP 2001). Most, moreover, enjoy sufficient revenue to sustain exceedingly robust expenditure on their security apparatuses. In fact these expenditures are among the highest in the world. MENA states are the world leaders in terms of proportion of GNP spent on security. On average, MENA countries spent 6.7 percent of their GNP on defense expenditures in the year 2000, compared to a global average of 3.8 percent; 2.2 percent in countries represented in the North Atlantic Treaty Organization (NATO); 2.8 percent in non-NATO European countries; 3.3 percent in east Asia and Australasia; 4 percent in sub-Saharan Africa; and 1.6 percent in the Caribbean, Central, and Latin America (IISS 2002: 304). MENA states are among the biggest spenders in terms of arms purchased. Seven MENA countries (Saudi Arabia, Iran, Egypt, Israel, the United Arab Emirates, Kuwait, and Algeria) alone accounted for 40 percent of all global arms sales in the year 2000.[11] Finally, the percentage of population engaged in various branches of the security apparatus is high by world standards. The average MENA country counts 16.2 men per thousand under arms compared to 6.31 in France, 3.92 in Brazil, and 0.33 in Ghana. In Syria, for example, the number is

26, in Bahrain it is 33.8, in Saudi Arabia it is 9.86, and in Egypt it is
10.87.[12]

How do these countries sustain such elaborate coercive apparatuses? Here is where access to rent comes into play, a quality that has
long distinguished the region (Anderson 1987: 9–12; Luciani 1990:
85–99; Crystal 1995; Chaudhry 1989; Vandewalle 1998; Ross 2001).
Many, though not all, MENA states are major recipients of rentier
income. Their rent derives from different endowments: petroleum resources, gas resources, geostrategic utility, and control of critical transit
facilities. From the more than $30 billion that the Saudi state earns each
year in oil revenue to the $2 billion that Egypt receives annually from
the United States in foreign aid, many MENA states are richly supplied
with rental income (Henry and Springborg 2001: 30–44).[13] This gives
them access to substantial discretionary resources so that even if the
country is in poor economic health overall, the state is still able to hew
to conventional economic wisdom and "pay itself first," that is, give
first priority to paying the military and security forces. Thus, while government spending on education and welfare may remain flat and economic crisis may cut into infrastructural investment, expenditure on the
security apparatus remains very high (Henry and Springborg 2001:
106).[14] In Egypt, for example, an economic crisis forced the regime to
sign an International Monetary Fund accord that required a reduction in
the subsidy of basic goods by 14 percent. This did not prevent the
regime from increasing the military budget by 22 percent that very same
year (Droz-Vincent 1999: 17). Similarly in Algeria, although civil war
has ravaged the country's economy, the army is always paid. The military apparatus remains intact thanks to Algeria's reliable dole of oil and
gas rents. In short, exceptional access to rents has nurtured a robust
coercive apparatus in many states across the region.

With regard to international support, the MENA region is exceptional for the unique position it enjoys in the international arena. As in
other regions, authoritarian states in the Middle East and North Africa
profited from the Cold War, reaping patronage from Eastern and Western great powers (sometimes simultaneously) in return for the promise
of reliable alliance in the fight for or against communism. But in contrast to other regions, the authoritarian states in the Middle East and
North Africa did not see their sources of international patronage evapo-
rate with the end of the Cold War nor with the United States' subsequent
reanimation with democracy. That is because Western interest in the
region has been driven by multiple security concerns that have survived
the Cold War. Two key concerns are assuring a reliable oil supply, a
strategically crucial resource to increasingly dependent member countries

of the Organization for Economic Cooperation and Development, and containing the Islamist threat, a menace that proved ever more alarming as Islamist radicals turned their fury toward U.S. targets at home and abroad.[15]

Both of these concerns have provided a compelling rationale to Western policymakers to persist in providing patronage to many authoritarian states in the region. As Roosevelt said about Somoza, "they may be sons of bitches but at least they are our sons of bitches."[16] Authoritarian regimes in Saudi Arabia, Egypt, Jordan, Tunisia, and Algeria have received Western support, at times in very generous proportions, because of the belief (perhaps mistaken) among Western policymakers that these regimes would be most likely to deliver on Western security concerns, assuring regular oil and gas supplies to the West and containing the Islamist threat. In short, the MENA region is exceptional in that the Cold War's end has not signaled great power retreat from patronage of authoritarianism, as has been the case in Latin America, Africa, and elsewhere (Henry and Springborg 2001: 32). Playing on the West's multiple security concerns has allowed authoritarian regimes in the region to retain international support. The West's generous provision of this support has bolstered the capacity and will of these regimes to hold on.

With regard to the third variable, patrimonialism, in most MENA countries the coercive apparatus, like the regimes themselves, is governed by patrimonial logic. Although not universal (the military in Turkey, Egypt, and Tunisia are highly institutionalized), many of the regional powerhouses, such as (preoccupation) Iraq, Syria, and Saudi Arabia, as well as lesser forces such as Jordan and Morocco, have coercive establishments shot through with patrimonialism. Personalism pervades staffing decisions. In Jordan and Morocco the king regularly appoints his male relatives to key military posts to guarantee against military rebellion (Kamrava 2000: 89). In Saudi Arabia and Syria entire branches of the military and security forces are family affairs (al-Yassini 1985; Hinnebusch 1990). Political reliability supersedes merit in promotions. In Jordan, Palestinians cannot rise above the rank of major or lieutenant colonel in combat units (Bligh 2002: 150). In Syria, an air force commander was appointed who was not even a pilot (but who was a trusted friend of Hafez al-Assad) (Zisser 2002: 118–122). Ethnic ties are used to guarantee loyalty. In (preoccupation) Iraq the elite units were overwhelmingly Sunni. In Syria they are Alawi (Rubin 2002: 7–8). Inter- and intracorp discipline is maintained by relying on balanced rivalry between primordial groups. The Syrian regime carefully balances Alawi, Sunni, and Christian leadership to maintain control. The Jordanian and Saudi regimes rely on tribal and bedouin loyalties to balance power between different corps (Satloff 1986: 60–62; Wilson and Graham 1994). The distinction between public and private is not always scrupulously observed. In Iraq and Syria the military has served as a key route to personal enrichment. It has not been unusual for generals to turn their units into personal economic fiefdoms (Zisser 2002: 119–120).

Of course not all security establishments are equally corrupted. The Jordanian military is much more rule governed than is its counterpart in Syria or (preoccupation) Iraq. Moreover, patrimonialism should not be confused with professional incompetence; many of these apparatuses are professionally well trained and equipped to handle the most modern military materiel. But patrimonialism does spell a strong personal linkage between the coercive apparatus and the regime it serves; it makes for the coercive apparatus's personal identification with the regime and the regime's longevity and thus fosters resistance to political reform.

Why this resistance? Given these patrimonial conditions, the prospect of political reform represents the prospect of ruin for the elite of the coercive apparatus. Political opening and popular accountability would deprive the Alawi officer in Syria of his special perquisites, if not his very life. Regime change would jeopardize the predominance of favored tribal elites in the Jordanian and Saudi militaries. Furthermore, few of these officers could expect to ride electoral politics to power, Roh Tae Woo style, because of the failure of these patrimonially driven apparatuses to deliver on national goals as brilliantly as did Roh Tae Woo. To the contrary, these officers have every incentive to close ranks behind the old authoritarian system, shoring it up even when natural calamity provides an opportunity for opening. This was evident in the case of Syria where the ruling dictator's final surrender to old age and illness might have created an opportunity for political opening in that country had the leaders of the coercive apparatus not closed ranks around the old system and persuaded the dictator's son that the country's best interests lay with the persistence of the ancien régime.

The prevalence of patrimonialism is by no means exceptional to the MENA region. Similar logic governs regimes in Africa, Asia, and beyond. But the low level of institutionalization in the region's coercive apparatuses constitutes one more factor explaining the robust will of so many to thwart political reform.

As for our fourth variable, popular mobilization on behalf of political reform remains weak. Nowhere in the region do you see mammoth, cross-class coalitions mobilizing on the streets to push for reform as in South Korea. Consequently, in most MENA countries, the costs of repression are relatively low. And even where mobilization has been higher, as in Syria in the 1980s or Algeria in the 1990s, when Islamists

managed to mobilize impressive numbers on the side of political reform, the state proved able to lessen the costs of repression, that is, the
potential loss of domestic legitimacy or international support, by playing on the special threat posed by these particular forces. Because the
mobilized had an Islamist face, the regime could cast the mobilization
as a threat to order and security for both domestic and international constituencies. And this approach succeeded. The Algerian state was able to
count on continued French patronage for quite a few years by emphasizing the danger of the Islamist menace. And even Assad's brutal massacre at Hama won him some popular support on the grounds: "Better
one month of Hama than fourteen years of civil war as in Lebanon"
(Friedman 1989: 101).

The low level of popular mobilization for political reform is not
limited to the MENA region and to some extent it is a consequence of
some of the absent prerequisites of democracy such as poverty and low
levels of literacy. However, there are additional factors that reduce popular enthusiasm for democratic reform in the MENA region. First,
experiments in political liberalization are historically identified with
colonial domination rather than self-determination (in contrast to the
experience in India). Earlier half-hearted attempts carried out under
British and French mandates were more window dressing for foreign
domination than substantive experiments in self-rule. Second, there is
no prolonged prior experience with democracy that might have put in
place the institutional foundations for popular mobilization, such as
mass-based parties or labor unions (in contrast to the experience of
many Latin American countries). Third, a counterparadigm exists that
offers an ideologically rich and inspiring alternative to the liberal democratic vision (in contrast to the experience of Eastern Europe after the
fall of communism). Although Islamist ideologies need not be posed as
an alternative to liberal democratic world views, they often are developed in this way for reasons of political expedience. Fourth, the presence of this nondemocratic Islamist threat demobilizes much of the traditional constituency for democratic activism, namely the secular and
educated elements of the middle class.

But no matter the explanation, low levels of popular mobilization
for democratic reform are a reality in the MENA region. They lower the
costs of repression for the coercive apparatus and increase the likelihood that the security establishment will resort to force to thwart reform
initiatives.

Of course there is one dramatic example in the MENA region where
popular mobilization for political reform did succeed in bringing on
regime change. That is the case of Iran. Millions of Iranians participated

in mass protests to bring down the shah, and popular mobilization played a key role in the revolution's success, not least for the profound impact it exercised on the military. Although the military retained the physical capacity to repress the protestors, its will was sapped by the potentially enormous cost of repression, not least to the institutional integrity of the military itself. Faced with masses of civilians bearing flowers and chanting religious slogans, many soldiers refused to shoot, desertions mounted, and outright mutinies against the upper ranks multiplied. Fearing for the institutional integrity of the armed forces, the chief of staff declared the military's "neutrality" toward the revolution and sealed the fate of the old regime (Kurzman 1996: 165). In short, high levels of popular mobilization in Iran raised the cost of repression sufficiently to undermine the coercive apparatus's will to repress.[17]

A fifth variable, the existence of a credible threat, has been suggested by some to explain the robustness of the coercive apparatus in many MENA countries. Given the centrality of the Arab-Israeli conflict to the politics of the region, some analysts link the robustness of the region's authoritarianism to the existential threat posed by Israel to its Arab neighbors and to the subsequent construction of large military apparatuses by many Arab states in order to face down that threat. No doubt the prevalence of interstate conflict in the region (including but not limited to the Arab-Israeli conflict) has played an important role in reinforcing authoritarianism in the region.[18] But analysts who champion this explanation must account for the fact that the robustness of coercive apparatuses in Arab states correlates neither geographically nor temporally with the threat posed by Israel. Geographically, the arc of authoritarianism in the MENA region far exceeds the fly zone of the Israeli air force—that is, MENA countries far removed from the epicenter of the conflict (e.g., Saudi Arabia, Morocco) still share the region's propensity for robust coercive apparatuses. Temporally, reduction in the existential threat posed by Israel has not spelled commensurate decline in the size of the coercive apparatus. Egypt, for example, has known twenty-five years of cold peace with Israel, yet this threat reduction has not been matched by any comparable reduction in the size of the country's military budget (Droz-Vincent 1999: 17).

Conclusion

The exceptionalism of the Middle East and North Africa lies not so much in absent prerequisites of democracy as in present conditions that foster the robustness of authoritarianism and especially a robust and politically tenacious coercive apparatus. Some conditions responsible for the robustness of this authoritarianism are exceptional to the Middle East and North Africa; others are not. Access to abundant rent distinguishes the region and subsidizes much of the cost of these over-developed coercive apparatuses. Multiple Western security concerns in the region guarantee continuous international support to authoritarian regimes in the Middle East and North Africa even in the wake of the Cold War. But added to this are factors by no means unique to the region, such as the prevalence of patrimonialism in state structures and the low level of popular mobilization. Together these factors reinforce the coercive apparatus's capacity and will to prevent democratic reform.

For other regions, the experience of the Middle East and North Africa draws our attention to the persistent importance of structural factors and, most important, the character of state institutions, in charting a country's susceptibility to democratic transition. The sudden and pervasive turn toward democracy in Latin America during the 1980s played a key role in discrediting socioeconomic determinism in theories of democratic transition, highlighting the centrality of elite choice and voluntarism in establishing democracy (Remmer 1989). The dramatic transition to democracy that swept sub-Saharan Africa and Eastern Europe in the 1990s drew attention to the important role popular mobilization can play in bringing down authoritarian regimes (Bratton and van de Walle 1997; Banac 1992). But the stubborn persistence of authoritarianism in the Middle East and North Africa highlights an equally powerful lesson. Where patrimonial institutions are wedded to coercive capacity, authoritarianism is likely to endure. In this context, regime elites possess both the will and the capacity to suppress democratic initiative. And where international support and financing is forthcoming to the authoritarian regime, rapid regime change in unlikely (Brownlee 2002b; Snyder 1998).

Given this analysis, some may be tempted to argue that removal of the coercive apparatus, perhaps by decisive external intervention, could end authoritarianism and spell democracy in regions so plagued. Unfortunately, the analysis presented here does not support this view. The four variables identified above explain the robustness of the coercive apparatuses in many MENA countries and their will to suppress democratic initiative. This analysis says little about the conditions necessary to implant democracy itself. For while the removal of democracy-suppressing coercive apparatuses is a necessary condition for democratic transition and consolidation, it is not sufficient. A host of conditions including a minimal level of elite commitment, a minimal level of national solidarity, a minimal level of per capita GNP, and perhaps most important of all, the creation of impartial and effective state institutions must be present. Effective bureaucracies, police, and judiciaries that can deliver a predictable rule of law and order are essential for democracy to flourish. To a large degree, order is prior to democracy. Democracy cannot thrive in chaos.[19]

Sadly, countries with a history of patrimonial rule are greatly disadvantaged in this institutional endowment. Personalistic regimes, by definition, privilege government by the ruler's discretion, not the rule of law. Generally, patrimonial regimes do not have the effective and impartial bureaucracies, police, and other state institutions that are essential for a robust democracy. This is why successful consolidation of democracy in postpatrimonial regimes is especially challenging (Chehabi and Linz 1998a: 48).

In the absence of effective state institutions, removing an oppressive coercive apparatus will not spell democracy but rather the rise of authoritarianism of a different stripe or, worse, chaos. To anchor democracy in the region, political reformers must focus on building effective, impartial state institutions, nurturing associations that reach across ethnic lines and unite people around common economic and cultural interests, as well as fostering economic growth that will tip per capita GNP into the magic zone of democratic possibility—statistically between $4,500 and $5,500. This challenge is gargantuan but is little different from that facing countless countries around the world. In facing this challenge, as in so many ways, the MENA region is hardly exceptional at all.

Notes

I gratefully acknowledge the critical comments of Lisa Anderson, Michele Penner Angrist, Mia Bloom, Jason Brownlee, Jose Chebub, Larry Diamond, Kenneth Erickson, Gregory Gause, Barbara Geddes, Daniel Gingerich, Steven Heydemann, Michael Hudson, Samuel Huntington, Alan Jacobs, Pauline Jones-Luong, Vickie Langohr, Ellen Lust-Okar, Nelson Kasfir, Augustus Richard Norton, Susan Pharr, Marsha Pripstein Posusney, Bruce Rutherford, Paul Salem, Benjamin Smith, Lily Tsai, Lucan Ways, Carrie Rosefsky Wickham, the members of the Harvard University Research Workshop on Comparative Politics, and two anonymous readers at *Comparative Politics*. Thanks also to Theresa House for assistance in researching this chapter.

1. The Middle East and North Africa is defined here to include the countries of the Arab world plus Iran, Israel, and Turkey. This includes twenty-one countries: Algeria, Bahrain, Egypt, Iran, Iraq, Israel, Jordan, Kuwait, Lebanon, Libya, Morocco, Oman, the Palestinian National Authority (PNA), Qatar, Saudi Arabia, Syria, Sudan, Tunisia, Turkey, the United Arab Emirates (UAE), and Yemen. I have excluded four countries that are members of the Arab League

but whose geographic remoteness disqualifies them from conventional conceptions of the MENA region. They are Somalia, Mauritania, Djibouti, and the Comoros Islands.

2. Israel and Turkey meet the standards of electoral democracy today, defined as a regime that chooses its government through regular, free, competitive elections. In 1972 Lebanon did as well (Freedom House, "Freedom in the World: 2002," www.freedomhouse.org, 7). For the distinction between electoral and liberal democracy, see Diamond (1996).

3. Freedom House, www.freedomhouse.org, 5–7. Note that Freedom House's division of the world places Turkey in Europe and the PNA in a separate category called "Disputed Territories." Thus, neither country appears in Freedom House's statistics for the MENA region. I have diverged from Freedom House's convention and included both Turkey and the PNA in my MENA counts.

4. The UN's Arab Human Development Report 2002 reports that government expenditures as a percentage of gross domestic product average at 30 percent in the Arab world, though this is likely an underestimate given that many oil-rich states such as Saudi Arabia and the UAE were not included in the count.

5. For poverty levels and illiteracy rates, see Economic Research Forum for the Arab Countries, Iran, and Turkey (2002: 23, 102). Note that the illiteracy rate cited excludes Israel, which registers 4 percent adult illiteracy. For human development data, see UNDP (2001). Interestingly, according to Page (1998), "the MENA region has the lowest regional incidence of extreme poverty with less than 2.5% of the population living on or below $1/day." In fact, MENA countries have, on average, one of the most equal income distribution in the world, although even this distribution spells significant income inequality. See UNDP (2001: 90); and World Bank (2002: 230–235).

6. Recall the pronouncements of Singapore's prime minister Lee Kuan Yew that "Asian values" are contrary to democracy. See also Pye (1985); Wiarda (1974); and Huntington (1991: 72–85). For an excellent overview of the debate on political culture and democracy, see Diamond (1993) and Diamond (1999: 161–217). Perhaps the most powerful critique of any deterministic association between religious tradition and authoritarianism, and specifically between Islam and authoritarianism, is made by a nonspecialist in the region, Al Stepan. In his piece "Religion, Democracy, and the 'Twin Tolerations,'" Stepan (2001) emphasizes the multivocality of all great religious traditions (including Islam) and their potential for reconciliation with democratic ideals. He provides empirical support for the possibility of Islam's reconciliation with democracy by pointing to both Muslim majority countries that nonetheless sustain electoral democracies (Indonesia, Turkey, Bangladesh) as well as to the millions of Muslims who reside in established democracies in India, Europe, and the United States, without injury to their religious identity.

7. In Egypt, for example, the president retains control over promotions above brigadier, has a final say over the military's budget, and has proven able to dismiss popular military leaders such as Abu Ghazala when the later proved *too* popular. At the same time, the military retains control over independent sources of financing, seems to be exercising veto power over the designation of Hosni Mubarak's successor, and has saved the regime from fatal attack on at least three occasions. See Droz-Vincent (1999); Sobelman (2001); and Sfak-

ianakis and Springborg (2001). Similarly, in Syria, the balance of power is unclear. The late dictator Hafez al-Assad was able to dismiss powerful Special Forces commander Ali Haydar over a difference in policy, but Assad also had to court the favor of the military to ensure the succession of his son Bashar to the presidency. See Brooks (1998).

8. Mohammad Harbi is the author of this motto, cited in *Le Soir de Bruxelles,* January 11, 2002. Thanks to Reda Bensmaia for alerting me to this. Droz-Vincent (1999: 16) identifies this as Mirabeau's original insight.

9. The impact of such a shift is evident even prior to the end of the Cold War. See Snyder (1998: 73) and Booth (1998: 148).

10. Popular mobilization should also not be confused with the variable "civil society" in that it encompasses and exceeds this variable, embracing more spontaneous and short-lived movements such as demonstrations and riots and not limiting itself to the more institutionalized components of associational life such as labor unions, businessmen's associations, and NGOs.

11. According to the IISS (International Institute of Strategic Studies), "the MENA continues to be the world's leading arms market . . . in absolute terms" (IISS 2002: 119).

12. Compiled from Ibid, 128. Note that the size of the coercive apparatus alone does not spell the relative robustness of authoritarianism. A country may boast a very large military and still be democratic, as is the case in the United States. Similarly, Israel manages to sustain a democratic political system despite the very large size of its military in relative terms (i.e., measured in terms of military expenditure as share of GNP or percentage of population under arms). So long as the coercive apparatus is subject to civilian control, large size is compatible with democracy.

13. Henry and Springborg (2001) give a very substantive account of the diverse rents harvested by MENA countries. Although they detect a declining trend in rents earned by MENA countries in recent years, this income is still substantial. For example, oil income alone accounted for more than 50 percent of government revenues in about half of MENA countries in the late 1990s.

14. The very high level of government expenditure on the military is documented for eighteen MENA countries in Henry and Springborg (2001: 106). In many MENA countries 25 percent (or more) of government expenditure is spent on the military and in some the proportion is significantly higher, including the Sudan (55 percent), the UAE (48 percent), and Saudi Arabia (37 percent).

15. Preserving the security of Israel might be a third concern, although this seems to be a more U.S. than a fully Western preoccupation. See Hawthorne (2001).

16. Thanks to Steve Levitsky for reminding me of this salty quotation.

17. Of course high levels of popular mobilization were not the only reason the military folded. Also at work were the weak administrative structure of the military (which was left "headless" after the shah's departure) as well as the sense among the generals that the United States had abandoned the shah. For more, see Arjomand (1988: 121–129).

18. Besides providing rhetorical legitimation for coercive regimes, persistent conflict has rationalized the prolonged states of emergency that stifle civil liberties in many MENA countries. For more on the role of interstate conflict and its relation to authoritarianism, see Gause (1995: 283–306).

19. Again, no single variable is ever universally necessary or sufficient to determine an outcome as complex as democratic transition or consolidation. But thirty years of experience tracking democratic transitions suggests that the chances for democracy are favored when per capita GNP rises above $5,500, when there is popular consensus about national solidarity, and when elites are persuaded that democratic institutions are the least-worst way to handle conflict. See Bellin (2003); Carothers (2002); and Ottaway et al. (2002).

3

Political Crisis and Restabilization: Iraq, Libya, Syria, and Tunisia

JASON BROWNLEE

Authoritarian rulers in the Middle East have operated very similarly to autocrats elsewhere—they have tried to stay in power when challenged and have often responded to domestic opposition with brutal crackdowns. What distinguishes Middle Eastern regimes is that these responses have occurred in a context of independence from foreign pressure to respect human rights and enable democratization. Consequently, regimes from North Africa to the Persian Gulf have survived for decades while similar governments in other parts of the world have collapsed. The cause is not cultural, but political, and originates in the capacity of rulers to repress their opponents through unrestrained violence.

When one looks at the Arab states of the Middle East in comparison to countries around the world, the endurance of their authoritarian systems seems extraordinary. Although personalistic regimes have fallen throughout sub-Saharan Africa, for example, the Middle East displays a wealth of similarly corrupt dictatorships that remain in power (Bratton and van de Walle 1997; Geddes 1999a). Yet long periods of political continuity in the region also contain significant episodes of contestation between rulers and proponents of change. These crises have not been treated in the comparative politics literature on regime change, giving the impression that the durability of Arab regimes stems from factors unique to the region. Explanations have tended to focus on religious culture or political traditions before exhausting conventional analysis of incumbent leaders and their challengers. An investigation into opposition attempts at ousting authoritarian rulers provides an alternative and less particularistic account: autocratic leaders have actively prevented domestic political transformations by deploying coercive organizations to suppress their foes. Hence, the salient difference between the Arab World and other regions is not the culture of the local population but the strength of the state's repressive apparatus.

As in other parts of the world, oppressed groups in the Middle East have regularly worked to end dictatorial rule. They have, however, been less successful than similar movements elsewhere, primarily because the regimes in power have proven more willing and able to deploy violence against their opponents. This propensity for unleashing violence to stay in power, and the consequent outcome of regime endurance, does not represent an exceptional causal pattern. Rather, when viewed along with cases of authoritarian breakdown elsewhere, Middle East states provide examples linking high levels of repressive capacity to low values in regime change. This unsurprising formula behind Arab regimes' resilience bolsters the wealth of evidence behind mainstream theories of change that consider institutions and the strength of competing factions.

This chapter elaborates on this nonparticularistic explanation for sustained authoritarian rule in the Middle East, presenting evidence from four crises survived by Arab regimes in which power is concentrated in a single leader: Syria (1982), Tunisia (1987), Iraq (1991), and Libya (1993). These regimes were just as arbitrary and corrupt as dictatorships outside the region, but the repressive capacity brought to bear against their challengers was not as constrained by an external patron. Consequently, they were able to survive crises, while similar regimes elsewhere fell. Thus, personalistic authoritarian rule, when unrestrained by patron states, can *enable* regimes to withstand challenges that would otherwise lead to transitions. The case studies replicate the format of conventional accounts in the transitions literature, considering the strength of forces supporting the regime (hard-liners) and those involved in the typical countercoalition (soft-liners and oppositionists). Their record indicates the importance of external backers restraining state repression, a factor that may have been underemphasized in studies of successful regime change.

In this chapter, I discuss how the regime change literature's lacuna regarding Middle Eastern authoritarianism can be filled. Comparativists can bridge exceptionalist accounts, which disregard the region or invoke culturalist variables to explain its politics, by recognizing that regime stability provides valuable empirical contrast to studies of change. Giving explicit attention to hard-liners as actors in the two possible transition scenarios—change versus restabilization—enables us to integrate Arab autocracies into a holistic and parsimonious account of political development during the recent era of democratization known as the "third wave" (Huntington 1991). I then present each episode of regime survival and conclude with implications for domestically driven regime change during the international war on terrorism. Lending support to the argument presented in Chapter 2 by Eva Bellin, the critical variables accounting for authoritarian durability in these cases prove to be extensive repressive capacity and minimal externally imposed constraints on its use.

Connecting Transitions Studies and Middle East Research

The literature on regime change has tended to treat the Middle East as an oddity on the map of worldwide democratization. Arab states that have known tremendous political continuity have either been excluded from comparative work or explained through culturalist approaches that had earlier lost currency in the field. On one hand, projects dealing with political transitions have focused primarily on cases of change and implicitly left the Middle East aside. On the other, studies addressing Middle Eastern states have not related examples of authoritarian durability to instances of authoritarian breakdown elsewhere. The natural result is an analytical gap that prevents dialogue between these two literatures. This fissure in explanations can be easily mended, however, by applying the tools of transitions studies to the countries of the Middle East. Examining the processes and outcomes of major opposition challenges enables comparativists to evaluate competing hypotheses (e.g., culturalist, institutionalist) in terms of how well they explain new cases. When one reviews earlier projects on democratization, the absence of explanations for Middle Eastern regime outcomes is striking. The foundational works in the field took political change as a criterion for case selection and either implicitly or explicitly excluded the Middle East (O'Donnell and Schmitter 1986; Diamond, Linz, and Lipset 1988; Higley and Gunther 1991). This approach ran counter to methodological conventions regarding variations in outcomes (Geddes 1990; King, Keohane, and Verba 1994) and hindered a causal explanation of the breakdown of authoritarianism. The focus on cases that experienced the phenomenon of interest (regime change) fundamentally impaired explanation of that outcome. Without cases of continuity to provide the needed contrast, comparativists cannot adequately answer the question why change here, but not there? How are we to know, for example, whether the factors that purportedly sparked transitions from authoritarian rule in southern Europe were not also present in North Africa, a region where authoritarianism persisted? Scholars had reacted to the differences the Middle East exhibited in comparison to other regions by isolating it rather than incorporating it in otherwise regionally diverse projects. The Middle East was deemed peculiar, while the unusual method of case selection that excluded Middle Eastern regimes was widely accepted. Nor was this tendency limited to the study of regime change. The Arab states and Iran constituted only 3.4 percent of the cases covered in three major comparative politics journals from 1982 to 1997 (Hull 1999: 120).

Recent studies have taken this supposed Middle Eastern exceptionalism as a starting point for analysis. Several prominent works have revisited culturalist explanations that had lost currency during the rapid spread of democracy around the globe (for the shift away from culture and preconditions, see Rustow 1970; O'Donnell and Schmitter 1986; and Anderson 1999). Invoking Islamic culture or Arab political traits, projects have looked at macro-level correlations between society and national-level regimes (Fish 2002; Berman 2003; Stepan and Robertson 2003). This research, however, has not provided a complete causal chain linking the explanatory variables to the outcome of interest and does not closely attend to the political actors and conflicts that were the focus of earlier regime change studies. Consequently, renewed attention to the Middle East has not necessarily filled the literature's gaps.

Transitions studies lacked Middle East cases. Culturalist explanations of Middle Eastern authoritarianism have suffered from the opposite fault, neglecting the actors involved in struggles for change. By considering opposition challenges that drew regimes into crisis, students of Middle East politics can strengthen the transitions literature. While doing so they can also determine whether the region's regimes are best explained through the idea of local antidemocratic traditions or instead through less unusual variables, such as political institutions and state capacity.

Regime Crises Without Transitions

Cases of change select themselves (e.g., Cuba 1959, Iran 1979, the Philippines 1986), but the task of finding counterfactual "crises survived" falls to the researcher. Comparativists can look beyond moments of stasis and continuity and choose those historical instances when the regime could have fallen but did not—when the leader could have gone the way of Cuban dictator Fulgencio Batista, the shah of Iran, or Philippine president Ferdinand Marcos, but instead withstood the revolt raised against him. For the field of regime studies and democratization, this approach means considering the stability of some authoritarian regimes alongside the replacement of others by new political systems. Moments of political contestation that resulted in regime restabilization rather than collapse provide the appropriate contrast cases to examples of change (Garfinkel 1981: 21–25). Public challenges to authoritarianism in the Middle East help scholars evaluate why the region has known such long-lived dictatorships.

This study covers four episodes that threatened authoritarian breakdown but did not force the regime from power. Viewed along with the extensive literature cited above, these cases counterbalance instances of change with crises survived. The method and format extends the approach applied in earlier transitions studies to cases of regime continuity. I look at the actions of those involved, recognizing that democracy often arises as an unintended by-product amid struggles between forces not ideologically committed to democracy (Rustow 1970). Additionally, I treat moments of potential authoritarian breakdown as the first contest in a multistage process of breakdown, transition, and consolidation. The end of a dictatorship is a necessary but insufficient condition for the inauguration of representative democracy. It follows that an explanation for the lack of democracy in the Arab World should begin with an explanation for the lack of regime change, namely, regime survival of domestic political conflicts.

The contestants in such challenges include both the pro-change opposition coalition and those forces trying to prevent the regime's collapse, loyalists in the state's political and military organs. Transitions projects have tended to focus on regime soft-liners and societal opposition forces as the key agents of political change. Yet, just as scholars measure the strength of soft-liners and opposition activists for bringing about transition, one should also weigh the regime's ability to *resist* change and *avert* breakdown. Committed incumbent hard-liners also played a role, albeit a losing one, by seeking to maintain authoritarian rule in the successful transition cases (O'Donnell and Schmitter 1986: 19).

In personalistic regimes, those systems in which a legal-rational order is subordinated to the whims of a central leading figure who rules arbitrarily, the critical determinants of hard-liner strength are the regime's penetration of state and society and its level of independence from externally imposed pressure. State penetration refers to the ability of the regime's most committed elements to subordinate state military and bureaucratic institutions to their agenda. For example, to what extent has the leadership "undermined the autonomy of the armed forces through patronage (for example, by subverting its organizational hierarchy and replacing it with a hierarchy based on loyalty to his person, and by dividing the officer corps)?" (Snyder 1998: 53). Penetration of society involves the extension of regime control to the monitoring and management of nonstate political activity. "When the dictator's patronage network is inclusive, penetrating deeply into society, political space for opposition groups is narrow because these vertical patron-client linkages both co-opt elites and extend the reach of the state's surveillance and control" (Snyder 1998: 55). As Richard Snyder writes, personalistic "dictators are often dependent on foreign patrons, who supply critical *military aid and material resources* that can help fuel their domestic patronage networks" (1998: 58, emphasis added). At the same time, these external backers may limit the incumbents' options when facing opposition.

The following studies of Syria, Tunisia, Iraq, and Libya illustrate how regimes use force to maintain power and why such repression can produce restabilization rather than transition. These four highly corrupt and arbitrary regimes represent personalistic dictatorships, the collapse of which has been analyzed elsewhere (Snyder 1992, 1998; Bratton and van de Walle 1998; Geddes 1999a). The accounts of short-term, serious crises show that while a regime's networks of control may foment dissent, they can also help it endure these challenges when they arise. Specifically, when external powers do not limit the repressive capacity of a neopatrimonial regime, the personalization of state institutions enables rulers to survive the threats their despotism sows. Contrary to claims that the corruption of legal-rational procedures undermines authoritarian regimes (Chehabi and Linz 1998a: 5), it is the *constraint* upon personalistic rulers—mainly by an external superpower—that often brings their downfall. And it is that limitation, rather than certain non-Arab cultural qualities, that the Middle East has lacked.

The Hama Revolt in Syria

From 1970 through 2000, Hafez al-Assad ruled Syria through a system of repression and personal networks. Security organizations and a pervasive cult of personality surrounded the president and strengthened his grip (see Wedeen 1999). He filled the military and upper-level offices with his extended family and focused patronage upon his Alawi allies in Syrian society. This combination provoked broad dissent. But when opposition arose, Assad was unfettered by foreign backers demanding restraint (Ahmad 1982). He brutally suppressed his most active opponents, the Muslim Brotherhood, when they challenged his forces in the city of Hama. Heavy repression ended the opposition's effort to change the regime. Since then Syria has seen twenty more years of continued authoritarianism, including Bashar al-Assad's assumption of the presidency after his father's death.

While real political power rested in Assad's "absolute presidency" (Perthes 1995: 139), Assad, like other neopatrimonial leaders, cloaked his authority in institutions of so-called democratic and populist governance. These included presidential elections affirming Assad with over 99 percent of the vote (EIU 2000c: 6) and the maintenance of the Baath Party tradition that began in 1963 (Heydemann 1999: 6–7). Yet Assad actually ruled through his extended family. His brother, Rifa't, headed the armed forces until he led a failed coup attempt in 1983. And most of Assad's other chief ministers came from his religious sect, the Alawis, which make up 11 percent of the population (Batatu 1982: 20). Religious and familial affiliation offered crucial access to power (Perthes 1995: 180). Financial and political resources flowed mainly to the Alawis, who held key posts in the "officer corps, the internal security forces, and the Ba'ath party" (Drysdale 1982: 4). Such patronage linked the "fate of the Alawi community to [Assad's] personal fortunes," driving a wedge between the regime's partisans and its potential opponents (Michaud 1982: 30).

Assad allied with the Soviet Union, but his regime was never as dependent upon Soviet backing as a satellite state as was, for example, Romania. During the Cold War, Syria received military aid and equipment from the Soviet Union (EIU 2000c: 8). However, Arab countries also gave $600 million annually to Syria because of its role as a front-line state against Israel (Perthes 1995: 33–34). Consequently, Assad was not beholden to one particular patron and was free to deploy his military against domestic opponents. Assad's greatest domestic threat arose when the Muslim Brotherhood rebelled in the town of Hama.

The Syrian Muslim Brotherhood grew in the late 1970s as a branch of the Egyptian Muslim Brotherhood. Their program called for political reform, including citizens' rights, an end to torture, and the rule of law (Batatu 1982: 13–14). Syria's professional unions—potential allies in the struggle for change—also pressed for political liberalization, but they were forcibly disbanded and their leadership incarcerated (Perthes 1995: 137). The Brotherhood's campaign consisted of guerilla raids on government officials and public buildings (Batatu 1982: 20), but in the spring of 1982 they challenged the regime even more directly.

In February 1982 the Brotherhood ambushed a Syrian army unit searching the town of Hama for members of the opposition. Suddenly emboldened, Brotherhood activists and supporters mobilized to take control of the city and hold it. Assad responded by laying siege to Hama with a force of twelve thousand soldiers, some of whom were withdrawn from Lebanon for the battle. Yet the fighting stretched on for more than two weeks, as the Brotherhood's resistance posed "a severe challenge to the regime" (Lawson 1982: 24). Assad's forces blocked off the city, barraged it with "heavy artillery, tanks, and helicopter gunships" (Drysdale 1982: 9) and obliterated entire residential sections. In Patrick Seale's words, it became "a last-ditch battle which one side or the other had to win and which, one way or the other, would decide the fate of the country" (Seale 1988: 332–333). Although well organized and determined, the Brotherhood was still fighting a regime that spent 30 percent of its total budget on the military and could deploy its force internally. In the end the opposition was simply overpowered (Drysdale 1982: 7). Syria's armed forces numbered two hundred thirty thousand. (In comparison, Brazil's military was only two hundred seventy-four thousand, while its population was thirteen times that of Syria.) The regime's siege eventually crushed the Brotherhood's resistance movement, taking the lives of between five thousand and twenty-five thousand civilians (Lawson 1982: 24; Perthes 1995: 137) as well as another one thousand soldiers (Batatu 1982: 20).

Assad's dictatorship stirred unrest, but it also proved capable of repressing the largest challenge that erupted. As despotic and nepotistic as other autocrats, he averted the overthrow of his dictatorship through an unrestrained use of force.

The Constitutional Coup in Tunisia

Tunisia's experience presents the continuation of an authoritarian regime despite a leadership transition from one personalistic ruler to another. Although Tunisia's crisis in 1987 resulted in Habib Bourguiba's removal from power, the regime reconsolidated around a new presidential figure. Therefore, the Tunisian case differs from that of Syria, because the regime's survival and restabilization coincided with a limited change in its head elite. In fact, the conditions producing Prime Minister Zine El Abidine Ben Ali's 1987 "constitutional coup" show that the leadership was ill-prepared to handle domestic opposition when it came. Shallow penetration of the state's military and civil society meant Bourguiba faced threats from outside the regime as well as from soft-liner elites who could move against the ruler. But moderate dissidents and soft-liners did not join forces. Subsequently, military and civilian soft-liners removed the regime's head but did not turn over power to the opposition. In the years since, President Ben Ali has rebuilt and strengthened the regime, which now allows little room for dissent.

After assuming the presidency in 1956, Habib Bourguiba centralized power in an overtly patrimonial style. Although he officially led as president, Bourguiba assumed the title of "Supreme Warrior" and encouraged a public cult of personality (Moore 1970: 330). He considered himself the incarnation of the Tunisian nation and shaped the government into a presidential monarchy (Moore 1965: 46, 71). When asked about his role in the Tunisian political system, Bourguiba once answered, "System? What system? I *am* the system!" (Moore 1970: 330). He often shuffled cabinet members and top officials in order to cut off alternate bases of power. Political influence depended on personal connection to the president, and Bourguiba's secretary held more clout than some cabinet members (Moore 1965: 93–94). A majority of Tunisians looked to Bourguiba to provide them with jobs and essentials (Waltz 1991: 31), and the president often entertained such supplications directly, allowing personal audiences to make requests (Moore 1965: 82).

Unlike the Baathist regime of Assad, Tunisian politics under Bourguiba was not saturated by secret police and parallel militaries. With a 98 percent Arab Muslim population, Bourguiba did not face, nor could he exploit, the ethnic and sectarian divisions of Syrian society. But by the end of his third decade in power, Bourguiba's links to Tunisian society had begun to weaken, and popular discontent rose (Paul 1984: 3). During economic adjustment, Bourguiba received minimal support from the United States and none from the Soviet Union. Instead, he leaned toward the Arab World and also relied upon the European Community, especially France (Deeb and Laipson 1991: 222). Drawing upon multiple external backers, Bourguiba maintained his resolve, unhindered from the outside when he faced insurgents in the aftermath of an economic crisis.

Pressured by the International Monetary Fund to reform Tunisia's largely state-supported economy, Bourguiba's government reduced subsidies on bread and other dietary staples at the end of 1983. Subsequently, prices for bread doubled in the first week of 1984 and spontaneous riots erupted nationwide. The regime then announced a state of emergency and sent in the police, National Guard, and army to suppress the protests (Seddon 1984: 7). The crackdown killed 150 Tunisians and wounded thousands more, but the unrest continued until Bourguiba announced the reintroduction of subsidies and the extension of other social safety nets (Paul 1984: 5). For Tunisia's Islamic Tendency Movement (Mouvement de la Tendance Islamique, or MTI), which sought nonviolent political reform but had been denied government approval to form a party, the 1984 riots demonstrated how the regime's modernization program had failed to provide for its citizens' needs (Boulby 1989: 591).

Excluded and discontent, the MTI escalated its struggle against Bourguiba in 1987. The movement organized a series of strikes among university students, a major base of its support (Boulby 1989: 606). The regime responded harshly. Interior minister Ben Ali arrested and incarcerated an estimated 1,270 Islamists, with unofficial estimates placing the figure at three thousand. But the opposition pressed on, holding another seventy to eighty protests in the wake of the mass arrests (Hermassi 1991: 195). Despite government efforts at suppression, the MTI remained the "best organized and most politically influential" (Boulby 1989: 602) opposition organization in Tunisian politics. This incessant pressure on Bourguiba led him to appoint Ben Ali prime minister in September 1987 (Boulby 1989: 611). Ben Ali's experience in containing the Islamists qualified him for resolving the tension between the regime and the MTI. Yet popular unrest grew further as Bourguiba became obsessed about the fate of Islamist leaders already in custody. On the night of November 6, 1987, Ben Ali gathered a group of physicians who declared Bourguiba physically unfit to rule. In accordance with Tunisia's Constitution, Prime Minister Ben Ali assumed the presidency the following day (Murphy 1999: 77–78).

The MTI, most Tunisians, and the international community welcomed Ben Ali's constitutional coup, and the new president soon proposed a "National Pact" that seemed to accommodate the opposition's calls for authentic multipartyism. Ben Ali thus resolved Tunisia's crisis by replacing the regime's leader and preparing the country for political liberalization. Structural change was illusory, though, and it soon became clear that Ben Ali's surface modifications masked fundamental continuities. In retrospect, the National Pact seems to have been a strategic ploy that appeased the MTI while Ben Ali stabilized his own position. Continuation of the Tunisian regime under Ben Ali thus differs from the crisis survived by Assad since Bourguiba himself lost power. The absence of a viable alliance of soft-liners and moderates may stem from the lack of a formidable radical movement (maximalist opposition) that could otherwise have pushed Tunisia's soft-liners into a more substantial alliance with the moderate opposition (Bermeo 1997).

The 1991 Uprising in Iraq

Until his removal from power in the spring of 2003, Saddam Hussein's regime relied on the same kind of pervasive personalism found in infamous dictatorships like Papa Doc's Haiti and Mobutu Sese Seko's Zaire. Yet those states never endured the kind of broad dissent Hussein confronted in 1991. Shortly after Iraq withdrew from Kuwait, Shia in the south rose up against Iraq's president, and Kurds in the north soon joined them. Weakened by defeat in the U.S.-led Operation Desert Storm, Hussein's forces faced uprisings on two fronts. Still, his Republican Guard units did not retreat or turn upon their leader but instead repressed both movements and reestablished control over the country. In this way Hussein's regime proved itself able to withstand the kind of widespread revolt that toppled other leaders. Hence, Iraq illustrates how arbitrary rule provokes internal crises but may also enable the regime to repress challenger movements. Autonomy from external powers enabled a loyal military to defeat the opposition, prevent domestically driven regime change, and sustain a personalistic dictatorship. The regime would last until international war removed Hussein from power over a decade later.

Saddam Hussein's domination of state and society knew few peers. Hussein succeeded his uncle in 1979, assumed the presidency, and quickly concentrated power in his own hands such that, as one former Baathist recalled, "All discussion began to revolve around the person of Saddam" (Makiya 1993: 63). The regime fortified itself as Hussein executed past allies and placed immediate family members in the government's most vital positions. Hussein's sons, Udai and Ousai, controlled the "security apparatus and wide-ranging economic interests" and appeared to be groomed to succeed him (EIU 2000a: 5). Under the façade of a republic, Iraq's National Assembly (parliament) offered another instrument for the regime to attack its enemies. The Baath Party also cloaked a patrimonial system in which Hussein's clansmen, the Tikritis, help stabilize his control (Batatu 1978: 1084, cited in Quinlivan 1999: 139). Tikritis filled the ranks of Hussein's Republican Guard, a paramilitary force responsible for domestic security that provided the main retaliatory institution deployed in 1991 (Quinlivan 1999: 145).

Like Assad, Hussein combined family-centered rule with institutions of repression to maintain minority (here Sunni) control over a population composed mainly of Kurds and Shia. At least five overlapping intelligence agencies ensured the watchers were themselves monitored (al-Khafaji 1992: 16). Hussein also maintained a professional army and a parallel militia force for both "enemies from abroad and . . . enemies from within" (Kamrava 2000: 91). Unlike in Syria, however, Hussein's patronage spread beyond the ruler's extended family. A "vast network of informers" permeated Iraqi society (al-Khafaji 1992: 16), and he even bought off potential allies to turn them against one another. One Kurdish leader admitted that he had not helped his fellow Kurds when the army repressed them in 1975, 1988, or 1991, because he had been bribed by the regime and feared joining with forces that would probably fail (Makiya 1993: 85).

Hussein's relations with external powers fluctuated. During the 1980s the United States heavily supported Iraq and Iran in an attempt to prevent both states from expanding their influence in the region. However, the extent to which U.S. support for Iraq in the 1980s prepared Hussein for the invasion of Kuwait and his internal campaign in 1991 remains unclear (Colhoun 1992: 35–37). Hussein was not an active client of the U.S. government at the time of Desert Storm. Compared to dictators like Iran's shah or Ferdinand Marcos in the Philippines, his dependence on external patrons was minimal when Iraqis rose against him in the days after the Gulf War.

In the last days of February 1991 Iraqi tanks were retreating from Kuwait when several soldiers and commanders spoke out against Hussein. One account describes how an army commander declared, "What has befallen us of defeat, shame, and humiliation, Saddam, is the result of your follies, your miscalculations, and your irresponsible actions." From his tank, the man blasted away a mural of Hussein in the middle of Basra. A crowd grew and began chanting, "Saddam is finished." Suddenly "the barrier of fear was broken" for many Iraqis (Makiya 1993: 59–60, 62). Shia, who make up over half of Iraq's population, began demonstrations in the town of Basra. They soon gained support in other Shiite strongholds like Najaf and Karbala (al-Jabbar 1992: 8). The rebellion in the south quickly escalated into attacks on public buildings and institutions and, finally, against Hussein's agents (al-Jabbar 1992: 8). Less organized than the Muslim Brotherhood in Syria, the would-be revolutionaries still took nearly a dozen cities through strength of numbers. However, because they directed their fight against not just Saddam Hussein but also regime personnel whose loyalty was wavering (Nakash 1994: 277), their anti-regime stance reduced support among army defectors who otherwise could have bolstered their ranks (Makiya 1993: 92).

Kurdish forces in the north joined the rebellion with their own revolt. Better organized than the Shia, the Kurds were "in a position to forge a wider unity" (al-Jabbar 1992: 11–12), even letting Kurds that had worked with Hussein join them in seeking the limited goal of regional autonomy within a federal Iraq. "The rebels' own armed actions were carefully limited to punishing security servicemen and leading Ba'th cadres" (al-Jabbar 1992: 11–12). Adopting this moderate stance, they accepted deserters, who numbered in the thousands, more readily than Iraqis in the south had. The Kurds thus played the role of a classic moderate opposition force in both their goals (autonomy in a post-Hussein Iraq) and tactics (cooperation with the army defectors).

Existing Kurdish resistance organizations were also better prepared than the Shia to physically engage Hussein's forces. They occupied city after city in northern Iraq, eventually claiming Kirkuk, which lies just three hours' drive from Baghdad.

Both the Kurdish and Shiite opposition suffered, however, from a critical lack of information and did not even know which areas had risen up against Hussein (al-Jabbar 1992: 12). They also failed to connect in Baghdad, due in large part to Hussein's prior success at quelling dissent around the capital through fear and intimidation. Opposition groups from the pro-Iranian Islamic Call to the pro-Syrian Baathists remained on the sidelines as Hussein prepared to strike back. When no significant resistance arose around Baghdad and Iraq's center, the Kurds and Shia lost a crucial geographic link for their struggle. Despite the second front opened in the north, Hussein's forces marshaled a crippling response.

Akin to multiple Hama offensives, the regime's Republican Guard Units retaliated in the south with napalm bombs and scud missiles, followed by helicopter gunboats supporting a ground assault (Makiya 1993: 96). U.S. troops, amassed on the other side of the Iraqi border, stood by and watched as the Shia were suppressed (Nakash 1994: 275). Najaf fell on March 13 while the longest holdout in the south, Samawa, lasted until March 29. Kurdish forces were pushed back a few weeks later. Despite desertions and organizational disintegration following the Gulf War, four Iraqi divisions crushed resistance in the south and, later, the north.

Hussein's brutal practices did not stop all Iraqis from challenging his rule, but he was able to repel the most serious domestic effort to overthrow his dictatorship. Unimpeded control of the military's special forces and an extensive reach into Iraqi society enabled the regime to restabilize during the crisis of 1991 rather than succumb to change.

The Army Rebellion in Libya

While Muammar Qaddafi has ruled Libya since deposing its king in 1969, he has not tied Libya's military as effectively to his own position as his peers in Syria and Iraq did. Hence, he has faced threats from within the elite that Assad and Hussein largely avoided. The regime was recently shaken by an army rebellion as well as scattered attacks by the Militant Islamic Group. Qaddafi's domination of the Libyan masses—fortified by oil revenues—remains strong, but he has not undermined military autonomy as fully as Saddam Hussein had. Consequently, he has confronted—and thus far *defeated*—both a weak Islamist movement and a more formidable challenge from soldiers within his regime, who tried to remove him in 1993. Dissent arose from corners where the regime's patronage did not reach. And in both situations Qaddafi was unconstrained by foreign ties when he combated domestic foes.

Since seizing power in 1969, Qaddafi has occupied a variety of government positions yet always held ultimate authority in Libya. Institutionalized arbitrariness, a rhetoric of mass participation, and his apparent intention of passing power to his son all imbue Qaddafi's dictatorship with a distinctly personalistic character. In 1973, Qaddafi announced his alternative to capitalism and socialism, the "Third Universal Theory," which declares that "representation is deception" and the only true democracy is one in which the people rule directly (Qaddafi 1980). Subsequently, he instituted a dizzying system of committees and congresses in which Libyans serve and, on paper, govern their own affairs. In practice, Qaddafi constantly shifts the networks, ensuring that participants are ill-prepared to address substantive policy issues (Vandewalle 1998: 99). He thus strives for "statelessness," a declared aversion to codifying institutions and a practice that keeps citizens atomized and their demands disaggregated (Vandewalle 1998: 36). Behind the screen of public accountability, Qaddafi depends closely upon family members for maintaining security within his government. Following an abortive coup in 1975, Qaddafi placed relatives in top military and security positions. Like Saddam Hussein, he developed a parallel military as a check against Libya's professional armed forces, yet this "people's army" was never activated (Kamrava 2000: 82–86).

Libya's oil wealth fuels patronage on a grand scale. From 1973 until 1982 the country reaped an estimated $95 billion from oil exports, from which "virtually everyone profited, directly or indirectly" (Vandewalle 1998: 105). Serving as the central patron for the country's population, Qaddafi reduced both motive and opportunity for autonomous collective action and social dissent (Anderson 1995b: 229). Oil largesse also helps Libya maintain greater independence in its foreign relations than many other neopatrimonial leaders, even in the midst of U.S. sanctions. Far from depending on a superpower, Qaddafi has instead engaged in both ideological and military conflict with the United States. A series of U.S. bans on military exports to Libya and oil imports from Libya began in 1978. In retaliation for an alleged terrorist bombing in Berlin, the United States bombed Libya in 1986, killing an estimated thirty-seven civilians. In 1992, the UN imposed further sanctions on Libya after it refused to turn over suspects in the 1988 bombing of a Pan Am Flight over Lockerbie, Scotland, in which 270 people died (EIU 2000b: 5, 6, 12). In the spring of 2004, the United States began lifting sanctions and restoring diplomatic ties in response to Libyan reparations for the Lockerbie bombing and openness to international weapons inspections.

Since the mid-1980s, oil revenues have dipped. With reduced oil income, Qaddafi has faced several internal challenges. Accurate information on Libyan domestic politics remains limited by the regime's deliberate opacity and its restrictions on foreign researchers. Still, it is known that a half-dozen assassination and coup attempts were made against Qaddafi during the 1990s (EIU 2000b: 7). Each of these attacks offered moments for a potential change of regime, but Qaddafi's greatest threat came from his own military forces (El Fathaly and Palmer 1995: 170–171). In 1993 a splinter of the Libyan army rose up against Qaddafi and he was forced to deploy his air force to quell the ground troops' assault (Takeyh and Rose 1998). The Libyan regime survived, but the revolt showed that Qaddafi's limited penetration of the military made him more susceptible than Assad or Hussein to challenges from his own elite (El Fathaly and Palmer 1995: 170–171).

Other attacks have come from domestic Islamist movements. Since 1995, the Militant Islamic Group and the Islamic Martyr's Movement have waged an escalating insurgency campaign (EIU 2000b: 8). Fighting between the regime and Islamists in Benghazi left thirty dead in 1996 (U.S. Department of State 1996), and in 1998 Qaddafi was injured during an assassination attempt (Freedom House 1998). Still, just as the country's leader survived, so has Libya endured these opposition attacks rather than falling into a widespread civil conflict.

Explaining Authoritarian Durability

Middle East politics has been relatively isolated from the comparative study of regime change, reinforcing the impression that standard social science theories fit the region poorly. But this brief examination of specific contests for power shows the area's peculiarity has been overstated. The preceding case studies illustrate a pattern familiar to most political scientists: authoritarian regimes withstanding domestic challenges through the unrestrained use of repression. As prosaic as these accounts may seem upon reflection, this scenario has been missed by a predominant focus on completed transitions. Unsuccessful campaigns for change in Syria, Tunisia, Iraq, and Libya show that strong rulers have forcefully suppressed domestic insurrections, thus enduring the discontent their arbitrariness provoked. In this pattern the regime's independence from externally imposed limitations on the use of force is a critical permissive condition. Treated as unexceptional, the record of long-lived authoritarianism in the Arab states holds the potential for substantial insights into the conditions of both regime durability and regime change. This study, along with the other chapters in this book, is a contribution to such research. Several observations may be drawn from the above accounts of regimes surviving crises.

Perhaps the most striking finding is that brutal rule can make a regime more, not less, durable. While familial patronage and government corruption may create the background conditions for contentious collective action, subsequent opposition efforts will not successfully install a new government unless the repressive capacity of the regime is hampered. In all four crises survived, hard-liners strove to prevent regime change and, with the exception of Tunisia, where soft-liners saved the regime and then reconsolidated it, they succeeded. Strong hard-liners, those with extensive patrimonial networks and few constraints in their domestic application of force, are difficult to overthrow. Hence, in situations of independence from a foreign patron, one observes a curvilinear relationship between personalism and regime longevity. An intermediate level of patrimonialism may not undermine state institutions and civil society sufficiently to insulate the ruler, but extensive efforts at weakening the military's autonomy and extending patronage in society may sustain dictatorship. The Libyan and Tunisian regimes survived efforts at change but, with weaker patrimonial networks, did so more tenuously than Syria and Iraq. Qaddafi used one set of armed forces to crush the other, and Ben Ali replaced Bourguiba before then replicating his methods. This study thus yields a compelling, if troubling, lesson for transitions and stability: in a time of internal crisis, extensive personal rule and corruption do not weaken the regime unless constrained by external patrons.

International Support and Domestic Stability

Beyond the domestic dynamic of personalistic rule extends the regime's relationship to foreign states. The record of failed rebellions and defeated insurgencies in the Middle East suggests that the role of external powers in constraining the use of force by autocratic leaders may have been underemphasized in studies of successful transitions. In Syria, Tunisia, Iraq, and Libya independence from foreign pressures for restraint left the regimes free to suppress domestic insurgencies. These states were generally not reliant on foreign backing at the time of crisis, but even those Arab governments that count on the support of the United States or another significant external power are not necessarily vulnerable.

Here it is vital to disaggregate situations of dependence on foreign backing from those instances when the patron limits the regime's ability to deploy violence. U.S. political leverage over regimes stems from the regimes' reliance on U.S. patronage, but the use of that leverage as restraint or support varies. For example, the current Saudi Arabian and Egyptian regimes receive large amounts of military and, in the case of Egypt, economic aid with few political strings attached. They may therefore exhibit the same kind of broad capacity for repression as the cases with weaker ties to the United States. Human Rights Watch describes their relationship as follows:

> Saudi Arabia . . . imposes strict limits on civil society, severely discriminates against women, and systematically suppresses dissent. But Western governments to date have contented themselves with purchasing Saudi oil and soliciting Saudi contracts while maintaining a shameful silence toward Saudi abuses. Egypt . . . features a narrowly circumscribed political realm and a government that does all it can to suffocate peaceful political opposition. Yet as a "partner" for Middle East peace, Egypt has secured from the U.S. government massive aid and tacit acceptance of its human rights violations. (HRW 2002a)

Thus, while independence from foreign patronage may be a sufficient condition for the restabilization of a heavily patrimonial regime, it is not a necessary one. Future research on regime change can examine the factors distinguishing dependence on a foreign patron from constraints imposed by one.

Such work could start with a comparative examination of U.S. policy stances toward different authoritarian regimes, recognizing that the U.S. government adopts distinct postures toward regime change depending on the target of aid or criticism. Thomas Carothers has candidly addressed this variance, "When democracy appears to fit in well with U.S. security and economic interests, the United States promotes democracy. Where democracy clashes with other significant interests, it is downplayed or even ignored" (Carothers 2000: 3). For example, even before September 11, 2001, U.S. support for pluralism rarely extended to Muslim states in the Middle East, especially when Israel, oil resources, and a perceived Islamic threat were involved (Gerges 1999: 17; Entelis 2000). Consequently, authoritarian states in the region may present regimes where "the status quo is so vital to American interests that it must not be disturbed" (Whitehead 1986: 41; see also Hawthorne 2001).

The U.S.-led war on terrorism appears to have further boosted the international legitimacy accorded to domestic repression as regimes receive a green light to crack down on political opposition movements, regardless of their tactics and goals. As reported by Human Rights Watch, the coalition's "leading members have violated human rights principles at home and overlooked human rights transgressions among their partners. They have substituted expediency for the firm commitment to human rights that alone can defeat the rationale of terrorism." The implication of this double standard is that "whatever its success in pursuing particular terrorists, the coalition risks reinforcing the logic of terrorism unless human rights are given a far more central role" (HRW 2002a; see also HRW 2002b). When questioned about the lack of progress on democratization in Egypt the U.S. ambassador recently replied "that the United States considers Egypt to be a friend and we don't put pressure on our friends" (Welch 2002).

Placing Culture in a Conventional Framework

As they have been traditionally proposed, cultural accounts are poorly suited for explaining the levels and outcomes of collective contentious politics in the Middle East. Where claims about the incompatibility of Islam and democracy predict complicity with dictators, one finds instead dissent and activism. Local factors such as religious ideologies are better treated as intervening variables in the maintenance of authoritarianism. The impact of political Islam, like that of other ideational programs around the world, is mediated through the interests and ideologies of participant groups. For instance, Islamist opposition projects may receive little support from Western states that would pressure autocrats elsewhere to reform. It follows that if states backing nondemocratic regimes prefer dictatorship to representative government in which Islamists will participate, then an Islamic-centered message would presumably diminish opportunities for external aid and reduce the chances for domestically driven regime change. Thus, the relationship of so-called Islamic cultures, often conceived in antiquated terms as monolithic and uncontested belief systems, to regime outcomes is not mechanistic. Rather, it is filtered through the outlooks of the multiple actors involved in the maintenance or breakdown of an authoritarian regime. Opposition groups in Syria, Tunisia, Iraq, and Libya have framed their projects in terms of Islam, but they did not generate the conditions for durable authoritarianism. On the contrary, Islam provided a set of ideas for mobilizing *against* dictatorships.

Yet the ideological framing of such campaigns for change may be employed by local rulers and U.S. policymakers in an ongoing and contested discussion over the conflict or compatibility of U.S. interests with those of Islamist leaders. When Islamist movements are perceived (or portrayed) abroad as embracing an anti-Western stance, their efforts are less likely to be bolstered by antiauthoritarian pressures from abroad. Consequently, even if rulers like Assad or Qaddafi do not depend on superpower patronage, they may count on the United States' unwillingness to support Islamist groups during popular uprisings (al-Sayyid 1991: 722–723).

It follows that what may have appeared as a regional exception is instead an unpuzzling product of conventional political dynamics. For a variety of reasons Arab leaders have enjoyed freedom from external pressure for change and reaped the correspondent political benefits within their regimes. When opposition has arisen, power holders have forcefully defeated alternative social forces. The issue of external constraints or support is essentially a political variable, rather than a religio-cultural or region-specific factor. Placed in the context of past assistance to non–Middle Eastern autocrats such as Somoza García and Mobutu Sese Seko, the current trend of U.S. support for the status quo in the Middle East does not make the region extraordinary or "exceptional." On the contrary, the Middle East's political landscape is typical to the extent that its regimes, like others around the world, are influenced by the signals and relationships the United States extends to incumbent leaders and opposition movements.

Conclusion

Before adopting exceptionalist theories for Middle Eastern authoritarianism, students of politics should first exhaust the analytical tools in common usage. Such work is essential to the collective and cumulative enterprise of understanding social phenomena. The evidence gathered in this study suggests that comparative political analysis can go a long way toward explaining the contrasts between durable authoritarianism in the Middle East and the breakdown of nondemocratic regimes in other parts of the world.

The above cases of restabilization draw attention to the under-researched role of externally imposed constraints on repression for explaining full transitions. Authoritarian rulers and their confederates use tightly managed repressive organizations and can be tenacious when challenged. Such regimes prove resilient when incumbent elites can crush internal revolts. These general patterns have been observed outside of the Middle East and prove equally valid within the region. When antiauthoritarian insurgencies arose in Syria, Tunisia, Iraq, and Libya, rulers deployed internal security organizations against their foes and held onto power. Their endurance illustrates the capacity of authoritarian incumbents, when unconstrained by foreign patrons opposing the use of repression, to stop opposition movements working for change.

In addition to considering the role of external states in the repression of domestic opposition, this study has emphasized the need to consider regime loyalists when evaluating transitions scenarios. Comparativists can approach the difference between change and continuity through direct attention to the actors involved, so long as hard-liners are included and one considers their capacity and constraints when trying to *prevent* transition. Authoritarian regimes in the Middle East employ a common set of practices (extensive patronage, nepotism, the undermining of formal institutions, etc.) and share an underlying susceptibility to challenges by those groups excluded under arbitrary rule. For a transition to occur, however, these factors must trigger sufficient protest among political actors—"causers" of regime change—to overpower incumbent leaders (Huntington 1991: 107). Contrary to claims about the debilitating effects of arbitrary rule, the Middle Eastern cases indicate that it is only when networks of personalism are weakened do regimes collapse. The erosion of institutional autonomy in a regime's military and the penetration of civil society through personalistic patronage networks, rather than portending the overthrow of dictatorships, preserved authoritarian rule in Syria, Tunisia, Iraq, and Libya. Once active, opposition movements faced repressive institutions that were highly integrated into the regime and defended their own survival along with that of the dictatorship. These agencies were not constrained by external dependencies that could have otherwise tempered their resort to force. Thus, the cases support an approach to regime collapse and survival that considers regime incumbents as political actors who try to stop change just as vigorously as reformists work to bring it.

Note

Portions of this chapter previously appeared in "And Yet They Persist: Explaining Survival and Transition in Neo-Patrimonial Regimes," *Studies in Comparative International Development* 37, no. 3 (2002), reprinted by permission of Transaction Publishers.

For constructive feedback on earlier versions of this chapter, I thank Michele Penner Angrist, Nancy Bermeo, Mac Brownlee, Ellis Goldberg, Fred Greenstein, Atul Kohli, James Mahoney, Marsha Pripstein Posusney, Dan Slater, Richard Snyder, David Waldner, and two anonymous reviewers at *Studies in Comparative International Development*.

4

Contestation Without Democracy: Elite Fragmentation in Iran

ARANG KESHAVARZIAN

This chapter asks why the Islamic Republic of Iran has main-tained its form of authoritarian rule. Authoritarian endurance in Iran is particularly intriguing because a number of factors, most notably long-standing elite fragmentation and contesta-tion, suggest that regime collapse is likely and imminent. The chapter explains the longevity of the Islamic Republic by argu-ing that the institutions of the state foster cleavages among elites and allow for a degree of pluralism, yet these same insti-tutions ensure regime maintenance and undermine democratic transition.

If in the 1950s and 1960s policymakers and analysts viewed "moder-nity" and "development" as the principle objectives for the developing world, the 1970s and 1980s ushered in "stability" and "strong states" as the focus, and in the wake of the end of the Cold War these teleolog-ical ends and normative goods have given way to "democracy." Conse-quently, a voluminous literature and wide array of think tanks have mushroomed to ponder the preconditions for consolidation of democ-racy and the modes of transition from authoritarian to democratic rule. With this flurry of intellectual energy and political ambition focused on democratization, an obvious but crucial point is sometimes slighted; that is, the path to democracy must set out from an authoritarian regime (Linz and Stepan 1996). Whether democratization takes the form of a mass movement, a negotiated elite pact that ensures that transition is mutually beneficial to both rulers and opposition groups, or a liberating foreign invasion that replaces an authoritarian system, the question of democratization is inextricably related to the constellation of institutions and actors that have maintained authoritarian rule and inscribed the opposition that seeks to transform it. A long-standing argument is that elite cohesion and consensus building ensures regime longevity (Moore 1966; Skocpol 1979; Herb 1999). In recent years the inverse proposition, that elite divisions precipitate regime decay and collapse, has also been presented. Guillermo O'Donnell and Phillippe Schmitter emphatically write that "there is no transition whose beginning is not the consequence—direct or indirect—of important divisions within the authoritarian regime itself, principally along the fluctuating cleavage between hard-liners and soft-liners" (1986: 19).

Given this prescription, over the past few years the prospects for an authoritarian breakdown in Iran have been auspicious. The revolution of 1979 was based as much on the principles of freedom and republicanism as it was on Islamic politics and anti-imperialism; and the Islamic Republic's mode of legitimation pivots on popular participation and refers back to a century of constitutionalism. Moreover, since the late 1980s leading politicians in the regime have been engaged in serious debates about reforming the political and economic system in order to diminish the state's monopoly and encourage citizen participation in certain facets of the regime's reconstruction and development projects. With the necessary institutionalization of the regime after the end of the war with Iraq (1988) and the death of Ayatollah Ruhollah Khomeini (1989), elite conflicts have come to the fore and alternative platforms have been espoused. Rooted in the fundamental ideological divisions within the establishment, rivalry among the regime's leadings figures resonated in the gradually more open political environment of the 1990s and in a society that has high levels of literacy, education, and urbanization. Supported by an independent press, emerging civil society organizations, and widespread electoral participation in the presidential elections in 1997 and 2001 and the parliamentary elections in 2000, this trend resulted in the self-proclaimed "reformist movement" coming to power with the explicit mandate to reform the political system by supporting the rule of law, deepening and expanding the role of civil society, and protecting fundamental civil and political rights.[1]

With the electoral debacle in the 2004 parliamentary elections, even the leaders of the reformist movement have acknowledged that their movement has been unsuccessful and defeated. If by "transition to democracy" we mean a domestically driven and relatively nonviolent restructuring of the political order from an authoritarian system to one based on participation and inclusion of citizens in policymaking and implementation (as opposed to regime change brought about by foreign invasion or revolution), at present the prospects for a transformation of the Islamic Republic from an autocracy to a democracy seem grim.

Rather than analyze these political dynamics by asking why Iran has not democratized,[2] this chapter sets out to understand the current structure of the Islamic Republic of Iran that has endured for more than a quarter century. The question is key because regime resilience has come under conditions that are believed to be debilitating, namely persistent and deep-rooted elite conflicts. The Islamic Republic is a regime that subsumes principles of republicanism and mass participation into a particular interpretation of Islam privileging clerical rule and limiting the scope of politics. Its constitution and political trajectory have institutionalized elections for parliament and the presidency as well as the position of "the Leader" and the Guardian Council that are believed to protect the will of God and enforce the interests of state-affiliated clerics and their lay allies.[3] From these diverse political and religious threads, political elites weave strong definitions of the true meaning of "Islamic Republic" that counter one another. Hard-line conservatives support the absolutist powers of the Leader and related unaccountable institutions, while soft-line reformists seek more expansive powers for republican institutions. The situation has been termed "factionalized authoritarianism" (Chehabi 2001).

Given the combination of participatory and authoritarian structures, what type of political system is the Islamic Republic? Given that political tensions and cleavages within the ruling oligarchy have been protracted and public, how has the regime survived? Why hasn't there been an authoritarian breakdown? In other words, how does the Islamic Republic *both* generate interelite conflict *and* resist complete regime breakdown? These are the central questions I address here.

The explanation for this puzzling situation cannot be found solely in the economic structure, political ideology, or religious nature of the Islamic Republic. Instead, I argue that the Islamic Republic's brand of authoritarianism is grounded in a highly fragmented state that generates and nourishes elite factionalism and public contestation but all along allows hard-liners to monitor and manage political forces, ensuring that conflicts among elites persist without unraveling into an authoritarian breakdown or a full-fledged democratic transition. Elite cleavages are not an aberration in Iran's authoritarianism and should not be taken as an indication of regime incapacity or weakness; instead discord is an essential component of the regime, which I describe as "fragmented authoritarianism." Thus, this constellation of state institutions bends— in order to accommodate rapid swings from more inclusionary to more exclusionary modes of interest representation—without breaking the authoritarian status quo.

The chapter proceeds as follows. I begin by first outlining the factors that predict regime crisis and breakdown of the Islamic Republic.

Next I will discuss the nature of the regime and posit that the fragmented nature of the state is critical for the manner in which it rules. In the subsequent section, I explain the resilience of the regime in the face of social mobilization and oligarchic contestation by arguing that the same qualities of the state that institutionalize elite conflict dampen prospects for regime breakdown. I conclude by briefly reflecting on the particular impediments to democratization generated by this political order, which points to organization building as a critical step in addressing the shortcomings of the reformist movement to date.

By focusing on the immediate factors that have generated regime stability in the context of elite pluralism, my analysis sidesteps an important strain in the study of regimes highlighting more macrostructural factors such as configurations of class relations, levels of industrialization and modernization, and international logics. While these factors are surely necessary to push back the chain of historical causation and to identify the menu of constraints and opportunities involved in constructing and consolidating a democracy in Iran,[4] the purpose of this chapter is to look at the specific factors preventing the demise of the Islamic Republic and the short-term factors that limit authoritarian breakdown and a democratic opening. Hence, my analysis here is informed by the more voluntarist strand of the study of regime change that privileges the role of political elites, specific political institutions, and political contingencies.

Is Regime Collapse Imminent?

"The grip of fear is broken, it is the beginning of the end" of the Islamic Republic, claimed Richard Perle, a Middle East policy adviser to President George W. Bush in early 2002 (Nixon Center 2002). By making this prediction he was repeating what many Iranians living in Los Angeles, London, and elsewhere have done since 1979. At the first sign of either internal dissent, conflict among the ruling clergy, or Western pressure, expatriates and anti-regime pundits have envisioned an unraveling of the regime. But it is not just wishful thinking to expect authoritarian decay and possible transition to democracy. Several prominent theories of transition would support this view, thus highlighting the paradox of authoritarian endurance in Iran.

First, dissatisfaction with the political, social, and economic status quo abounds. There does remain an ideologically committed core of support for the current form of the Islamic Republic, and there is a group of well positioned Iranians benefiting from state patronage and economic policies. However, journalistic accounts, election results, low turnouts, and periodic public demonstrations make it clear that the majority of Iranians want significant changes necessitating a refashioning of the political relations. These grievances have also been transferred into collective action and public mobilization. During the 1980s and 1990s, the Islamic Republic, probably more so than any other regime in the Middle East and North Africa, has been confronted by civil disobedience and violent political protests. University-based protests and activism against the policies and the authoritarian nature of the regime have been the most dramatic (Mahdi 1999). While these recent student protests and political activism have received the greatest attention abroad, many other sectors of Iranian society have mobilized and publicly demonstrated against economic hardships and state policies. For example, in one week in 2004, schoolteachers, retirees, and heads of medical colleges all held public gatherings to protest work conditions and unfulfilled government commitments (*Sharq* 20 Esfand 1382 [March 10, 2004]). The urban poor have protested living conditions, industrial workers have challenged privatization policies, and in a number of cases city dwellers have clashed with authorities over redistricting of provinces and other local disputes. These mass protests signify diverse issues that have galvanized and politicized citizens and are reflected in parliamentary debates, newspaper editorials, and public consciousness. Yet neither grievances nor mass mobilization have toppled the Islamic Republic's officialdom.

Second, the Islamic Republic has lacked international patronage, a factor that, as Eva Bellin and Jason Brownlee note in their respective chapters in this book, has helped maintain many regimes in the region, including its monarchical predecessor. If anything, Iran has been burdened by political and economic pressures from regional foes and world powers alike. Also, the eight-year war with Iraq that resulted in a bloody stalemate represented the sort of military failure that helped undermine authoritarian regimes in Argentina and Greece.

Third, the concept of the rentier state that applies to oil-exporting states such as Iran suggests that the Islamic Republic would be particularly vulnerable to popular opposition. Theories about rentier states, or states that are dependent on revenues from external windfalls known as rents, argue that the existence of these external rents forms a set of political relations between the state and its citizens that—unlike in states that must rely on taxes and domestic sources of revenue—discourages the development of democracy despite relatively high levels of wealth and development (Luciani 1990; Ross 2001). In addition, the theory suggests that these authoritarian regimes may in fact be quite unstable and susceptible to overthrow; the rentier state theory has often been cited as an explanation for the demise of the Pahlavi monarchy in 1979 (Skocpol 1982; Shambayati 1994). The resilience of the rentier state is understood to be tied to its ability to allocate revenues and co-opt pivotal groups via patronage (e.g., issuing select import licenses) and placate entire social strata through public goods (e.g., subsidized consumer goods) (Mahdavy 1970). Thus, political instability is expected when there is a downturn in oil revenues and the state's allocative capacity dries up (Luciani 1995). In addition, states that are dependent on rents are underinstitutionalized because they do not develop the wide array of domestic institutions necessary for domestic resource extraction and redistribution (Chaudhry 1997; Karl 1997). Therefore, they are believed to be weak states and less able to withstand external shocks. Since the 1980s, Iran has experienced major swings in the price of oil, the decline of oil revenue on a per capita basis, and a persistent dependence on oil revenues, yet the regime has withstood these pressures far better than those in Algeria, Indonesia, Nigeria, and Venezuela.

Finally, relative elite pluralism and persistent contestation have characterized the Islamic Republic's political oligarchy. In the initial years a semblance of cohesiveness was probably fashioned among a core of Khomeini's supporters through an unwritten cultural compact rooted in their common experiences in seminaries, the prison, and a host of familial and communal networks. But soon after the revolution it was evident that the new elites were unable to maintain a consensus for extended periods of time and never across policy areas, factionalism was rife. Even with Khomeini as a charismatic arbitrator and the Islamic Republic Party (IRP) as a supposed single party, differences and swings in policy were common, with the ruling oligarchy having particularly impetuous debates regarding foreign and economic policy. Khomeini was frequently drawn into these disputes and forced to mediate and balance the powers of different personalities and political tendencies with the central aim of neutralizing, though not completely suffocating, differences. Thus, the regime's rather clumsy method of diminishing discord among officials featured broad slogans against foreign enemies and domestic traitors and populist politics that sought to mask class-based and corporate politics (Abrahamian 1993).

Since Khomeini's death, even the semblance of elite cohesion has faded. Little in the way of effective consensus building occurs, as there is no single party or social institution, such as a dynastic royal family, that obliges elite negotiation and limits conflict (Herb 1999). Seditious squabbles and factional fortitude have only increased over the years, with distinct organizations and personalities splintering off of one another and developing shifting, strategic alliances. The internal divisions have been variously labeled as splits between revolutionaries and pragmatists, the radical left, Islamic left, modern right, and traditional right, and most recently reformists and conservatives. For the purposes of this chapter, it is sufficient to simply focus on two categories that I will interchangeably refer to as conservatives and reformists, or hard-liners and soft-liners.

The hard-liners consist of both clerics and lay figures who want to preserve the status quo that places a large degree of formal authority and discretionary power in the hands of the Leader, unelected councils under his supervision, and state-affiliated religious charities and economic foundations. They tend to support the interests of capital and have a more traditional understanding of religion and the social roles of women and youth. Reformers, in contrast, seek to empower and expand the jurisdiction of the republican institutions of the regime, institutionalize greater citizen participation, and have a higher tolerance for contestation and pluralism. Because many of the leading figures of this faction have their intellectual origins in Islamic leftist interpretations of the revolution, they are less associated with pro-capitalist development strategies, although their support for greater transparency and meritocracy has attracted private economic interests that have been shut out of Iran's crony capitalism.[5] Without serious research on the social roots of these elite groupings or the development of political associations with organized and specific social bases, it is difficult to precisely map these elite divisions onto Iran's social typography. Yet recent electoral results suggest that political positions of soft-liners have greater support among Iranians living in Tehran, the younger generation, women, and the educated population, while hard-liners tend to have greater support in provincial capitals, among the older population, and those directly benefiting from the revolutionary organizations discussed below (e.g., various economic foundations, bonyads [charitable foundations], and the Islamic Revolutionary Guard Corps [IRGC]).

This cleavage among elites deepened after a self-proclaimed and popular group of reformists took over the executive and legislative branches of government in the late 1990s by reaching out to student associations, more independently minded political activists, women, and university and high school students. In practice the reformist president Mohammad Khatami and the Second of Khordad Front (named after the Persian date of his first electoral victory on May 23, 1997) acted and were treated by hard-liners as the opposition—an opposition, however, that was located in the government and shared a history with their political opponents.

Given the heterogeneous nature of the revolutionary forces and the existence of some republican institutions and norms, the prevalence of political contestation and a drive for democratization is less surprising than the endurance of authoritarian rule. The literature on democratization uniformly identifies elite fragmentation as a necessary condition for authoritarian breakdown (Haggard and Kaufman 1995: 31; Huntington 1991). The logic behind this analysis is found in Dankwart Rustow's seminal article, where he writes, "the dynamic process of democratization itself is set off by a prolonged and inclusive political struggle" that "is not a lukewarm struggle but a hot family feud" (1970: 352). Rustow emphasizes the familial nature of these confrontations because conflict among those who view their rivals as people with whom they must live are an essential aspect of the preparatory stage toward democracy. But since the 1990s, in newspapers, elections, courtrooms, and the parliament, the founding leaders, ideologues, and technocrats of the Islamic Republic— a number of whom share kinship relations—have battled each other over state power. Shifting fissures and alliances among elites have made postrevolutionary politics volatile, if not completely unpredictable, and contentious, if not fully representative. Yet elite cleavages also have not led to authoritarian breakdown.

What Is the Islamic Republic?

What is this political system that creates such a divided elite? When discussing political systems, we are inclined to think in terms of regimes (democratic, authoritarian, and totalitarian) or their subtypes, described as liberal democracies, single-party autocracies, and sultanistic or personalized autocracies. By political regime, I mean a system of rules that define the methods of gaining access to state power, excluding citizens from state power, and exercising authority in order to devise and enforce binding decisions. By democracy, I refer to a system that has established guidelines that ensure competition for access to state power and accountability of rulers; an authoritarian regime has more limited pluralism among those with state power and in contrast to totalitarian regimes lacks an elaborate ideology shared by governing elites and extensive and intensive capacity for political mobilization in society (Linz 1975: 264). Fitting any regime into these ideal types is difficult, but this is especially true of the Iranian case. Under the Islamic Republic's constitution, sovereignty belongs to God but is delegated to all humans (Article 56). Executive and legislative power is formally divided between popularly elected branches of government and unelected offices and councils that function as the pious legal experts entrusted with maintaining the dominion of God. After Khomeini's death, the religious standing of the Leader and clerical leadership was greatly diminished and the disparity between mosque and state has been more pronounced; consequently, the theological premise of overlaying popular sovereignty with clerical representation of God's will has become suspect. Hence, Saeed Hajjarian (1380 [2002]), a leading reformist ideologue and journalist, speaks of the Islamic Republic as suffering from a "dysfunctional dual sovereignty" because the Islamic and republican dimensions have not been synchronized and stabilized.[6]

Like democracies, the Islamic Republic is in part based on institutions through which citizens participate in making and executing rules that govern their lives through representatives who are assumed to represent their will. Elections for various offices and levels of government are regularly held and largely free of violence and vote rigging at the election booth. Given the populist and revolutionary roots of the regime and existence of universal suffrage, voter participation has become an integral component of the regime's repertoire of fashioning legitimacy with ballots described as a "vote for Islam" and elections as moments when the state calls upon citizens to be "ever-present in the political arena" and demonstrate their opposition to the "enemies of the Islamic Revolution." Indeed voter participation in presidential and parliamentary elections is often substantial even if at times it is uneven and varies across region. Moreover, parliamentary debates over policies are heated, and criticism of various branches of government is common with the parliament frequently exercising its power to reject presidential appointments and censure ministers. Finally, there is a growing and boisterous civil society that reflects a significant and politically active segment of citizens. Although, as we will see below, numerous unelected governmental posts exist, elections have been a means for citizens to either punish the establishment by voting incumbents out of office or expressing displeasure by not voting and implicitly bringing the populist platform of the regime under question.

However, these democratic practices and the tenacity of republican institutions are limited and undermined by a whole host of mechanisms that limit contestation and participation, while divisions of power deaden the capacity for citizens and their representatives to meaningfully participate in politics. First, the election process is such that competition is highly regulated. The registration of candidates is closely controlled at the local and national levels to ensure only partial participation by opposition groups. Whereas in the early years of the Islamic Republic liberal nationalist and leftist candidates were deemed unfit to run, in more recent elections Islamist candidates who call for strengthening the republican institutions and are hostile to the conservative circles that supervise the vetting process are (not surprisingly) disqualified.

Furthermore, despite the constitutional tenets (Articles 19–42) and the claims of official discourse to protect many of the principles of democratic rule, such as freedom of assembly, speech, and press, administrative regulations and extra-legal practices result in the systematic disregard for civil and political rights. A complex and opaque court system has developed to convict political activists, journalists, academics, artists, and even members of the government that the hardliner–controlled judiciary deems as threats to the regime or their individual interests. These legal and administrative impediments to free and fair public participation in politics are reinforced by the use of targeted violence and indiscriminate intimidation by a multilayered law enforcement apparatus and vigilante squads seeking to control and monitor many dimensions of public and private life. As such, public space has been highly dominated and regulated by the regime.

Finally, the republican institutions are themselves straightjacketed by antidemocratic institutions. Over time the doctrine of *velayat-e faqih,* or the mandate of the jurist, developed by Khomeini in the decade prior to the revolution, has come to be defined in personal and absolute terms, wherein the Leader (Khomeini, 1979–1988, and 'Ali Khamene'i, 1988 to the present) wields extensive supervisory and executive powers. Article 110 of the constitution (amended in 1989) stipulates that the Leader is authorized to "determine the general policies" of and "supervise over" the regime, declare war and peace as the supreme commander of the armed forces, and appoint and dismiss the heads of the judiciary, chief of the joint staff, and the commanders of the IRGC and the armed and police forces. While Khomeini's charismatic authority empowered this post with particular authority to impose his will upon the entire system, with the support of conservative allies in other branches of government the less religiously authoritative Khamene'i too has wielded decree powers, for example, to end parliamentary debates over liberalizing press laws and discussions over relations with the United States. Through appointed "representatives," the Leader oversees activities in military, economic, and religious organization and ministries.

In addition, the Leader directly appoints half the members of the Guardian Council; the remaining six are selected by the parliament from a list of nominees drawn up by the head of the judiciary, who himself is appointed by the Leader (Article 91). The Guardian Council is entrusted with two critical responsibilities. First, it reviews all legislation to ensure that it is compatible with Islamic law and the constitution. When the Guardian Council rejects the parliament's bills, the legislative dispute is resolved by the Expediency Council, an unelected body composed of all branches of the government, including representatives of the Leader. Second, the council is authorized to "supervise" presidential and parliamentary elections (Article 99); it is with this approbatory power that it has vetted candidates. Thus, these and other institutions are a de jure and de facto trump against popular sovereignty, reflected imperfectly in the legislative and executive branches. This is so much the case that even during the heady months immediately after Khatami's 1997 presidential victory, one of the leaders of the reformist factions felt it necessary to remind citizens not to expect a "miracle" given that the president only controls "between one-tenth and one-fifth of the [state] power" (*Salam,* 10 Shahrivar 1376 [September 1, 1997]).

In conclusion, following Robert Dahl's frequently cited two dimensions of democratization—contestation and participation—Iran falls somewhere in the mid-area between closed hegemony and polyarchy, in what can be termed as a limited polyarchy (Dahl 1971; O'Donnell and Schmitter 1986). The Islamic Republic is neither a military nor a single-party dictatorship, and since the death of Khomeini the regime lacks the highly personalistic nature that would make it somewhat similar to sultanistic regimes, and therefore various neologisms have been offered to describe the regime; Houchang Chehabi, for instance, describes the system as a "doubly hybrid semipresidential and quasitheocratic" (1991: 78–99).

The State of Iran's Authoritarian Rule

Iran is thus a "hybrid regime" that combines democratic and authoritarian elements (Collier and Levitsky 1997; Carothers 2002). Most scholars studying these regimes add modifiers to democracy or autocracy and have coined terms such as "limited democracies," "tutelary democracies," or "illiberal democracies" on the one hand and "inclusionary autocracies," "illiberal autocracies," or "competitive autocracies" on the other. By adding these adjectives authors seek to accurately describe the diversity of regimes that is not captured by the ideal types of democracy or authoritarianism and to avoid overextending our understanding of these terms in ways that lead to "conceptual stretching" (Collier and Levitsky 1997).

One way to capture the complexities of systems of governance is to modify our understanding by shifting the overarching concept from regime to state (Collier and Levitsky 1997: 444–448). The nation-state is the distinctive collection of institutions that claims exclusive sovereignty over a given population and territory. As Ira Katznelson points out, "How they exercise their sovereignty, which institutions they deploy, and how they justify their rule are the distinguishing, and contested, hallmarks of stateness" (2003: 108). Thus, the analytically more macro-level notion of "stateness," as much as "regime," plays a crucial role in shaping how regimes function, reproduce their authority, and adjust to pressures from elites and masses. Introducing the structure of the state into discussions, therefore, allows us to avoid stretching the concept of either autocracy or democracy while acknowledging that regimes differ in how they are authoritarian and how they distribute coercive and infrastructural powers.

Even though the nation-state is the entity that is to be democratized, the literature on democratization has paid little attention to the structure of the nation-state (Carothers 2002; Bunce 2000) and has only been raised in the context of discussions of democratization in ethnically diverse and divided societies and when disputes over state borders and territory exist (Dahl 1971; Rustow 1970; Linz and Stepan 1996). Ana-lyzing the Islamic Republic reminds us that the manner in which state institutions distribute power, legitimize groups, and structure political opportunities are foundational for understanding how regimes are authoritarian and remain in power. I argue that not only is sovereignty divided, but also Iran's state is highly fragmented. It is this quality that enables the regime, or more specifically hard-liners within the regime, to reproduce its power and control society, and it is *because* of this structure and *in spite* of elite fragmentation and contestation that the Islamic Republic has survived. I will thus refer to the Islamic Republic as a "fragmented autocracy," which is shorthand for a "fragmented state with an autocratic regime."

To quote two recent studies of the Islamic Republic, with the Islamic revolution the Iranian nation-state is "institutionally balka-nized" (Kamrava and Hassan-Yari, 2004) and has taken on a highly "diffused nature" (Moslem 2002: 11). A patchwork of parallel institu-tions create overlapping authorities, competing interests, and checks and balances. This is in sharp contrast to the Pahlavi monarchy, when the state was ostensibly a monolithic and centralized entity that placed all decisionmaking powers in the hands of the monarch (Fatemi 1982: 9). Conversely, the postrevolutionary state, even though its regime is neither pluralistic nor corporatist in its interest representation, consists of multiple and competing institutional bodies. Below the office of the Leader of the Revolution a disjointed and overlapping bureaucratic grid persists, allowing ideological factionalism to flourish and engendering elite competition—all within the confines of state institutions.

For instance, at various moments in time, the army coexists with the IRGC; the police with Islamic Revolutionary Committees; the Ministry of Housing and Urban Development with the Housing Foundation of the

Islamic Revolution; the Ministry of the Construction Crusade with the Ministry of Agriculture; the Red Crescent with the Imam Khomeini Relief Committee; the Ministry of Energy with the Ministry of Oil; the Literacy Movement with the Ministry of Education; and the Supreme Council of Cultural Revolution and the Organization for Islamic Propaganda with the Ministry of Culture and Islamic Guidance. In legal matters the judiciary is composed of heterogeneous courts, with alleged press violations being directed either to branches of the revolutionary court or the press court. An article in the leading economic magazine in Iran complained about the existence of parallel bodies in the area of economic policymaking by stating that as many as twenty organizations and councils participate in economic decisionmaking (*Eqtesad-e Iran* no. 59, Bahman 1382 [February 2004]), 20–21). Additionally, a large number of parastatal economic foundations and commercial units in ministries participate in the production and distribution of goods. Even the power associated with the office of the Leader has been fragmented in the years since it has been occupied by the less religiously qualified and politically powerful successor to Khomeini. The power at Khamenei's

> disposal falls far short of the power he would wield were he to be regarded as the embodiment of the spirit of the constitution or in a position to exercise the absolute power of the ruling jurist. After the death of Khomeini, representation of the spirit of the constitution was not transferred to his official successor but to the totality of the influential members of the clergy who held various top positions in the government [e.g., Guardian Council and the judiciary] or who controlled life in the religious academics in Qom and elsewhere. . . . The absolute power of the ruling jurists prevails throughout the whole country now as before, even if that power is not wielded solely by the leader. (Schirazi 1998: 79–80)

This constellation of institutions makes it almost impossible for a single ministry or institution to decide and execute major policies unilaterally or without criticism from interested parties.

What are the origins of this highly fragmented state structure? The fragmented state has its roots in a number of factors emanating from the diverse ideologies, social classes, and competing agendas of the revolutionary forces and founders of the Islamic Republic. The mass revolution brought together nationalists, Islamists, and leftists into an effective weight to topple the Pahlavi monarchy. Yet once that objective was achieved, little organizational or ideological glue united the disparate revolutionary leaders or classes; consequently, the Pahlavi regime was not replaced with a robust, single party or a ready-made government in exile. One of the young Islamic revolutionaries, who today is a member of the reformist camp, Emad ad-Din Baghi, recalls that in the first year after the revolution, schisms among Islamists led to groups establishing organizations to counter competitors. He explains that he and other young, and implicitly more "modern," Islamists joined the Islamic Revolutionary Guard Corp as a response to the local revolutionary committees that they believed to be under the control of more conservative clerics and local toughs (Behnoud 2004).[7] Moreover, the initial creation of parallel bodies was due to the revolutionaries' mistrust of the ancien régime's institutions and their decision to hastily create countervailing military, economic, political, and cultural institutions (Kamrava and Hassan-Yari, 2004).

This revolutionary statecraft was institutionalized through a constitution that married republicanism with Khomeini's interpretation of religious government, generating what one observer has called "dissonant institutionalization" (Brumberg 2001). The constitution essentially legitimated the system of dual sovereignty that is reflected in the clustering of loci of power under both the republican institutions of the regime (the legislature and the presidency) and its unelected institutions (the Leader, Guardian Council, and Expediency Council) (Schirazi 1998). Mehdi Moslem argues that the framers of the constitution "designed the Islamic state in such a way that left the door open for institutional conflict and factional rivalry" (2002: 31). Therefore, the state was highly fragmented from its inception.

A strong single party might have added cohesion to this decentralized form of authoritarianism, but no such organization emerged. The Islamic Republic Party was established shortly after the revolution by clerics who were close confidants of Khomeini in order to unify the revolutionary forces. This party, however, did not develop into a single party regime such as those of the Institutional Revolutionary Party (Partido Revolucionaro Institucional, or PRI) in Mexico or the Baath Party in Syria. From the outset the IRP merely acted as an umbrella organization, and powerful political associations, such as the Society of the Combatant Clergy and the Organization of the Mujahidin of the Islamic Revolution, remained active and cultivated their own constituents even if they officially deferred to the IRP. The party was unable to create consensus among its select membership or impose a uniform platform on important issues let alone mobilize the masses, which was left to local Islamic associations, Friday prayer leaders, and revolutionary-era committees. Once opponents to the Islamic Republic were effectively neutralized and intraparty battles over economic policy and elections for the third parliament came to a head, the party was disbanded in 1987.

Finally, some have suggested that the absence of formal ecclesiastic hierarchy and the historic independence of individual Shiite clerics from one another have fueled the fragmented nature of Islamic Republic (Buchta 2000: 6). Given that the Shiite clerical hierarchy was decentralized and composed of independent circles (Fischer 1980; Mottahedeh 1985), it was always difficult for the Islamic Republic to ensure that the clergy within and beyond the government would and could act in unison. Despite some initial attempts by leaders of the new regime, especially Motahhari, the Islamic Republic could not create a centralized chain of command within the clergy and link the minority of clerics working for the state and those remaining in the mosque (Chehabi 1991). Hence, there was a degree of political space for religious, if not secular, critics to dissent and refrain from throwing their support behind the regime. Initially clerics such as Zanjani, Shariatmadari, and Khoii and more recently Montazari, Sanei, Shabestari, and Kadivar have taken advantage of the amorphous religious structure to challenge the state by speaking out about their interpretations of Islam.

This discussion of the origins and persistence of elite conflict is meant to question the functionalist explanation that such pluralism is simply due to the incapacity of the government to suppress all dissent and monopolize the public discourse. Rather, the political roots and socioeconomic dimensions of the creation of the regime unleashed centrifugal force that marks Iran's brand of authoritarianism. Hence, the ideological factionalism and disunity of the elite found an institutional expression in the state's decentralized web of parallel organizations and authorities.

Institutionalizing Elite Cleavages

The balkanized state translates into a segmentation of state agents and the institutionalization of elite factionalism. These governmental bodies are not empty shells but are distinct organizations with administrative authority and their own employees. The Guardian Council, for instance, hires two hundred thousand persons to investigate potential parliamentary candidates (Ehsani 2004). In many cases, the government positions are not well paid and often do not keep pace with the cost of living but are attractive in tight job markets and because they provide social and private benefits. Over time and through ties to particular university faculties and patronage networks, these state institutions have also developed institutional cultures and reputations of their own that reinforce the bureaucratic divisions.

The existence of parallel state organizations comes with a whole host of lower-level departments, research centers, and offices that are largely only accountable to their immediate supervisors. They may develop as think tanks for soft-liners or security agencies for hard-liners, they may differ in terms of their ideological persuasion or their political loyalty, but in all cases they act like gray areas (Buchta 2000: xii) that house clusters of actors often protected by senior clerical figures acting as patrons. Often these areas are unaccountable and unsupervised by the popularly elected branches of the government. In recent years agents of hard-line cells have been responsible for the murders of intellectuals and attacks on student organizations and reformist members of the government.

Meanwhile, these organizations are also spaces in which politicians, intellectuals, and technocrats can come together to formulate agendas and critique opposing factions and government policy. During the late 1980s and early 1990s, many of the prominent members of what would become the reformist political movement found refuge in the Presidential Center for Strategic Studies, which was established in 1989 and officially linked to the Ministry of Foreign Affairs. Thus, former young revolutionaries such as 'Abbas 'Abdi and Saeed Hajjarian, who were previously in the IRGC and the Ministry of Intelligence and National Security, were able to come together and develop new conceptualizations of Islamic government that are now challenging the conservatives. Similar circles formed around the Ministry of Culture and Islamic Guidance, which was headed by Khatami from 1982 to 1992. Conversely, the IRGC, the Radio and Television Organization, and the Center for Strategic Research (under the Expediency Council) were incubators for authoritarian interpretations of the Islamic Republic. More recently, the Supreme Council of the Cultural Revolution has been an important organization in producing some of the younger members of the conservative faction that controls the Seventh Parliament (*Iran* 6 Esfand 1382 [February 26, 2004]). The large number of bureaucratic safe havens preserves regime insiders whose political stock may rise and fall depending on power struggles or electoral outcomes.

Compounding the political divisions among the elite are nonideological divisions based on clientelism. In the context of divisions among elites, patronage is often used to solidify support for one faction or another (Waldner 1999). In the beginning, diverse distributive organizations were a means to solidify mass support for the regime, but also to divvy outside payments to allies. The rentier nature of the state, of course, exacerbated this modus by enhancing the financial centrality of the state. The many state-affiliated organs are a nontransparent means for members of the hierarchy to distribute patronage and create cronyism by allocating jobs, hard currency, and political protection to family members, ideological allies, and past employees. As one official in an economic organization self-consciously told me, the diverse bodies are an excellent means for political allies to establish bonds by "lending each other bread." It is probably safe to assume that these institutionally embedded circles of state agents compete with one another to gain access to state coffers and that ideological and institutional fissures are given a pecuniary dimension, too.

Finally, it should be noted that the various elite circles have been able to reproduce and regenerate themselves. The fragmented state with multiple offices and regularized elections has ensured that elite politics in the Islamic Republic is not a winner-take-all scenario. When established figures of the regime are pushed out of power—as the Islamic left was after its 1992 electoral defeat and disqualifications, or discredited, as hard-line conservatives were after successive electoral defeats in the late 1990s—they have been able to survive, modify their positions, and produce new elites. The old Islamic leftists have become the current soft-liners by transforming their slogans supporting "the downtrodden" and denouncing "American Islam" into a platform calling for transparency and rule of law. Revolutionary clerical leaders of anti-imperialist students gave way to their protégés, who are now as prone to discuss civil society and Bonapartism as they are to quote Khomeini and Ali Shariati. More recently, in the 2004 parliamentary elections when the Guardian Council prevented reformist candidates from running and conservatives were poised to sweep the elections, they nonetheless felt it necessary to put aside older leaders of the highly reactionary Islamic Coalition Society and present a list of little-known younger conservatives who spoke of the people's real economic needs rather than the language of Islamic values. These examples are not meant to necessarily symbolize substantive political transformations, although that may be a reality in many cases; rather, I want to illustrate that the regeneration and differentiation of factions from one another takes place *within* the diffuse state structures.

The varied state apparatus has housed and created clusters and circles of political elites with differing interpretations of the regime, working relations, and immediate institutional interests. In the Islamic Republic the production of political elites takes place within a diverse array of state organizations, rather than a single party or military hierarchy. The topography of the state, however, is such that elites differentiate themselves from one another and electoral losers remain active within the state. These auxiliary organizations allow elite conflict to persist by preventing one faction from completely suffocating opposing elites even if they are marginalized.

Divided They Rule and Survive

In theory, fragmentation among elites of an authoritarian regime opens the possibility for the collapse of the regime and its control over society because it leaves autocrats vulnerable to overthrow from within and without. In the first case, a faction among the elite can seize power and initiate a radical transformation of the regime, a shift that may lead to a more democratic order or a new authoritarian system. Also, the mere threat that soft-liners may split from hard-liners also raises the risk of using heavy-handed measures and can precipitate a democratic opening. In the second case, opposition groups outside of the regime could take advantage of the internal strife to seize the state. To date neither scenario has happened in Iran, and the institutional structure of the Islamic Republic has remained largely unchanged since its establishment. Ironically, the same factors that have fragmented the ruling elite of the Islamic Republic have circuitously fostered the survival of the regime by effectively controlling the formal political process and limiting the organization of soft-liners and their potential societal supporters.

The wide assortment of safe havens and institutional veto points has been an important means of preserving the power of hard-liners in the government and preventing a radical transformation of the regime. Iran's fragmented state, which limits the power of the president and checks the power of the parliament, frustrates soft-liners such as the more technocratic supporters of the 'Ali Akbar Hashemi-Rafsanjani administration (1989–1997) or the champions of political reforms in the Khatami administration (1997–2005) by impeding restructuring through institutionalized policymaking. While the Guardian Council, the office of the Leader, and the judiciary are on the forefront of blocking substantive and procedural policies aimed at moving Iran toward democracy, the more minor state organizations mentioned above reinvigorate the conservative forces intellectually and mollify protest through patronage. Thus, hardliners are well situated to withstand short-run political losses and are assured that electoral defeat will not be catastrophic.

As Eva Bellin points out in Chapter 2 of this book, oil revenues are a valuable resource because they flow directly to the state and finance the coercive and monitoring apparatus of the state even during instances of social unrest. In the Iranian case, oil-financed coercion can also withstand elite disunity. Unlike a military regime with a fairly uniform and centralized chain of command, the Islamic Republic has developed a coercive apparatus that has disparate and often independent branches that escape supervision by the parliament and the international monitoring agencies. Alongside the law enforcement forces, the judiciary and the IRGC operate their own secret detention centers and intelligence services, which are free of monitoring by the Organization of National Prisons and hold detainees without pressing charges, incommunicado, and in solitary confinement. Nonuniformed members of these agencies work in conjunction with vigilante groups to disrupt political gatherings, arrest dissidents, and attack and incite students and protesters at major political events. Because hard-liners control these autonomous institutions, they can crack down on opposition within and outside the regime. Whereas elite conflicts and splits will weaken military regimes, if not paralyze them, the hard-line elements in the Islamic Republic can crack down efficiently even without elite cohesion. Finally, multiplicity of organizations allows the different hard-line coercive cells to easily select fall guys and deflect public anger from one person or institution to another.

The use of force is made more effective and less risky because the soft-liners in the government and supporters of reform in society at large are highly fractured. The democratic opposition has been more of a free-floating and informally cobbled constituency than an organized political entity. Indicative of the heterogeneous and organizationally amorphous nature of the reformist faction are a number of factors that capture the breadth and depth of opposition to the conservative forces and hence in some lights may be viewed as strengths of the movement. Yet the large number of publications, the variety of old and new parties and professional associations that make up the front, the variety of issues, and the bringing together of technocrats, old revolutionary clerics, religious intellectuals, and human rights advocates result in a cacophony of voices that are brought together under a porous umbrella and with little deliberation, agreement over tactics, and prioritization of objectives. Since 1997, when reformists have held positions in the executive and legislative branches, these divisions have resulted in battles over a host of issues including support for student activism, the priority of economic reforms, and the response to the ever-increasing defiance of the judiciary and Guardian Council. Rather than being able to integrate the diverse forces, elected officials have lost ties with the student movement (*Middle East Report* 2003) and have not cultivated ties with religious nationalist parties (*Yas-e No* 7 Bahman 1382 [January 27, 2004]). These factors have limited their ability to transform the deep cleavages among elites into a purge of hard-liners or establish a powerful position from which to bargain for a transition away from the status quo.

Elite divisions are also given voice in the print media. Once limitations on the press were lifted, political elites and intellectuals, who were able to maneuver around obstacles, expressed and publicized their ideological positions and engaged in debates in a whole host of publications. Since the late 1980s, different positions were presented in periodicals such as *Kian, Keyhan-e Farhangi, Howzeh, Goft-o-Gu, Iran-e Farda, Shalamcheh,* and *Shoma;* daily newspapers such as *Salaam, Resalat,* and *Entekhab;* and the series of reformist newspapers and online publications that grew out of *Salaam* and the previous journals. Each of these journals constitutes what are often called circles, cells, societies, wings, and groups (*halqeh, dowreh, mahfal, jenah,* and *goruh*) and describes small clusters of personalities that publish and write in a specific journal, attended a specific seminary, or share a common discourse.[8] These journalistic and scholarly writings have played an important role, especially in the reformist camp, in introducing and developing a democratic discourse as well as engaging in investigative reporting to uncover atrocities and publicize particular issues. Nonetheless, as a leading member of the Sixth Parliament admitted, the activities of the newspapers have not been coordinated with each other or with the reformist members of the parliament (*Yas-e No* 7 Bahman 1382 [2004]).

These problems are exacerbated by the simultaneous atomization of Iranian society. Since the 1930s, the process of modernization (i.e., urbanization, expansion of education, and industrialization) and specific state policies since the revolution have undermined and reconfigured communal forms of organization and identity, while more individualizing tendencies have become more pronounced (Adelkhah 2000; Kazemipur and Rezaei 2003; Varzi 2002). Second, the type of interest representation has contributed to this atomization of society. Unlike more corporatist regimes such as those in Latin America and in Egypt and Turkey between the 1940s and the 1960s that engaged society as a set of economic and social classes, the Islamic Republic practices clientelism on a more personalized basis. Because the state is fragmented, the lines of patronage tie diffuse and isolated state agents to particular social clusters and have consequently produced vertical divisions in society. Third, the authoritarian nature of the regime leads social groupings to remain purposely small and informal to escape the sight of the state and continue to maneuver, undetected, through and around the administrative maze in order to receive publishing licenses, entry into elections, or engage in other forms of associational activity.

Hence, social activity, whether personal or political, tends to be opaque and creates distrust. "In every association in Iran there are two people: those whom everybody knows and those whom nobody knows. The association needs people that nobody knows, whose work is hidden," commented a student member of the university-based Office of Fostering Unity (*Christian Science Monitor,* November 22, 1999). I witnessed and participated in the concrete consequences of this atomization and distrust after the tragic earthquake in Bam in December 2003. There was mass confusion regarding to whom to donate funds. Many Tehranis mentioned that they did not completely trust state organizations such as the Imam's Relief Committee and the Red Crescent. While some turned to an account in the name of the recent Noble Peace Prize winner, Shireen Ebadi, others including the Noble winner herself warned against fake accounts and relief organizations. Most people I met decided to give their contributions to acquaintances from Bam or the province of Kerman. Several members of the Tehran Bazaar mentioned that they planned to send aid through Kermani merchants they knew and trusted, rather than channel their charity through the bazaar's Islamic associations. Socially insulated and isolated groupings of families and friends mirror the intellectual circles and political factions; hence, their capacity for coordinated and extended mass action to pressure hard-line conservatives is limited.

In this manner fragmented authoritarianism helps block regime decay and collapse that is often associated with elite cleavages. It has done this to date by confining elite conflict within the state, which has robust authoritarian procedures and unaccountable bureaucracies that retard the potential transformative capacity of soft-liners. Meanwhile, the combination of effective repression and disunity among pro-reform forces has limited their ability to create organizations necessary to translate elite conflicts and public opinion into political power to push elite politics beyond this stalemated stage. The opposition cannot create a uniform front to raise the cost to hard-liners of using coercion or support soft-liners in their bargaining with hard-liners. These factors combined to undermine the reformists' momentum acquired through electoral victories and the initial opening of the public sphere.

Prospects for the Democratization of a Fragmented Autocracy

After a recent authoritarian backlash, the Guardian Council's barring of reformist candidates from running in the 2004 parliamentary elections, Kaveh Ehsani remarked, "This is a period of transition, requiring a politics of transition. Thus far, the reformers have not been able to formulate such a politics, preferring always to focus on the individual stages of their own participation" (2004). This politics of transition will require an acknowledgment that authoritarianism in Iran is embedded in a highly fragmented state that will require specific opposition tactics that "fit" with the structure of the state (Skocpol 1992). What are the particular impediments for democratization that are created by a fragmented autocracy, such as Iran's regime? I focus on two models of transition to democracy that have been distilled from the Latin American and Eastern European experiences: elite-based pacts and mass mobilization reform movements.[9] Of course, many geopolitical, historical, and cultural differences exist between Iran and recent democratizing states, but if Iran is to move away from authoritarianism without another mass revolution or foreign intervention, one of these two trajectories, or combinations of the two, will probably be central.

Under the pacted transition model, democracy is "crafted" and "negotiated" by elites through a series of compromises that transforms the institutions of the regime allowing for greater participation of opposition groups but does not uproot all the powers of hard-line autocrats at once. For hard-liners to accept soft-liners, they will have to believe that once soft-liners are in power they will not attack their material interests or eradicate them from the political arena. Thus, in return for hard-liners relinquishing some power, reformers must signal this guarantee and demonstrate that they are able to control radical elements. A pacted transition, which was the cornerstone of the Spanish, Venezuelan, and Uruguayan transitions, requires the development of "a viable system of mutual security" to build consensus and "lower the costs of tolerating opposition" (Dahl 1971: 36). Under fragmented authoritarianism, however, we have seen that coordinated action among elites as a whole, and among soft-liners in particular, is made more difficult by multiple countervailing and competing centers of power and circles of actors. The diverse and institutionally scattered hard-liners and soft-liners are in no position to make credible commitments, for instance, that the IRGC will not organize a military coup or that reformists will not enact sweeping reforms that put the entire system of Islamic Republic under question. The risk of tolerating each other and the cost of creating a system of mutual security increases as the polity is more fragmented because it is necessary to bargain with a larger, and by definition more heterogeneous, collection of political competitors.

In Eastern Europe, mass mobilization played the crucial role of strengthening the bargaining position of soft-liners in the government and precipitating an authoritarian breakdown from the existing elite divisions. Mass movements in Poland, Serbia, and the former Czechoslovakia increased the costs of hard-liners using force to suppress opposition and thus discouraged a hard-line backlash against prodemocracy activists. Yet the fragmentation of soft-liners in Iran and the atomization of society, both of which are partly produced by the structure of the state, make this potential counterweight to authoritarian reentrenchment unlikely. In Iran, electoral victories by reformists in 1997, 2000, and 2001 led to antidemocratic backlash by the centers of hard-line power. Although students and intellectuals protested and challenged abuses of the law and the use of violence, their actions were isolated and uncoordinated, with politicians and organizations of the reformist Second of Khordad Front unwilling or unable to connect the issues and activities of the various groups that were willing to vote repeatedly in favor of these regime soft-liners. Thus, the coercive apparatus was able to identify vocal dissenters and crush protests, while the electoral majority remained immobilized.

Both theorists and soft-liners, including President Khatami, have often been wary of encouraging social mobilization and have preferred a more "moderate" tactic of confronting hard-liners. However, referencing a multitude of cases in southern Europe, Latin America, and East Asia, Nancy Bermeo demonstrates that democratic transition, including via elite pacts, is possible even when masses or popular classes are mobilized and active (Bermeo 1997). What she describes as the "moderation argument," or the thesis that too much popular mobilization threatens democratic transition because it can trigger a hard-line backlash, ignores important mass mobilizations such as labor, student, or leftist activism that under certain contexts not only did not impede transition but strengthened the position of reformists. Thus, under certain contexts and with particular forms of framing, mass politics may not necessarily be construed by hard-line elites as extreme or threatening.

It is in the shadow of the dilemmas of democratization and the exacerbating effect of a fragmented state that we fully appreciate the importance of soft-liners having a deeply rooted, strong organization or political party. Without one, elite disunity and the atomization of society cannot withstand repression or bargain with hard-line forces that are institutionally well placed. This has been the case with the current reformist movement that has shunned such organization building. When Khatami came to power, Hajjarian stated that the reformist faction aimed at "strengthening civil society and developing *an ensemble of autonomous institutions* that absorb and channel the torrent of social activity" (Ehsani 1999: 40, italics added) and functioned as a "front, rather than a party. At this point the leaders have insisted on a broad platform. They want to avoid rigid discipline in order to create a broad base" (Ehsani 1999: 42). The capacity of the reformists to maintain pressure on hard-liners was undermined by their strategy that did not actively engage its social base to coordinate activities of potential supporters (e.g., students, teachers, industrial workers, family members of political prisoners, and others).

Most reformist leaders have only viewed the role of citizens as voters. "Asked by a journalist why the reformers have failed to firm up a base in political parties and labor unions, Behzad Nabavi, deputy speaker of the Majles, replied that, in his opinion, popular support should be limited to people showing up regularly to cast their votes" (Ehsani 2004). The mainstream reformists have come to describe their strategy as "civil resistance" and "active pacifism" (*Sharq* 2 Ordibehesht 1383 [April 21, 2004]).

This strategy is shortsighted, if not naïve, for it assumes that public opinion and political will translate into political power. It is a particularly ineffective strategy given that hard-liners were well positioned in parallel institutions and thus the control of the presidency and legislature did not carry over through the entire regime. With a fragmented state structure with little control by elected officials over the bureaucracy and key executive powers, elected soft-liners cannot "translate electoral preferences into public policies that are then implemented" (Bunce 2000, 713). This became more evident as public apathy increased. What's more, the lack of a party or strong set of opposition institutions made it difficult to rejuvenate the energies of supporters at key moments. This was obvious in January 2004 when dozens of parliamentary members participated in a monthlong sit-in at the parliament in protest against the Guardian Council's disqualification of almost half the candidates for the Seventh Parliament, including eighty reformist candidates who were sitting members of parliament (MPs). Despite these dramatic events, threats of mass resignation by government ministers, and verbal support from university professors, students, newspaper writers, and other groups, there were no large demonstrations in front of the parliament, strikes, or other forms of collective action at the societal level. What is more, Mohsen Mirdamadi, a prominent reformist MP, admitted that reformists did not share the exact same tactics, nor did they have a committee for coordinating activities with likeminded groups in society (*Yas-e No* 7 Bahman 1382 [January 27, 2004]). Fortunately, since 2000, it has become evident to some members of the reformist camp that their position has been weakened by the lack of institutions to mediate their relationship with the society.[10]

Institutionalized political organizations will always help coordinate activities of group members. In the context of democratization, opposition groups that are centralized and hierarchical, even autocratic, tend to be better able to signal commitments to the rules of the game and thus negotiate an elite pact with hard-liners (Kalyvas 2000). However, political organization will also allow pro-reform forces to resist hard-line backlashes with timely political mobilization. These qualities are particularly wanting in the context of Iran's fragmented authoritarianism, and this suggests that organization building should be on the top of the agenda for those who wish to see a more democratic Iran.

Conclusion

Preservation is a creative matter. In this chapter, I have argued that the endurance of authoritarianism is a process that must be studied in its own right. Politics in authoritarian settings are neither aberrations of incomplete state control nor are they a stage to some democratic resting point. The Islamic Republic's authoritarianism is reproduced by elites and through state institutions that have patterned, although not determined, politics more generally. In Ellen Lust-Okar's analysis of Jordan and Morocco during economic crises in this volume, the Islamic Republic has created a "divided environment" where only certain elites are allowed to participate in formal politics, yet contestation has been sustained, ironically through state institutions themselves. This analysis of the Iranian case suggests that even in contexts where the opposition has unequal access to state power, oppositional mobilization is possible and indeed incubated by the state structure. This conclusion, however, is consistent with Lust-Okar's more general observation that a highly divided environment allows rulers to survive, even in the face of opposition from members of the ruling oligarchy. The case of the Islamic Republic demonstrates that elite conflict may be a necessary factor in a transition to democracy. Yet without taking into consideration the institutional context of these divisions, it is unclear if soft-liners will have the bargaining power to push through reforms, or if social forces will be sufficiently organized to push back an authoritarian backlash. The lesson from Iran is that without organizational power, democratizing forces cannot transform public opinion for democratization into political leverage to negotiate or force through an authoritarian breakdown.

Notes

I would like to thank Tamir Moustafa, Heather Fussell, Michele Penner Angrist, Marsha Pripstein Posusney, Ali Rezaei, and Nazanin Shahrokni for their thoughtful comments and suggestions on earlier drafts of this chapter.
    1. The reformist movement is composed of a coalition of parties and associations, principle among them are the Islamic Iran Participation Front, the Executives of Construction, the Association of Militant Clerics, the Organization of the Mujahidin of the Islamic Revolution, and the Islamic Iran Solidarity Party.

2. A few months after the 2004 electoral defeat of the reformists, the pro-reformist Islamic Association of the Faculty of Law and Political Science and Faculty of Social Science at Tehran University organized a two-day conference, "Transition to Democracy," that included lectures by leading reformist politicians and ideologues and university professors. At the opening, the secretary of the conference stated that the organizers of the conference believe that "Iran is a society in the process of transitioning to democracy" (*Sharq* 22 Ordibehesht 1383 [May 11, 2004]).

3. The terms *rahbar-e enqelab* and *vali-e faqih* are used interchangeably and are often translated as "Supreme Leader," "Leader of the Revolution," or "ruling jurisprudent." For the sake of simplicity, I will use "the Leader" to designate the office of the highest official of the Islamic Republic.

4. With high levels of urbanization and literacy, a moderate level of industrialization, and a fairly large middle class, Iran meets many of the preconditions commonly sited for democratization.

5. For a more thorough analysis of these groups, changes over time, and differences and similarities in other areas, see Baktiari (1996); Moslem (2002); and Mortaji (1378).

6. On the nature of sovereignty in Iran, see Schirazi (1998).

7. On the disparate groups that came together to constitute the IRGC, see *Hamshahri* 3 Ordibehesht 1383 (April 22, 2004).

8. On the role of "circles" in prerevolutionary Iran, see Bill (1972).

9. For an overview of pacted and mass mobilization models of democratization in Latin America and Europe, see Karl and Schmitter (1991) and Bunce (2000).

10. For examples, see comments by Hajjarian in *Yas e No* 27 Ordibehesht 1382 (May 16, 2004) and in *Sharq* 27 Day 1382 (January 17, 2004) and Behzad Nabavi in *Sharq* 2 Ordibehesht 1383 (May 21, 2004). Also see Razjou (1382 [2003]).

Part 2

Challenges to Authoritarian Rule

5

Multiparty Elections in the Arab World: Election Rules and Opposition Responses

MARSHA PRIPSTEIN POSUSNEY

This chapter discusses contested legislative elections that were held in a number of Arab countries from the 1970s through 2000. Arguing that electoral competition alone does not constitute democracy, it shows how the election rules were manipulated by the incumbent authoritarian executive rulers in order to ensure the emergence of loyal parliaments. The elections thus presented a strategic dilemma for opposition forces working to weaken or unseat the incumbents.

The 1990s and early 2000s saw a significant number of Arab countries initiate or expand multiparty competition for elected legislatures. Contested parliamentary elections were held in Tunisia, Algeria, Morocco, Egypt, Jordan, Yemen, Kuwait, Lebanon, Bahrain, and the Palestinian Authority (PA).[1] Incumbent executive rulers invariably tout these elections as evidence of domestic legitimacy and popularity, often anointing their countries as democracies in their wake. Among Middle East scholars, however, there is virtual consensus that despite this increased contestation, the political process in these countries, albeit to different degrees, falls short of today's generally accepted criteria for modern representative democracies.[2] Executive authority typically remains an uncontested, if not completely unelected, post,[3] as well as one that commands extraordinary powers, while the authority of the judicial and legislative branches is sharply constrained. Opposition parties have only limited access to the media and are usually restricted in their campaigning activities, new political parties must receive government permission to become legal, votes in support of the incumbent elites may be coerced (*tadakhkhul*, or interfered with), and a variety of means of falsifying the actual vote count (*tazwir*) are available. Thus, these countries are commonly considered to be more pluralist variants, but still in the category of authoritarian regimes.[4] Many scholars see their political openings as strategies for regime survival that are intended to forestall, rather than encourage, further pressures for democratization (see, e.g., Brumberg 1995; Dillman 2000; Talbi 2000).

Considerably less agreement exists, however, about the prospects for these openings to evolve into genuine democratic transitions. While much of the literature is pessimistic,[5] a spate of 1990s studies found in the region forces at work and processes similar to those that undermined authoritarian rule elsewhere in the world (inter alia, Brynen, Korany, and Noble 1995; Korany, Brynen, and Noble 1998). Some scholars have particularly emphasized the proliferation of nonstate, voluntary organizations, which are expected to promote greater tolerance for political debate and/or expand the organizational skills and resources available to citizens for challenging state power (esp. Norton 1995, 1996).

This civil society literature is, however, ambivalent about the significance of "pseudocompetitive elections" in the democratization process (Abu Khalil 1997).[6] The Western concept of civil society, albeit somewhat ambiguous, generally excludes political parties (Foley and Edwards 1996: 38–39; Chazan 1992: 287); thus, its evocation as the engine of democracy in Arab countries implies a denigration of partisan politics there.[7] In this context, opposition parties are often faulted for undemocratic internal operations (Abu Khalil 1997: 158–159; Harik 1994: 49); and, in some countries, party leaders are also criticized for being octogenarian, opportunistic, and out of touch with the masses.[8]

This chapter examines legislative elections held in the Arab world from the 1960s through 2000, with emphasis on those held in the 1980s and 1990s. It rests on the premise that *gradual* democratization is possible in these countries and that the elections themselves are an important arena of struggle. Holding contested elections foregrounds the principle that citizens have a right to self-selected political representation. Polls that are carefully controlled by governments can still provide a forum for diverse segments of society to publicly debate their collective future, as well as new opportunities for political mobilization. In addition, even legislatures with limited power often become the focus of press attention, so an opposition presence in parliament can provide a means for critics of the ruling regimes to promote their arguments via the official media.[9]

Therefore, I see the controlled contestation described here as a significant departure from earlier practices in these countries when elections, if held at all, featured little or no actual choice and were routinely reported by the governments to have almost universal voter turnout. "Pseudodemocracy" also distinguishes these countries from neighbors in the region, which remain as single-party states or monarchies devoid of elected legislatures altogether. The Arabic term commonly applied to these political openings, *ta'adudiyya,* meaning pluralization or multi-partyism—but not full democratization—captures these distinctions.

There is comparative evidence that democratic transitions can emerge from prolonged periods of controlled contestation. Both Samuel Huntington (1991) and Donald Share and Scott Mainwaring (1986) describe a situation in which opposition forces, originally weak at the time of regime-initiated openings, are able to gradually gain influence and ultimately negotiate democratization with reluctant incumbent authoritarians.[10] Mexico (Martinez 2000) and Senegal (Vengroff and Cheevey 1997; Vengroff and Magala 2000; Vengroff and Mozaffar 2002) provide examples of such protracted processes.

My approach presupposes the existence of secular opposition forces working within the electoral arena, and possibly Islamists as well. In suggesting that these groups can play a role in furthering the democratization process, I reject the argument that the forces in the region committed to Western democratic models are insignificant, so that the only real threat to incumbent authoritarians comes from radical Islamist movements that are equally antidemocratic (Waterbury 1994; Salamé 1994). The secular and moderate Islamic opposition forces identified and privileged here may be relatively small in number, but there is evidence that their actions can affect the political opening process. Moreover, even if some of these groups themselves exhibit authoritarian tendencies, their propaganda and actions in struggling against the incumbent regimes may nevertheless help to erode the latter's legitimacy.[11] Comparative research has identified the loss of regime legitimacy as key to the demise of authoritarian rule (Shin 1994: 152).

But suggesting the *possibility* of a phased and gradual transition to democracy is not meant to imply its *inevitability*. Against the optimistic teleology—reminiscent of the earlier "modernization theory"—of some civil society literature (esp. Ibrahim 1995; Kubba 2000), I emphasize political institutions and the influence of human agency. This chapter focuses particular attention on the institutional framework of these elections and the strategies that opposition forces adopt in relation to them. My purpose in this is not to diminish the potential role of nonpartisan civic associations in democratization;[12] rather, I wish to correct for the paucity of studies of electoral politics in the Arab region.[13]

Indeed, while the recent third wave of democratizations has spawned a considerable literature on what institutional designs are most conducive to the *consolidation* of new democracies (inter alia Mainwaring 1993; Lijphart and Waisman 1996; Linz and Stepan 1996), scant attention has been devoted to the possible role of institutional change in creating the conditions for democratic transitions to occur.[14] My claim here is simply that electoral struggles can play a role in helping to undermine authoritarian rule and that electoral systems influence the shape of electoral politics. Electoral structures may not be the unique or even the primary determinant of authoritarian election results, but they still "structure political interactions and in this way affect political outcomes" (Thelen and Steinmo 1992: 13). Even under controlled contestation, electoral systems will affect the number of political parties that operate in a country, their internal dynamics, and the strategies they adopt.

The following section shows that Arab rulers have consciously resorted to election engineering in order to produce loyal legislatures.[15] More subtle than *tadakhkhul* or *tazwir,* manipulating electoral design offers incumbents another way to control electoral outcomes in an immediate sense and partisan politics in their countries more broadly. The recent configuration of electoral systems in the region shows a preference among regime elites for winner takes all (WTA) voting,[16] which has proven especially beneficial for regimes pluralizing from a single-party situation.

I then explore the strategies through which nonviolent opposition forces—legal political parties as well as unrecognized groups that nevertheless manage to operate in the electoral arena—seek to diminish the authoritarian regimes' hegemony within the constraints posed by the electoral institutions. Election boycotts, organized election monitoring, and challenges to the existing electoral rules have all been attempted with varying degrees of success. Surmounting differences among the opposition forces in terms of ideologies, as well as short-term political goals and prospects, is a central strategic dilemma. For reasons explained here, the future is likely to see greater participation in campaigns by opposition activists, along with at least minimally cleaner elections as a consequence of opposition pressures. As regimes' resort to *tadakhkhul* and *tazwir* is restricted, electoral institutions will take on greater importance, and more struggles over election rules should result.

Electoral Engineering Under Controlled Contestation

Despite the sharp limits on the power of Arab parliaments, incumbent executives have exhibited a concern for ensuring compliant legislatures. Minimally, this will guarantee speedy passage of their legislative initiatives. In some cases these parliaments are also responsible for ratifying the rule of the government's head; even where the executive authority is not elected, loyal legislatures create the impression of a popular mandate for the incumbent leader. Thus, when they initiate contested legislative elections, executives try to guarantee parliaments dominated by their supporters (cf. Lust-Okar and Jamal 2002).

There is evidence in some cases that the executives designed the electoral rules at the outset to achieve the desired outcome. Both Morocco's first king, Muhammad V, and the PA's Yasir Arafat consulted international experts before settling on an electoral system, while Jordan's late king Hussein gerrymandered districts to diminish the influence of the Palestinian vote. But results may prove contrary to expectations, even when rigging and coercion are added for good measure. Jordan and Egypt represent two cases of regimes altering the rules of the game after initial results proved threatening.

Egypt's late president, Anwar al-Sadat, first initiated party contestation for parliamentary elections in 1976. He implemented a WTA system under which two seats were contested separately in each district, using a majority runoff rule.[17] In these elections candidates could run as independents, or as affiliates as one of three "platforms" that were created by Sadat, prior to the poll, from different tendencies within the singular Arab Socialist Union. The self-proclaimed centrist platform, representing Sadat supporters, won 280, or 82 percent, of the 342 contested seats. Forty-eight of the remaining 62 were captured by independents.

The WTA system thus worked to the advantage of the government-backed platform; Mark Cooper (1982) estimated that its actual popular vote was only 60 percent. Nevertheless, as Hosni Mubarak prepared for new parliamentary elections in 1984, albeit under expanded party competition and a freer press, he initiated a new electoral law. It seemed designed to maintain the vote distortion in favor of the ruling party, now known as the National Democratic Party (NDP), while at the same time eliminating the threat from the independent candidacies. His choice was a party-list proportional system but with such a high threshold—8 percent—that it negated the advantages of proportional representation (PR) for most opposition parties. The threshold was particularly onerous because the law required that a party poll 8 percent of the vote *nationally* in order to win seats in any particular constituency, so that even if an opposition party earned enough votes in one or more areas to qualify for seats there, those seats would be lost if its national total of the vote fell shy of the 8 percent. Moreover, *any* votes that a small party won that could not be used to obtain seats would accrue to the most successful party instead.[18]

In the end, of 448 contested seats, the NDP won 390, or 87 percent, thus increasing the ruling party's parliamentary majority over the 1976 legislature. However, it captured only 73 percent of the reported popular vote. The distortion occurred because both the leftist Tagammu Party and an Islamist/nationalist rival, the Socialist Labor Party (SLP), came in under the 8 percent threshold, so their votes accrued to the NDP instead.[19]

Jordan's King Hussein decided to convene full national legislative elections after a twenty-two-year hiatus, along with some other measures of political liberalization, in 1989 (Jaber and Fathi 1990: 67–86; *Middle East Magazine,* October 10, 1989). The monarchy revived the at-large plurality system of British colonial days, creating twenty electoral districts returning between two and nine candidates each (Reynolds and Elkit 1997: 53–54). Although a thirty-two-year-old ban on political parties remained in effect, affiliates of underground parties could run as independents, while the Muslim Brotherhood was able to sponsor candidates because it was considered a charitable organization and not a party (Piro 1992: 39–44; *Middle East Economic Digest,* November 24, 1989).

One of the king's main concern was to limit the representation of critics of his friendly attitude toward Israel. Thus, Jordanians of Palestinian origin were deliberately disadvantaged at the outset by the apportionment of representatives to the voting districts. Rather than being done strictly by population size, it awarded more seats to districts whose population was predominantly East Bankers, so that East Bankers' votes, in effect, counted more (Reidel 1994: 53; Wederman 1993: 11). Nevertheless, the elections resulted in considerable representation of anti-Israeli forces because of other aspects of the electoral rules. The multiple vote feature permitted electors to seek simultaneous representation of several different political identities. Given three votes, for example, citizens were able to first choose someone from their tribe and then perhaps some government patron, with a vote still remaining to express an ideological preference. In Jordan, many of these tertiary votes went to candidates from the Muslim Brotherhood, who were opposed to the monarchy's pro-Western foreign policies. Out of an eighty-seat parliament, Brotherhood and Islamic-identified candidates won thirty-four seats, or about 42 percent, and an assortment of leftist and pan-Arabist candidates won about another twelve (Piro 1992: 39; Brynen 1998: 75).

The Brotherhood had an advantage in these elections because of its national recognition, which the long-standing ban on parties denied to other opposition forces. This advantage was then magnified by the plurality voting rule. The relatively large number—averaging eight per district—of candidates per seat meant that as little as 10 percent of the vote could be sufficient for victory in some cases. Brotherhood candidates actually earned less than 20 percent of the vote overall, and the other Islamic candidates likewise captured a greater number of seats than the proportion of votes they polled (Reynolds and Elklit 1997: 53).

The regime solved this "problem" with the next elections, held in November 1993. A year earlier, the monarchy had permitted the formation of political parties, and some twenty-four of them, many reflecting pan-Arab, pan-Islamic, or Palestinian nationalist views, had been legalized before the poll. However, the king's endorsement of the controversial Oslo accords made the Islamists' foreign policy stance more threatening to the regime. Thus, Hussein also decreed a change in the electoral rules, switching to a single nontransferable vote (SNTV) system in which each district would still elect multiple candidates by plurality rule, but now each citizen would only get one vote (Reidel 1994: 53–56; *Chicago Tribune,* November 7, 1993).

Considered semiproportional by numerous scholars, SNTV can solve the problem of minority vote dilution in at-large districts with a racially or ethnically polarized electorate (Reynolds and Reilly 1997: 51–52; Amy 1993: 186–187, 232–233; Engstrom 1992: 743–770). In the Jordanian context, however, its effect was to privilege tribal sentiments. As the monarchy anticipated, many citizens awarded their single vote to a tribal favorite rather than an ideological preference, and the resulting parliament had a sharply diminished opposition presence. The Islamic Action Front, a coalition dominated by the Brotherhood, took sixteen seats, and independent Islamists another four, so Islamist forces together now held only 25 percent of the seats. Another eight seats were captured by various leftists, leaving roughly a 65 percent majority to generally pro-regime figures (Reidel 1994: 56; *MEED,* November 19, 1993).[20] There was then stepped-up repression of opposition Islamists, Arab nationalists, and leftists following Jordan's signing of a peace treaty with Israel in October 1994. And shortly before the next elections in 1997, the parliament provisionally approved a draconian press law intended to sharply limit public expressions of opposition to the monarchy's foreign and economic policies. In light of this, but especially because the government rejected calls to return to the old election laws, more than half of the political parties in Jordan boycotted the 1997 elections (Hourani 1998; Khouri 1998: 27–33; HRW 1997).

Winner-Takes-All Elections

Today, almost all of the Arab countries practicing *ta'adudiyya* have winner-takes-all electoral systems. WTA offers particular advantages to incumbent regimes in countries pluralizing from single-party situations. While in advanced democracies WTA is associated with two- or three-party systems, in this authoritarian context its effect is to maintain single-party domination by distorting the popular vote earned by the ruling party (see Table 5.1).

Table 5.1 Contested Legislative Elections in the Arab World: Years and Electoral Rules, Unicameral or Lower House Elections, 1964–2000

Country	Election Years	District Magnitude	Electoral System
Algeria	1991	1	Majority runoff (MRO)
	1997	Varies (by governorate)	Closed party-list PR (CPLP) (5% threshold)
Egypt	1976	2, separately contested	MRO
	1984	10	CPLP, 8% threshold
	1987	10, divided (9 plus 1)	Same as 1984, but 1 seat per district by plurality w/21% threshold MRO
Jordan	1990, 1995, 2000	2, separately contested	
	1989	Variable	At-large plurality
	1993, 1997	Variable	Single nontransferable vote
Kuwait	1992, 1996	2	At-large plurality
Lebanon	1992, 1996, 1999	Variable	At-large plurality, must conform to confessional quotas
Morocco	1964, 1977, 1984, 1993, 1997	1	Single-member district plurality
Palestine	1996	Variable	At-large plurality
Tunisia	1989	—a	Party-block vote (PBV)
	1994	—	PBV, but 12% of seats reserved for opposition by CPLP
	1999	—	PBV, 20% of seats reserved for opposition by CPLP
Yemen	1993, 1997	1	Single-member district plurality

Note: a. No data were available for Tunisia.

Explanation of Voting Systems

■ Single Winner Systems

Single Member District Plurality (SMDP), also known as "First Past the Post." Voters cast a ballot for a single candidate, and the candidate with the most votes wins.

Majority Runoff, also known as the "Two-Round system." Like SMDP but requires that a candidate receive some minimum proportion, usually just over 50 percent, of the vote. If no one does, a second election is held between only the two top vote-getters.

■ Multiwinner Systems

At-Large Plurality, also known as the "block vote." Voters can vote for up to as many candidates as there are seats to be filled but can assign only one vote to each candidate. The candidates with the most votes win.

Single Nontransferable Vote. Like at-large plurality in that winners are determined by a plurality rule, but each voter can only choose one candidate.

Closed Party List Proportional (CPLP), Voters cast their ballot for a party, and parties are awarded a number of seats according to the proportion of the vote they obtain. Each party fills its seats according to a prearranged, ranked list. (In open list systems, voters have the opportunity to show some preference among party candidates, thereby influencing the order of the list.) The threshold refers to the minimum proportion of seats a party must win to qualify for representation under this system.

Party-Block Vote. Like CPLP, except that that party that wins a plurality of the vote gets *all* the seats for that district.

Sources: Electoral system descriptions drawn from Reynolds and Reilly (1997: 27–50); Reeve and Ware (1991: ch. 7); and Amy (1993: 225–233). Country data drawn from country sources cited in text.

The cases of Palestine and Yemen illustrate this point nicely and also provide insight into how a PR system might produce different outcomes. In Palestine, the same at-large system that proved problematic for Jordan's monarchy worked to the advantage of Yasir Arafat's Fatah

Party. Elections to the Palestine Legislative Council (PLC) were held in January 1996 under the auspices of the 1993 Oslo peace agreements. They resulted in Fatah supporters holding about 75 percent of the seats in an eighty-eight member council (Ghanem 1996: 526; *Jerusalem Post,* January 23, 1996; *DPA,* January 22, 1996).[21] The rules for the PLC election were developed by an electoral commission appointed by Yasir Arafat in November 1993; the resultant election law was approved by the Palestinian Authority cabinet in December 1995.[22]

As in Jordan, the design called for multimember districts, in this case sixteen, with citizens able to cast as many votes as there were seats to be filled in each district with the winners decided by plurality rule. Also as in Jordan, the multiple-vote system enabled Palestinians to select local patrons and/or family favorites and at the same time register support for one or more candidates based on ideology. In this latter category the plurality rule favored Fatah-backed candidates because of the party's history and national recognition. In all districts combined, candidates running on a Fatah slate received only 30 percent of the votes, but the distorting effects of plurality gave them 58 percent of the eighty-eight seats. Conversely, those opposition parties that participated captured 10 percent of the total votes but received only 3 percent of the seats, while independents (many of whom were Fatah activists who for various reasons had not been selected for the Fatah slate in their district) polled about 60 percent of the votes but got only the remaining 39 percent of the seats (Ghanem 1996: 526).

Fatah's position was enhanced by the fact that rival factions within the Palestine Liberation Organization, as well as many Islamists affiliated with Hamas, refused to participate in the elections, charging that this would imply acceptance of the Oslo accords. But as noted by Khalil Shikaki, the smaller parties' decision to boycott was encouraged by the choice of an electoral system that gave them little opportunity to capture seats (*Jerusalem Post,* June 16, 1995). Before the draft election law was approved, several opposition parties, as well as the Geneva-based International Commission of Jurists, had urged the PA to adopt a proportional system that would give greater representation to opposition forces (Ghanem 1996: 526; *Jerusalem Post,* December 7, 1995, January 19, 1996). Put differently, the *magnitude* of Fatah's victory was the consequence of intentional, plurality-based electoral architecture by the Arafat appointees who designed the election rules.

Yemen's 1993 elections followed the 1990 merger of two formerly single-party states, the People's Democratic Republic of Yemen (PDRY, South Yemen) and the Yemen Arab Republic (North Yemen); multipartyism was adopted in both countries just before unity.[23] The election law, promulgated in 1992, specified a single-winner district plurality system (Republic of Yemen 1992: 24).[24] Containing 80 percent of unified Yemen's population, the north got a similar proportion of the 301 legislative seats.

Prior to the 1993 elections, the north's General People's Congress (GPC) and the south's Yemen Socialist Party (YSP) colluded in designing electoral districts to limit the challenges each would face from independents. The YSP was more ideologically coherent and faced less partisan competition, but because of the demographic disparity, vote distortion in the 1993 elections mainly benefited the GPC. Each of these parties captured about 14 percent of the popular vote in the *other's* former mainstay. Within its own stronghold, however, the YSP, with an average 57 percent of the vote, claimed almost 95 percent of the south's fifty-seven seats. By contrast, the GPC averaged just 32 percent of the vote in the north, winning only 49 percent of its seats. But in the country as a whole, the YSP's 18 percent of seats just equaled its overall popular vote, while the GPC still enjoyed a 13 percent gap between its seats (123, or 41 percent) and its 28 percent vote.[25]

Because Yemen's 1994 civil war was precipitated in part by frustrations of some YSP members with the GPC-dominated parliament, it is worth considering how proportional representation might have changed the complexion of the legislature: the GPC's proportion of seats would have been reduced, and more smaller parties and independents would have been represented. In addition, both the GPC's and YSP's parliamentary delegations would have contained party members based outside of their territorial strongholds, possibly exercising a moderating effect on north/south tensions.

As it happened, the YSP-led secessionist uprising was defeated, and the former PDRY was occupied by northern troops that destroyed former government institutions, confiscated the YSP's assets, and imposed harsh political restrictions, reversing the gains of the unification period. The YSP's irredentist leadership fled, and the party, albeit now in the control of a new faction, was ousted from the governing coalition. This enabled the GPC and Islamic-oriented al-Islah, the former third party and now junior partner in the government, to push through constitutional reforms that increased the powers of the president. Amid persistent rumors that the two governing parties had plans to rig the vote, the YSP boycotted the 1997 election. The GPC again benefited from vote distortion, garnering 62 percent of the seats with only 42 percent of the popular vote, and proceeded to govern as the ruling party (Saqqaf 1998: Glosemeyer 1998: 35–43; Carapico 1998: 186–195, 149).[26]

Tunisia and Egypt likewise illustrate the distorting effects of WTA but also show the potential for opposition forces to affect electoral institutions.

Tunisian elections use a plurality-based, multimember system known as the party-block vote, in which citizens vote for a single party, and the party that obtains the most votes wins all the seats in that district.[27] The first contested elections were held in 1989, after then–interior minister Zine al-Abidine Ben Ali deposed the senile strongman Habib Bourguiba. Ben Ali initiated a political liberalization that included the recognition of several additional secular opposition parties. Nevertheless, the regime refused to legalize the largest opposition group, Hizb al-Nahda, and when it came time to devise a new code for the 1989 elections, the government overruled the opposition parties' demands for a PR system. Not surprisingly in light of the election rules, the ruling Constitutional Democratic Rally (Rassemblement Constitutionnel Démocratique, or RCD) then captured *all* of the seats.

The next five years saw the government backtrack on liberalization as the Islamic movement intensified its activities. Torture, preemptive repression, and military trials of both Islamist and leftist dissidents returned, and the government refused to extend recognition to any more political parties. Prior to the 1994 elections, however, in a concession to the six parties that had been legalized earlier, the regime agreed to set aside 12 percent of the parliamentary seats for the opposition, to be distributed on a proportional basis. The remainder of the seats were still contested by party-block vote, and the RCD again won all of these. Officially, the ruling party polled just under 98 percent of the vote, so that the ironic effect of the set-aside was to distort the ruling party's vote *downward,* albeit still allowing it a comfortable majority of 144 seats in the then-163-seat legislature. Moreover, Michele Penner (1999: 94–99) has suggested that, besides lending an aura of legitimacy to the RCD's monopoly of power, the entry of self-admittedly weak opposition parties into the parliament served Ben Ali's purpose by fostering tighter discipline among the RCD delegates.

To what degree this 98 percent figure represents the regime's actual popularity, as opposed to a combination of *tadakhkhul, tazwir,* the bankruptcy of the legally recognized opposition, and/or the exclusion of the Islamists, cannot be determined here. But in response to accusations of fraud and vote coercion, Ben Ali upped the number of proportional seats to 20 percent in the 1999 elections; after these the legal opposition held thirty-four seats in a 182-seat body. For these elections, which coincided with the country's first contested presidential race, he also agreed to opposition demands for representation at the ballot counting and an independent, national group of election supervisors. In addition, some press restrictions were eased and pro-government rallies outside of polling places, previously used to pressure voters, were prohibited.

With these measures in place, the RCD's officially reported vote tally fell to 91.5 percent in the 1999 poll. Although the opposition's total vote was thus still upwardly distorted by the 20 percent PR set-aside, it did increase by about 400 percent over the previous election.

Finally, Egypt's return to WTA was actually not the original choice of the president but was imposed by the courts. A legal challenge filed by two opposition lawyers charged that the prohibition of independent candidacies violated constitutional provisions for individual rights. In 1986, the regime preempted an anticipated ruling in their favor by disbanding the parliament and issuing a new electoral law. It set aside one seat in each constituency for independent candidacies, although parties were also permitted to nominate individuals for these seats. They were contested on a plurality basis, with a runoff requirement if the top candidate polled less than 20 percent of the vote. Otherwise, however, the old PR system remained in effect.[28]

The subsequent 1987 election did result in a more diversified legislature, with most opposition parties represented. While the NDP still enjoyed a comfortable margin above the two-thirds majority needed to ensure Mubarak's renomination to the presidency, its hold on the legislature had fallen to 79 percent. Thereafter, the regime continued to cling to the PR rules, and the lawyers revised and resubmitted their case (Khalid 1989), setting the stage for another court battle and short-lived parliament. In May 1990, Egypt's constitutional court ruled that the 1986 election law unfairly discriminated against independents and declared the parliament elected under the law to be "null and void." A new election law restored the majority runoff system used in the 1970s, and new elections were then held in December, 1990.[29]

Still critical of the law for its failure to guarantee independent supervision of the elections, all but one of the established legal opposition parties, along with the still-unrecognized Muslim Brotherhood and some small leftists groups, boycotted this poll. Nevertheless, there were about 3,000 candidates, or almost seven for each seat, including 789 who were affiliated with the NDP but ran without the backing of their party. For the NDP's parliamentary majority, the full WTA system worked as well as the previous poll. NDP-backed candidates won only 253 of the 444 seats, with some significant defeats for party secretaries in six governates. However, 95 of the party affiliates who ran as independents won, and almost all of these were quickly co-opted into the party's parliamentary committee. Thus, the NDP could again count on 79 percent of the legislature's votes.

The individual candidate process did, however, remove from party leaders some ability to manage *which* NDP members would sit in the legislature. This phenomenon may have been a contributing factor to the escalated violence that marred the next elections, held in 1995.[30] Several new parties were legalized, and the government agreed to double the limited amount of airtime available to the opposition. That, and promises by Mubarak and his interior minister that the voting would be free and fair, led all opposition groups to participate, and the number of candidates grew to almost four thousand, or an average of about nine per seat.

Thanks in part to a large-scale crackdown on the Muslim Brotherhood—more than 1,000 members and sympathizers were arrested on the eve of the election—the NDP managed to increase its parliamentary majority in spite of this enhanced contestation. In the election's first round, there were 138 winners, of whom 124 were NDP backed, and 11 of the 14 victorious independents were NDP affiliates; no opposition party candidates captured seats. NDP-selected candidates then claimed 183 of the 306 seats that went to runoff, with opposition parties taking only 13 seats.[31] All but 13 of the winning independents were again NDP loyalists, giving the ruling party a total of 417, or 94 percent, of the contested seats—its strongest parliamentary majority ever.[32]

Despite an election-monitoring effort mounted by several domestic NGOs (see next section), opposition activists maintain that an unprecedented level of repression and government interference was behind this result. There were also numerous violent clashes between camps supporting rival candidates loyal to the regime. Some charge that party leaders tolerated, if not encouraged, these confrontations because they questioned the loyalty of members who ran as independents when denied the party's backing (Kienle 1998: 230–331).

Egypt's "deliberalization" continued thereafter, with tighter restrictions on trade unions and professional syndicates, the aforementioned law on NGOs, further crackdowns on the Muslim Brotherhood, and the court-ordered disbanding of the SLP.[33] However, several months before the next scheduled parliamentary elections in the fall of 2000, the Supreme Constitutional Court supported a long-standing opposition demand that the polling must be supervised by judges, and Mubarak accepted the ruling. Thus, the regime once again proved itself somewhat vulnerable to domestic and international criticism of its electoral practices. Civil society, however, paid a high price for this victory: it was just a few weeks before the anticipated court ruling that Saad ed-Din Ibrahim, who had been a leader of the 1995 election monitoring effort, was arrested along with some two dozen associates. The arrests were widely understood as an attempt to discredit Ibrahim and silence his criticisms of fraudulent electoral practices. The Egyptian Organization for Human Rights, another mainstay of the 1995 monitoring effort, had also been intimidated from accepting foreign funding and was forced to cut back its activities; these factors combined severely hampered the informal monitoring of the 2000 poll (Langohr 2001).

With judges supervising the actual casting of ballots, observers say that the focus of government attempts to manipulate the outcome moved outside the voting booths; numerous incidents of soldiers or government-sponsored thugs preventing voters from getting to the polls were reported. Also, for the first time the regime arrested Muslim Brotherhood candidates, not just supporters, prior to the voting. Nevertheless, the vote itself was reportedly cleaner because of the judiciary's role, and the results show a diminished NDP majority in parliament—the ruling party captured 388 seats, or 87 percent. As before, however, a significant number of pro-NDP candidates ran as independents, and this time a much greater proportion of these won, while there were embarrassing losses for some notable NDP-selected candidates. What Jason Brownlee cleverly labeled "NDPendents" won 56 percent (218) of the NDP's total number of seats, up from 23 percent in the previous poll, which complicates the enforcement of party discipline. Opposition parties gained only 3 seats, but the Muslim Brotherhood captured 17 seats, despite fielding less than half the number of candidates it did in 1995.[34]

In sum, then, opposition forces were able to make some gains through challenging Egypt's electoral practices. The single-winner district electoral system, however, has worked to perpetuate ruling-party domination of the legislature as well if not better than the 1984 PR laws, albeit weakening the NDP internally. Opposition *parties* faired poorly under it, though, suggesting that for them, endorsing the return to WTA elections was a miscalculation.[35]

WTA in Non–Ruling Party Situations

Where a single, loyalist party does not exist, WTA is not necessarily intrinsically beneficial to ruling executives. The lack of a large, nationally based party appears to make preexisting religious, ethnic, and/or regional cleavages in a country more salient to electoral outcomes. This may make it necessary for incumbent executives to foster multiple loyalist groupings, and/or to make greater resort to other institutional manipulations, to ensure a compliant legislature.

The interaction of tribal identifications, the lack of a national party, and an at-large voting system has already been illustrated in the case of Jordan's 1989 elections. Lebanon is another example of this, although its confessional history and long years of interference by Israel and

Syria in its internal affairs make its political dynamics unique in the region. The at-large system there is modified by the requirement that the winning slate—and each voter's ballot—fulfill certain confessional requirements. To simplify voting and enhance their chances, elites within the different religious communities forge alliances and present complete lists, thus giving the elections the appearance of a choice among competing, party-like slates. However, independent candidacies are possible, and voters can split their tickets as long as they respect the confessional quotas that the winning slate must fulfill.[36]

In this situation, the design of the constituencies plays a key role in determining *which* communal group will constitute a plurality within a district, and can also favor supporters of one elite group *within* a religious community over others, thereby creating excluded political minorities within the different confessions. Critics have charged that the system perpetuates communal identities and impedes the development of large, national parties (Naaman 1998; cf. Harik 1999).

The 1992 election law, which resumed parliamentary elections under the auspices of the Taif accords, was widely criticized for gerrymandering to favor communal leaders allied with the Syrian-backed government. Christian opposition forces as well as many Muslims boycotted the elections, and about 90 percent of the winners were government supporters. This parliament then passed a similar election law shortly before the 1996 poll, prompting some anti-Syrian Christian groups to boycott again. With blatant intimidation of voters, encouraged by an open ballot provision in the law, the pro-government lists increased their hold to 95 percent of the seats (Salem 1997: 26–29; LCPS 1996; Khazen 1994: 120–136; Harik 1998: 127–156; wire services).

The 2000 elections, however, held after the death of Syrian president Hafez al-Assad and his replacement by his son, Bashar, may have changed this pattern.[37] Lebanese president Emile Lahoud and then–prime minister Salim al-Hoss were hand picked by Bashar after his succession, and the election was widely understood as a referendum on their leadership. Though several right-wing Christian parties again boycotted, some Christian opponents of the regime did participate, including, notably, the grandson of Phalange founder Pierre Gemayel and Nassib Lahoud, a relative but critic of the president. The regime was also challenged by some left-wing and nationalist forces who had become disillusioned with Syrian interference in Lebanese affairs, notably Druse leader Walid Jumblatt. Finally, billionaire Rafik Hariri, the former prime minister who had been ousted when Lahoud became president, mounted a well-financed campaign to reclaim his post.[38]

Results showed a dramatic setback for the regime. Amid accusations of extensive vote buying, but also in defiance of new gerrymandering in the Beirut area intended to weaken his chances, Hariri and his allies swept the Beirut poll, defeating al-Hoss; Hariri was appointed prime minister the following month. Nassib Lahoud was elected in the Christian Metn region, in spite of interference by the interior minister, himself also a candidate, and Jumblatt and his allies were also victorious, in spite of gerrymandering, in the Shuf area. Thus, Hariri's bankroll notwithstanding, these elections demonstrate that incumbent authoritarians are not invincible.[39]

Morocco has the longest history of contested legislative elections in the region, dating back to 1963. Single-member district plurality rules were regularly used. The previous two kings, Hassan II and his father, Mohammed V, both sponsored a succession of multiple loyalist parties, including one geared toward the country's Berber minority, while at the same time working to foster splits among opposition forces. When the monarchy nevertheless had difficulty ensuring loyalist victories through the standard means of gerrymandering and *tazwir,* it resorted to parliamentary suspensions, delayed elections, and indirect elections that favored regime clients.[40]

In the SMDP context, this strategy of fostering competing loyalist parties was risky: on the one hand, it gave the various opposition parties an incentive *not* to unite by offering each an opportunity to win seats with a very low proportion of votes, without having to compromise their ideological principles or political agendas.[41] But on the other hand, it meant that the opposition, if it could unify, would have an advantage over the competing loyalist candidates.

In addition to shifting popular sentiments, such cooperation was a factor behind legislative gains realized by the opposition parties in the 1993 and 1997 polls. By agreeing not to compete with each other in the same districts, the two main opposition parties, Istiqlal and the Socialist Union of Popular Forces (Union Socialiste des Forces Populaires, or USFP) gained 45 percent of the directly elected seats in 1993.[42] But they refused to accept junior positions in the cabinet, instead renewing charges of electoral fraud and coercion, as well as generalized repression. Hassan responded by granting a wide-scale political amnesty and establishing a Ministry of Human Rights. He then proposed a compromise constitutional revision: a bicameral legislature but with a fully directly elected lower house. The new upper house would be indirectly elected, mainly from local and provincial assemblies where the monarchy, thanks to patronage, enjoys more support. Most of the opposition agreed to support the change, which was put to a referendum in 1996 and passed by the customary wide margins (White 1997: esp. 393–399).

There are some indications that the late king was rethinking his electoral strategy before the 1997 vote. In a major speech, Hassan extolled the virtues of umbrella-type political movements and was reportedly urging unification of the disparate loyalist parties and individuals. However, this project encountered resistance from MPs and high-level civil servants worried about the risk to their sinecures and clientage networks.[43]

In 1997, the Istiqlal/USFP block, again with a noncompetition agreement, won a total of 102 seats in the lower house vote, compared to only 100 for the pro-government group. However, in the upper house, pro-regime parties took 76 seats to the opposition's 44. Afterward, the king offered the premiership and various other ministries to the opposition groups, which this time accepted, and USFP leader Abderrahmane Youssoufi became prime minister (Karam 1998; Assidon 1998; *MEED,* December 19, 1997). However, critics maintain that the USFP's victory was sanctioned by a monarchy seeking the opposition's cooperation and blessing (Assidon 1998) and that the authoritarian cast of politics in the country was not substantially changed, even after the death of Hassan and the ascension of his son, Mohammed VI (Catusse 2001; Maghraoui 2001b).

* * *

This brief overview demonstrates that electoral systems affect electoral outcomes, even under conditions of controlled contestation. Authoritarian executives have many resources at their disposal to ensure a loyalist legislative majority, but electoral rules influence the size and cohesion of that majority. They also affect the degree to which incumbent rulers must resort to *tadakhkhul* or *tazwir* to maintain legislative control.

The preceding sketches also refute the image of executive omnipotence. Incumbent authoritarians regularly resort to repression, coercion, ballot-box stuffing, and (at times) to redesigning electoral rules and gerrymandered districts. Nevertheless, democratic forces are not entirely powerless in this game and have made limited gains. This makes the strategies employed by opposition forces in relation to these elections worthy of study.

Oppositional Strategies Under Contested Authoritarian Elections

When authoritarian rulers initiate controlled multiparty contestation, it signals that they are vesting part of their legitimacy in a competitive electoral process and the constitutional framework that accompanies this opening. Though authoritarian executives retain extraordinary powers, this act nevertheless gives democratic forces cards to play. By withholding participation, exposing and challenging electoral violations, and/or critiquing the electoral rules themselves, independent activists and opposition parties can diminish the executive's credibility. Success in such campaigns may also result in an expanded opposition presence in parliament, giving greater voice to alternative legislative agendas.

There is a paucity of comparative literature on opposition strategies under pseudodemocratic conditions. This section seeks to begin filling the void by reviewing the various strategies that opposition forces in pluralizing Arab countries have employed. As with the previous section, this overview confirms the importance of institutional analysis. Because electoral systems affect the number of parties that operate, the likelihood (outside of *tadakhkhul* and *tazwir*) that these parties will win office and the degree of internal party cohesion play a role in shaping the opposition response to controlled contestation.

Election Boycotts

For independents and opposition parties, the invitation to participate in controlled elections represents both opportunities and risks. Campaigning provides a previously denied avenue, however narrow, for promoting their general programs and critiques of the regime. However, opposition activists risk being perceived as opportunistic for joining in a venture aimed at legitimating authoritarian rule and hypocritical if they criticize the electoral process too extensively even while participating in it. Campaigning may also drain their limited resources from other important grassroots activity.[44]

In contrast, formally abstaining from elections represents a strong challenge to ruling regimes, as it denies authoritarian incumbents whatever legitimacy they might claim from sponsoring contested elections. Opposition activists have suggested that boycotts are most effective when linked to specific demands for political reform.[45] Such a situation requires a cooperative effort by at least most of the opposition forces, though, and this coordination may be difficult to achieve.

One obvious problem is ideological: it is difficult to achieve cooperation among parties and individuals who compete with each other precisely because they disagree on important matters. Another is that parties may have different short- and long-term political goals depending on their size and history. Adam Przeworski (1991: 40–41) has suggested that under democracies, parties compete because of uncertainty about electoral outcomes; if they knew they were certain to lose, they wouldn't make the effort. But even in two-party democracies, third parties often contest elections solely as a vehicle for gaining greater popular recognition and awareness of their platforms. This same reasoning applies to newer, smaller opposition parties contesting authoritarian elections. For larger groups, however, actually winning seats and the mantle of being the main opposition voice in parliament may be more realizable and more important. The latter groups sacrifice more by nonparticipation and thus may be reluctant to join their smaller counterparts in such an effort; this happened in Egypt when the Wafd pulled out of an opposition coalition planning to boycott the 1984 poll.[46] Even among parties with compatible goals and equal prospects, election boycotts represent a classic prisoner's dilemma situation. While each would benefit from the embarrassment to incumbent elites if all join the boycott, if one party defects, it then gains sole access to whatever benefits—in terms of media attention and/or rewards from the regime for participation—come from being the sole opposition presence in parliament.

Parties also vary in their levels of internal cohesion, and boycotts can challenge party discipline and cause splintering. In countries whose electoral systems permit independent candidacies, individuals who disagree with their party's boycott decision will be tempted to break ranks. Such disagreements may be purely strategic but could also stem from opportunism: for prospective opposition candidates who place their personal political aspirations above their party's goals and are also popular enough to win seats, abstention means an opportunity to serve in parliament foregone. The boycott decisions in Egypt's 1990 elections were controversial, and numerous opposition figures defied their parties; the Wafd publicly cancelled the membership of fourteen party affiliates who had won seats running independently. Some individual Hamas members defied boycott instructions to run as independents in Palestine's 1996 poll; likewise, in Jordan's 1997 election, a few Islamic Action Front (IAF) members defected from their party's boycott, as did some members of the other abstaining parties.

For all these reasons, coordinated boycotts are likely to be rare, and the probability of success will vary inversely with the number of opposition parties and groups. The one effective opposition boycott shown here—the Istiqlal/National Union of Popular Forces (Union Nationale des Forces Populaires, or UNFP) abstention from Morocco's 1970 election—required the cooperation of only two parties. Significantly, it resulted in a subsequent constitutional revision involving concessions to the opposition. Otherwise, as the previous section showed, the terrain of Arab elections has seen numerous partial abstentions that failed to produce institutional change.

Excluded or abstaining parties, and/or independent dissidents, may ask voters to spoil their ballots rather than simply staying home from the polls.[47] A clandestine movement to this effect emerged during Egypt's 1987 campaign; numerous educated Cairenes reported purposely voting for all the parties as a means to show approval of none. This was intended not only to register disenchantment with the candidate field but also to prevent government functionaries from using unclaimed ballots to falsely vote for the ruling party. Although no one officially claimed credit for this tactic, it was obviously an idea that resonated: more than 5 percent of the total votes cast were disqualified, representing an increase of 64 percent over the 1984 poll, at a time when voter turnout increased by only 15 percent. Still, in the absence of a public and organized effort to promote deliberate ballot invalidation, governments can easily dismiss the voided ballots as simple voter error.

Participation Strategies

While both public and clandestine boycott attempts are apt to continue, the difficulties outlined above suggest that at least partial participation by opposition elements is likely to characterize authoritarian Arab elections in the near future. Choosing to participate presents democratic activists with a number of alternative strategies that can enhance their chances for capturing seats. These strategies aim at surmounting or lowering electoral thresholds, and/or restricting government-sponsored voting irregularities.

Electoral coalitions. Multiparty coalitions can take the form of joint slates (in party-list-based systems), or noncompetition agreements. As with boycotts, smaller coalitions among like-sized parties are easier to build and maintain than larger, more diverse ones. Morocco's Istiqlal/USFP noncompetition agreement, which resulted in an increased opposition presence in the 1993 and 1997 parliaments, is an example of this.

Again, however, differences in ideology, size, and short-term goals and prospects among parties—all mediated in part by the electoral system—present barriers to cooperation. These factors were operative when the larger, more popular Wafd refused to join a joint opposition slate proposed by smaller opposition parties for Egypt's 1987 PR elections. In 1984, the Wafd did form a temporary coalition with the Muslim Brotherhood, which was prohibited from forming a party but allowed to contest the elections via an alliance with a legal party, and this proved to be the only opposition slate that passed the 8 percent threshold. However, the arrangement broke down over ideological differences before the 1987 poll. A new alliance (*tahaluf*) between the Brotherhood and the Islamic/nationalist Socialist Labor Party and the smaller Ahrar Party was then formed; the secular and leftist Tagammu declined to participate because of ideological disagreements.[48]

Election monitoring. Because all opposition candidates suffer when a regime is able to coerce votes or falsify results, all stand to benefit from joint activities that restrict these practices. It is easier for ideologically diverse groups and individuals to cooperate on domestic election supervision than on coalitions, and parties of different size and prospects can unite on monitoring more readily than on boycotts. For all these reasons, domestic monitoring activities have been on the increase. This includes efforts initiated both by parties and by independent civil society organizations.

Egypt's 1995 elections saw opposition parties, human rights groups, and some individual democratic activists form a People's Committee for Election Monitoring, which trained about six hundred individuals as poll watchers and was able to monitor voting in 40 percent of the constituencies. The committee also investigated citizens' complaints elsewhere and ultimately issued a damning report of its findings. Although this activity did not seem effective in reducing the regime's resort to rigging and coercion, it did appear to have some effect afterward in discrediting the election outcome. The U.S. Department of State was obliged to issue an unusual statement of concern, calling on the Mubarak government to investigate the irregularities, and the courts subsequently nullified the results in eighty out of eighty-eight districts that the committee had cited (Ibrahim 1995: 2, 10; Egyptian Organization for Human Rights 1995: 3; *al-Ahram Weekly,* December 14, 1995; Reuters, December 1, 1995). The aforementioned persecution of Saad ed-Din Ibrahim and his associates is perhaps the best testament to the salience of the election-monitoring campaign.

Lebanon's 1996 and 1999 elections also had informal monitoring, by an independent group called Lebanese Association for the Democracy of Elections (LADE). Headed by an American University of Beirut political science professor, LADE reported numerous instances of security forces intimating voters in both polls. However, the group was too small to place people throughout the country or even to cover all the polling places within an individual district.

In Tunisia, as we have seen, Ben Ali agreed to opposition demands for representation at the ballot counting and an independent, national group of election supervisors for the 1999 poll, and the opposition performed better in these elections. The Moroccan opposition struggled unsuccessfully to have a committee of constitutional judges supervise the elections rather than the interior ministry. Before the 1997 poll, however, the regime did agree to the formation of a committee headed by a senior judge, with representatives from those parties serving in parliament along with the ministers of justice and the interior, to review complaints of procedural violations (Karam 1998: 5).

Monitoring by international organizations is more controversial. U.S. agencies that participate in this have been vilified in some opposition circles because of the lopsided U.S. support for Israel; European powers, while perceived as more evenhanded, are nevertheless tainted by their history of colonialism in the region. In Egypt, some opposition parties have relied on foreign journalists to report irregularities, and there was a request by some for neutral foreign observation of the 1995 poll. It was not supported by all democratic forces, though, and was denied by the government, which has used accusations of subservience to foreign powers as a means to discredit some opposition activists. Foreign monitoring of Palestine's elections was mandated in the Oslo peace agreement, but the flagrant foreign presence was suspect among some opponents of the peace accords, even though the monitoring was supposedly intended to protect their participation.

The effectiveness of foreign monitoring has also been criticized. In Morocco, the regime itself invited international observers in an attempt to legitimize the 1993 poll. The Istiqlal/USFP bloc nevertheless considered the results to have been rigged, and at least one foreign monitor found reason to validate this suspicion (Munson 1999: 37–39).

Changing the rules. Finally, opposition forces have at times struggled to influence the electoral rules themselves. In the case of districting, the results in the period under study have been mixed. Morocco's opposition bloc successfully negotiated a redrawing of district lines prior to the 1993 poll (Dillman 2000: 220), but the boycotts in Lebanon failed to undo gerrymandering there.

The same is true of electoral system change. In Egypt, as already noted, the opposition parties miscalculated in supporting a return to single-winner districts as opposed to fighting to maintain PR, but with a lower threshold. The Egyptian case nevertheless shows that authoritarian regimes claiming to uphold constitutionalism can be vulnerable to legal challenges. Elsewhere, Jordan's opposition did not win a repeal of the 1993 electoral rules, and in Palestine, small parties were rebuffed in their attempts to win PR. The region is, nevertheless, likely to see more struggles over election rules in the coming years because, as election monitoring programs spread and increase in effectiveness, regimes will have less resort to *tadakhkhul* and *tazwir*. This will make institutional engineering more important as a means of electoral control.

Opposition representation as a whole could be increased through the adoption of PR. This, in turn, could strengthen the opposition's ability to push for further democratic reforms.[49] Opposition forces may, however, have difficulty uniting behind a particular PR program. Smaller parties, as well as those that are geographically based, have reason to seek systems with a relatively low threshold that is applied on a district basis; larger parties with a national following might seek more stringent parameters. For independents, or parties contending in countries where voting is tribally based, preferential varieties of PR such as SNTV or cumulative voting seem most beneficial, although there appears to be less awareness of these possibilities.[50]

In the debate over the best institutional arrangements for the consolidation of new democracies, some scholars have cautioned against the use of proportional electoral systems. The large, umbrella-type parties typically associated with WTA are held to be crucial for building national unity, whereas PR systems, by encouraging small parties, are said to promote ethnic or other fragmentation (Lardeyret 1991: 30–48). Those who see economic liberalization as necessary for democratic consolidation have suggested that fragmented party systems are an obstacle to winning legislative support for economic reform programs (Haggard and Kaufman 1995: 166–174, 355–364; Diamond 1994: 16; World Bank 1995: 200–201, 211). Both sets of arguments can be contested on theoretical as well as normative grounds (Lijphart and Waisman 1996; Reynolds 1999). But even if one stipulates that the stability and efficiency of government associated with WTA systems is preferable for new democracies, the Arab countries analyzed here are not in that category. Supporters of democracy in these countries must rather consider what type of voting system will best help to *undermine* the stability of incumbent authoritarians regimes intent on forestalling further democratic reform.

To be sure, demands for PR by the opposition might serve to educate incumbent authoritarians about the benefits, to them, of maintaining WTA systems. But even when opposition demands for systemic change are rebuffed, simply calling for PR provides another way for activists to publicly expose the limitations of these regimes' supposed commitment to diverse representation. And that exposure, in turn, can help to erode whatever legitimacy entrenched authoritarians gain by sponsoring pseudoelections.

Conclusion

For democracy to come to the countries studied here, many reforms would have to follow the initiation of contested elections. Respect for individual and group freedoms must be instantiated and the extraordinary powers of the executive must be curtailed. In the monarchies, executive authority must become an elected, civilian post.

Multiparty legislative elections have been initiated by authoritarian Arab rulers not as a step toward making these changes but as a means to forestall them. Nevertheless, in associating their own legitimacy with electoral competition, authoritarian rulers have set the stage for democratic activists to contest not only the elections but also the constraints under which the opposition must operate. Thus, the limited electoral openings reviewed here can prove to be stepping stones toward greater democracy.

With ideological and political differences among opposition forces making unified boycott actions unlikely, opposition strategies can be expected to gravitate toward electoral participation coupled with challenges to the rules of the game. Over time, the results should be cleaner and fairer elections, with an increased, even if still limited, opposition voice in the parliaments. These are only modest gains, to be sure, but advances that can nevertheless signify, and make further contributions to, a gradual erosion of authoritarian rule.

Notes

I would like to acknowledge helpful comments on earlier versions of this chapter from Eva Bellin, Miguel Glatzer, Iliya Harik, John Kerr, Ann Lesch, Vickie Langohr, Rob Richie, Wendy Schiller, Jillian Schwedler, Joe Stork, Greg White, and especially Ellen Lust-Okar. I am also grateful for the research assistance of Myrna Atalla, Daria Viviano, Laurent Fauque, and Colleen Anderson.

1. For simplicity of writing only, the Palestine Authority is categorized here as a country. This is not intended to prejudge the outcome of any new peace negotiations.

2. Dahl (1971: 1–7) offers a commonly used checklist.

3. The exceptions are Algeria, as of spring 2004 and the 1996 presidential elections in the PA.

4. Diamond (1996) labeled countries of this type "pseudodemocracies." For more recent classification schema, see Carothers (2002); Schedler (2002); Levitsky and Way (2002); and Ottaway (2003).

5. This is especially true of the orientalist school, which sees Islamic culture itself as inimical to political pluralism. For a review and critique of this literature, see Sadowski (1993); Kramer (1997); and Anderson (1995a).

6. "Pseudocompetitive elections" was coined by Linz (1978a, esp. 60–65) in reference to historically analogous elections in Europe and Latin America.

7. Some authors, however, do consider Arab political parties to constitute part of civil society. Al-Sayyid (1995: 137) suggests that since Arab opposition parties have no real chance of capturing power, they are not functionally different from issue-oriented interest groups. Norton, in his 1995 introduction to the *Civil Society* volumes, includes parties as part of civil society, without comment.

8. See, for example, Abdelhaq and Heumann (2000) on Tunisia; and Maghraoui (2001a) on Morocco; this same criticism of Egyptian opposition parties has been made to me by numerous independent Egyptian intellectuals.

9. Jillian Schwedler contributed to the formulation of this paragraph.

10. See also Diamond (1996: 25). Baaklini, Denoeux, and Springborg (1999, esp. 30–33) use Share and Mainwaring's term "transaction" to describe the possibility of this occurring in the Arab world. Yet I believe that the loss of authoritarian control implied here makes their "extrication" (or "transplacement," in Huntington's [1991] typology) the more appropriate term.

11. On this point, see also Kramer (1992: 23).

12. It is worth noting, however, that as civic associations have become more of a threat to authoritarian regimes, they have come under increasing pressures to curtail their activities. During the 1990s, governments throughout the region have passed laws sharply regulating NGOs (Pitner 2000). At the same time, NGO leaders, like party heads, have been criticized from below for authoritarian and opportunistic practices; they are also accused of dependence on foreign donors. See Vickie Langohr's chapter in this book.

13. With minimal and only recent exception (notably, Baaklini, Denoeux, and Springborg 1999), political institutions and political strategies generally have been downplayed in the study of Arab countries. Another attempt to fill this gap is shown in Lust-Okar and Jamal (2002).

14. Shin (1994: 143) notes a general paucity of studies on the process of eroding authoritarian rule prior to the onset of transitions. Subsequent efforts to fill this gap, with an emphasis on the role of institutions, include Bratton and van de Walle (1997); Vengroff and Magala (2000); and Martinez (2000).

15. I focus on legislative rather that executive elections here, first, because there are more examples to use as evidence, and second, because there are more institutional manipulations available for parliamentary polls than for the election of a single individual.

16. Winner-takes-all voting is understood here to include all methods of electing a single winner and multimember elections using the at-large plurality method. For debate on the different systems' effects in a democratic context, see inter alia, Reynolds and Reilly (1997); Reeve and Ware (1991); and Amy (1993).

17. One seat per district was reserved for candidates identified as a worker or a peasant. Information on the 1976 elections throughout this chapter is collated from Makram-Ebeid (1996: 120–121); Auda (1991: 12, 18n); Waterbury (1983: 366); Hinnebusch (1985: 172–173); and Cooper (1982: 222–226).

18. Information on the 1984 elections is from Najjar (1989: 98–100) and Hendriks (1985: 11–18).

19. An alliance between the New Wafd Party and the Muslim Brotherhood was the only opposition grouping able to surmount the 8 percent barrier; it polled 15 percent of the vote, and got the remaining 13 percent of the seats. The Brotherhood was officially prohibited from entering the elections because the constitution forbids the formation of religious parties, but their participation was tacitly tolerated by Mubarak.

20. On Western interpretations of the implications of these and the subsequent Palestinian elections for the Oslo peace process, see Posusney (1999).

21. This figure combines the seats won by fifteen Fatah activists running as independents with those captured by Fatah members running on the party's slate.

22. The committee received advice from the European Union and the U.S.-based National Democratic Institute and International Foundation for Electoral

Systems. The U.S. organizations apparently supported these election rules and, as required by the Oslo agreements, Israel also signed off on them. See National Democratic Institute and the Carter Center (1997: 27–20).

23. Information on Yemen's 1993 elections is drawn from Carapico (1993: 2–6); Detalle (1993: 8–12); Glosemeyer (1993: 439–451), and Carapico (1998: 140–151).

24. I am grateful to Iris Glosemeyer for providing me with this text.

25. The computations of vote/seat ratios are mine.

26. The computation of vote distortion is mine.

27. Sources on Tunisia's elections are Gasiorowski (1992: 85–97); Penner (1999); Alexander (1997: 34–38); Tessler, Entelis, and White (1995b: 423–445); Wright (1999); Geisser (2000); Abdelhaq and Heumann (2000); Bras (2000); and *Africa News,* October 29, 1999. I also benefited from personal communication with Mark Tessler, Chris Alexander, Greg White, and Michele Angrist in April 1999.

28. Information on the 1987 elections comes from Najjar (1989: 100–109) and Post (1987: 17–22), which was written pseudonymously by me.

29. Information on the 1990 elections is from Auda (1991: 14–16); *Africa Economic Digest,* May 28, 1990; *Middle East Economic Digest,* September 28 and October 12, 1990; *The Guardian,* November 29, 1990; and an interview with Ahmad Adballa, April 1993.

30. Information on the 1995 elections is culled from Mustafa (1997); Makram-Ebeid (1996); Center for Human Rights Legal Aid (1996); Egyptian Organization for Human Rights (1995); Langohr (2001); *Al Ahram Weekly,* December 7–13 and December 14–20, 1995; and press coverage in Reuters, United Press International, and Deutsch Presse-Agentur

31. The Wafd earned six of these and thus reclaimed its earlier status as the leading opposition party in parliament.

32. Only one Muslim Brother was elected from among the 180 who ran.

33. Based on the reporting in *al-Ahram Weekly* and conversations with various intellectuals and activists during several visits to Cairo in 1999 and 2000.

34. Drawn from Brownlee (2001); Langohr (2000, 2001); an interview (in Providence, RI, May 6, 2001) with Bahgat Korany, a political science professor at the American University in Cairo; and regular coverage in *al-Ahram Weekly.*

35. It should be noted that Kamal Khalid, one of the lawyers who filed the court case against the PR laws, intentionally sought to encourage independent candidacies because he viewed the opposition parties as authoritarian and corrupt. Personal interview (in Arabic), in Providence, RI, October 1, 1998, and Khalid's comments at the conference on "Controlled Contestation and Opposition Strategies: Multi-Party Elections in the Arab World," Brown University, October 2–3, 1998. Hereafter referenced as the "Brown elections conference" (Khalid 1998).

36. This information is based on press accounts of the 1996 and 2000 elections and personal communication with Iliya Harik, June 18, 1999. This paragraph modifies (and slightly corrects) the information on Lebanon in Reynolds and Reilly (1997: 36–37).

37. Sources on the 2000 elections were Abu Khalil (2001); Gambill and Abou Aoun (2000); Shahin (2000); an interview with *Lebanese Daily Star* journalist Marlin Dick, conducted in Beirut by Myrna Atalla, January 24, 2001; and coverage in *The New York Times, The Financial Times, The Washington Post,* and Reuters.

38. Under the terms of the Taif accords, the prime minister is formally appointed by the president from among the Sunni Muslim delegates elected to parliament, after having obtained majority support in that body.

39. That Syrian influence was as damaged as the *ancien regime*—as some press reports proclaimed—is less certain, however, because Hariri himself had maintained strong ties with some Baath Party elites after his ouster. Jumblatt's rift with Damascus may be mendable, and in the predominantly Shiite south, the victorious slate, which promptly supported Hariri's bid to become premier, reflected a Hizballah-Amal alliance that was forged under Syrian pressure.

40. On Moroccan elections and parties through 1993, see Karam (1998); Mossadeq (1987: 59–83); Mednicoff (1994: 383–397); Tessler, Entelis, and White (1995a: 369–386); Bendourou (1996: 108–122); and Nelson (1985). I also benefited from personal communication with Gregory White, April 1998.

41. In the 1984 elections, for example, there were instances of candidates winning with less than 30 percent of the vote in their districts.

42. Together, they won 91 of the 222 seats open to direct contestation. Two smaller opposition parties gained an additional eight, giving the opposition all together a gain of 14 percent over 1984. See also United Press International, June 24 and 26, 1993; and *MEED,* July 9, 1993.

43. Interviews with Mohammed Dahbi, a Moroccan social scientist, Harvard University, April 20, 1998, and (in Arabic) Mohammed el-Gahs, a Moroccan journalist, Providence, RI, May 18, 1999.

44. For discussions of this dilemma in comparative context, see Linz (1978a); Middlebrook (1985: esp. 27); and Kinzo (1988).

45. This was the dominant sentiment in a roundtable on boycotts at the Brown elections conference, which brought together ten democratic activists from seven different Arab countries.

46. Examples used throughout this section draw on sources previously cited; to save space, only additional references are included here.

47. On the use of this tactic in Latin America, see Skidmore (1988: 114–116); Middlebrook (1985: 8–9); and Manzetti (1993: 101–102).

48. The *tahaluf* continued through the 1995 elections but was a source of conflict within the SLP. As well, its raison d'être was weakened by the switch to all single-winner district voting. The alliance broke up before the 2000 poll.

49. Vengroff and Mozaffar (2002) offer evidence that the partial adoption of PR during Senegal's pseudodemocratic period contributed to democratization there.

50. For example, Kamal Khalid, the Egyptian lawyer who fought for single-winner districts, was unaware of the nonparty-list methods of PR. See the website of the Center for Voting and Democracy, www.fairvote.org, for an explanation of these systems.

6

Party Systems and Regime Formation: Turkish Exceptionalism in Comparative Perspective

MICHELE PENNER ANGRIST

This chapter seeks to explain why competitive electoral politics emerged in Turkey and nowhere else in the post–colonial Middle East. In doing so, it suggests a new account of the historical origins of authoritarian and competitive regimes in the region and focuses on the nature of political party systems that emerged after the colonial period. Three characteristics of party systems prove to be critical: the number of parties, the degree of ideological conflict among them, and differences in their capacity to mobilize supporters in electoral contests.

Since 1950, competitive party politics and free and fair elections have, to a significant extent, determined who governs Turkey.[1] Yet of all the modern states to emerge in the twentieth century from the ruins of the Ottoman Empire, Turkey alone evolved competitive political institutions. Everywhere else in the Middle East, armies, families, hegemonic single parties, or monarchs came to dictate the rules and parameters of politics. What explains regime types in the region? How should Turkish exceptionalism be understood? Scholars typically explain Turkish pluralism by invoking either an externalist argument that Cold War–era international influences were pivotal or an internalist account that credits Turkey's middle class with political pluralization. The origins of authoritarian rule elsewhere in the region tend to be attributed to local political cultures, levels of socioeconomic development, or class structures.

This chapter articulates key liabilities of these rival hypotheses and takes a different approach, one that highlights the causal impact of party system characteristics on regime-construction processes. It argues that, upon the departure of the imperial powers from the region early last century, the nature of nascent indigenous party systems significantly affected the type of political regimes that eventually emerged after Middle East states gained their independence (see Table 6.1).

Three characteristics of party systems are pivotal: the number of parties, polarization levels, and the presence or absence of mobilizational asymmetry. In three countries (Tunisia, South Yemen, and Algeria), single preponderant parties monopolized the political stage at independence and immediately constructed authoritarian one-party regimes. The fate of countries where *multiple* parties existed at independence was influenced by how the remaining variables shaped events during transitional periods of political contestation that unfolded before stable founding regimes were established.[2] In six countries (Iraq, Iran, Jordan, Egypt, Syria, and Morocco), polarization and mobilizational asymmetry drove conservative parties—threatened by opponents' policy platforms, mounting organizational strength, and ideological appeal—to initiate vicious cycles wherein party behavior destroyed nascent competitive institutions, paving the way for the establishment of authoritarian regimes. In Turkey, such institutions survived and matured in part because its two-party system depolarized and became more mobilizationally symmetrical over time, generating a situation wherein all parties felt their core interests would not be jeopardized by the operation of free and fair elections.

Table 6.1 Number of Parties and Regime Outcomes

Country	Independence	Parties at Independence	Founding Regime	Type
Tunisia	1956	Single, preponderant	1956–present	Authoritarian (immediate)
South Yemen	1967	Single, preponderant	1967–1990	
Algeria	1962	Single, preponderant	1962–present	
Iraq	1932	Multiple	1968–present	Authoritarian (delayed)
Iran	(1941)[a]	Multiple	1953–1979	
Jordan	1946	Multiple	1957–present	
Egypt	1936	Multiple	1952–present	
Syria	1946	Multiple	1963–present	
Morocco	1956	Multiple	1965–present	
Turkey	1923	Two	1950–present	Competitive (delayed)

Note: a. Iran was never formally colonized, so "independence" means something slightly different in the Iranian case.

The cases considered here represent all members of a finite universe: the ten Muslim majority Middle Eastern countries where parties played an important, postindependence, regime-formation role.[3] To the extent that the argument helps account for outcomes in all of them, it is quite robust. Moreover, the cases control broadly for regional traits held in common as well as for world-historical time, with crucial regime-construction dynamics unfolding in all of them during the 1940s, 1950s, and 1960s. Finally, the cases provide for variation on both the independent variables (party number, polarization, and mobilizational asymmetry) and the dependent variables (immediate authoritarian regime, delayed authoritarian regime, delayed competitive regime) that constitute the article's central argument.

Preponderant Single Parties and the Path to Authoritarianism

Tunisia, South Yemen, and Algeria each entered the postindependence era with a single preponderant party present in the political arena. These parties were "preponderant" in that they were mass parties organized and exerting social control in all (or nearly all) rural and urban areas. The term "social control" refers to the fact that these parties commanded the loyalty of the majority of elite and nonelite actors in these areas.[4]

Single preponderant parties emerged in these countries for two primary reasons. First, preindependence party-building processes occurred in the absence of elective parliamentary bodies that gave indigenous elites some measure of real political voice. As Table 6.2 shows, such institutions existed in all but one of the other cases analyzed here and, it will be argued, spurred rival indigenous elites to create competing party organizations. France and Britain established pseudo-parliamentary bodies in Tunisia, South Yemen, and Algeria but these patently denied indigenous elites political voice. This meant that indigenous elites did not face an incentive to build rival competing parties in order to access policymaking power.

In Tunisia, for example, France created the Consultative Conference, a legislature-like body through which French colonists could express their preferences regarding economic policy and the budget to the protectorate administration. The French expanded the conference in 1907 to include a handful of Tunisian members—but these were *appointed* by the French. In 1922, a Grand Council took the place of the conference. The council included twenty-six elected Tunisian members; however, protectorate officials closely controlled Tunisian candidate

Table 6.2 Countries, Colonizers, and Party-Building Incentives

Country	Western Colonizer	Years Colonized	Independence Struggle	Imperial Intransigence	Indigenous Preindependence Parliaments
Tunisia	France	1881–1956 (76)	1920–1956 (37)	More	No
South Yemen	Britain	1839–1967 (129)	1950–1967 (18)	More	No
Algeria	France	1834–1962 (129)	1926–1962 (37)	More	No
Iraq	Britain	1920–1932 (13)	1920–1932 (13)	Less	Yes (1st parliament 1924)
Iran	n/a	n/a	n/a	n/a	Yes (1st parliament 1906)
Jordan	Britain	1921–1946 (26)	1928–1946 (19)	Less	Yes (1st parliament 1929)
Egypt	Britain	1882–1936 (55)	1919–1936 (18)	Less	Yes (1st parliament 1923)
Syria	France	1922–1946 (25)	1922–1946 (25)	Less	Yes (1st parliament 1928)
Morocco	France	1912–1956 (45)	1943–1956 (14)	Less	No
Turkey	n/a	n/a	1918–1923 (6)	n/a	Yes (1st parliament 1876)

Note: "n/a" indicates "not applicable."

lists. Similar to prior bodies, the council's only function was to examine and approve the budget; it did not discuss political or constitutional issues. These chambers' mainly French national membership and narrow policy purview meant that rival Tunisian elites were not moved to build competing parties to access policymaking power.

The second factor facilitating the emergence of single preponderant parties was that France and Britain behaved intransigently in the face of indigenous calls for independence. Of the cases analyzed here, Tunisia, South Yemen, and Algeria were among the earliest to fall under Western control (see Table 6.2). The colonial interlude was also longest in these three countries. Reluctant to take their leave, France and Britain responded to independence movements more stubbornly than they did elsewhere in the region. Their intransigence gave nationalist elites incentives to build broad-based, mass-mobilizing parties. These elites came to believe that only by mobilizing the masses in widespread acts of protest could they persuade the imperial powers to leave.[5]

Tunisia's Neo-Destour (ND) emerged in the 1930s and successfully constructed a territory-wide, mass-mobilizing political party. The party builders' intent was to force the French to rethink their decision to resist Tunisians' demands for independence, which had surfaced in 1920. Party leaders worked to recruit the entire Tunisian social spectrum into their organization, including businessmen, workers, students, peasants, tribal groups, artisans, and merchants. In the course of two decades, the ND established more than one thousand branches across the country and recruited more than three hundred thousand members. ND leaders used the party to organize the people in acts of civil disobedience and violence designed to raise the costs to France of maintaining the protectorate. By the mid-1950s this strategy had worked; Tunisia gained its independence from France in 1956.

The existence of single preponderant parties helped facilitate the immediate establishment of one-party authoritarian regimes at independence in Tunisia, South Yemen, and Algeria. When the colonial powers departed, these parties faced no significant challengers for power. What's more, they constituted extremely effective tools with which elites could construct and maintain authoritarian rule. Leaders used party organs to intimidate and suppress would-be rivals, take control of the state, and craft new rules of the political game in their favor. They then used party organizations together with state resources to direct patronage and punishments at society in such a way as to deter future organized challenges to their rule.

In postindependence Tunisia, ND chief Habib Bourguiba capitalized on the party's preponderant position as he crafted a one-party authoritarian regime. He used the party's mass organization as an instrument of intimidation to snuff out would-be rivals quickly and effectively.[6] He layered party members into all key positions in the state administration and security apparatuses, and he made sure that ND cadres monopolized the constituent assembly that was charged with drafting a constitution. These measures provided Bourguiba with pivotal political support as he established the rules of the game that defined Tunisia's single-party dictatorship—rules that weakened his opponents, created an authoritarian presidential republic, and centralized the president's control over ND operations.[7]

The existence of single preponderant parties at independence did not render authoritarianism *inevitable* in these cases; other variables such as elite preferences and cultural norms will also inevitably influence regime outcomes. The assertion made here is more modest: in a context characterized by a political vacuum, such as that which exists at moments of national independence, single preponderant parties enable nondemocratically inclined elites to quickly and effectively build authoritarian regimes. This is so because such parties face no substantial rival actors with which their leaders must contend in the elaboration of postindependence regime rules and because such parties are extremely effective political "tools" in leaders' hands.

The Multiparty Cases:
Explaining Divergent Regime Trajectories

In the seven remaining cases considered here, multiple important parties populated the political arena at independence due to two factors. In contrast to Tunisia, Algeria, and South Yemen, these were places that the imperial powers either were not as intransigent about leaving or failed to formally occupy at all (see Table 6.2).[8] In addition, in general these were places where, prior to independence, parliaments functioned that were peopled exclusively by indigenous elites and in which these elites wielded some measure of real influence. The attractions of parliament moved rival indigenous elites to build competing party organizations. They did so both to maximize their access to the personal gains and/or policy influence available in parliament and to optimize their respective political positions come independence. At the same time, because the imperial powers were comparatively quick to take their leave, these elites never concluded that building a single, mass-mobilizing party would be necessary to achieve independence.

Morocco is the exception in this group of cases because France did not establish an elective parliamentary body there in which Moroccans wielded influence. It therefore lacked this incentive for the establishment of competing indigenous party organizations. Indeed, Moroccan politics produced a would-be preponderant single party, the nationalist Istiqlal, which hoped to establish one-party rule at independence. At independence, however, Istiqlal was not preponderant: it did not command the loyalty of rural Morocco. Had France behaved more intransigently, Istiqlal would have had the time and incentive to broaden its political grip on the nation. Instead, Istiqlal's urban-only character meant that it possessed neither the number of cadres nor the territory-wide organizational presence it would have needed to prevail in the multiyear struggle it proceeded to engage in with Morocco's popular king for hegemony over postindependence politics.[9]

Given the existence of multiple important parties in these cases, no single actor could impose its will and craft the rules of a stable founding regime right away as had occurred in Tunisia, South Yemen, and Algeria. Instead, interim transitional periods unfolded during which the rules of the game were in flux. Multiparty elections and parliaments to a significant extent determined who wielded power during these periods, so it is contended here that Iraq, Iran, Jordan, Egypt, and Syria all had an opportunity to evolve competitive institutions.[10] In Morocco, multiparty elections and parliaments did *not* figure in immediate post-independence politics, a time when the king struck crucial blows in his contest with Istiqlal. Morocco therefore had significantly less potential for evolving a competitive founding regime and is excluded from the remaining analysis for this reason. Only Turkey, of course, managed to nurture a norm of political competition. Everywhere else, nascent competitive politics gradually gave way to authoritarian rule. The presence or absence of policy polarization and mobilizational symmetry in party systems helps account for these divergent trajectories.

The logic underpinning this claim begins with lessons taken from the "contingency school in explaining the initiation and institutionalization of democracy" (Waterbury 1997a: 383).[11] This perspective focuses on relationships among actors during periods of regime flux. Its crucial insight is that democratic regimes are difficult to construct because, by specifying that competitive elections and parliamentary politics will determine policy, they introduce levels of uncertainty into politics that are unmatched in authoritarian contexts. In a democracy, no actor can be sure that its rivals will not come to power. Democratic institutions therefore cannot survive unless all key actors are prepared to live with the fact that no guarantees exist as to the identity of those who will decide policy.

In democracies, elections are the route to power, and parties are the vehicles used by elites to gain the votes they need to defend their interests in parliament. As parties are pivotal to the processes that determine who will wield policymaking power, party-system characteristics will influence elites' calculations about their ability to defend their interests in a democratic context. If democracy is a bargain struck by elite actors—a bargain that no actor wishes to terminate—then party-system characteristics should bear greatly on actors' decisions as to whether or not they can tolerate democracy.

For a given party elite, this calculation entails two considerations. The first is an assessment of what rival parties bring to the table platform-wise. If opponents' policy platforms threaten a party's core interests, it will be less likely to remain allegiant to democratic institutions. High levels of polarization in party systems (i.e., when parties are at loggerheads over indivisible policy issues) thus will lower the probability that democratic rules can survive.

Parties must also consider what rivals bring to the table mobilizationally. In terms of ideological appeal and organizational strength, how well equipped are one's opponents to capture votes relative to one's own party? This question is important because its bears on the probability that one's opponents will have the opportunity to determine policy. If a party feels it is significantly handicapped relative to its opponents in the vote-getting arena (and thus that it is not up to the task of defending its interests democratically), it will be less likely to remain faithful to democratic rules—especially if polarization exists. Hence, in party systems characterized by mobilizational asymmetry—the existence of significant gaps in contending parties' respective abilities to attract votes—the probability that democratic rules will survive is low.

If polarization and mobilizational asymmetry are present in party systems, then each should independently lower the chances that a nascent democratic bargain will survive. Again, the claim is probabilistic. As these are not the only variables that bear on democracy's possibilities, not all nascent democracies possessing polarized and/or mobilizationally asymmetrical party systems will fail. However, these are pivotal factors that, controlling for other influences (external pressures, wealth levels in society, political culture, etc.), should make the consolidation of democratic bargains more difficult. The empirics of the cases presented here support this proposition.

Polarization, Mobilizational Asymmetry, and the Slide to Authoritarianism

Party systems in newly independent Iraq, Iran, Jordan, Egypt, and Syria were polarized, with conservative forces (large landowners, tribal leaders, wealthy merchants, etc.) interested in maintaining the political-economic status quo pitted against challenger forces interested in significantly altering the status quo. The parties that confronted one another in elections and parliaments fought over indivisible policy issues, property rights regimes being foremost among them (see Table 6.3). In addition, mobilizational asymmetry characterized these party systems. Conservative forces either failed to build parties at all or built nonideological parties on a limited base of patron-client linkages. Challenger parties, meanwhile, were building encompassing party structures (possessing branch or cell systems) and articulating strident ideological platforms. Both attributes enabled them to mobilize voters on a mass scale. In other words, the challenger parties were laying the building blocks for a capacity over the long term to outpoll conservative parties.[12]

Table 6.3 Empirics of Core Breakdown Cases

	Conservative Patron-Client Parties		Ideological Mass-Mobilizing Challengers	
Country	Names	Alternative Arenas	Names	Alternative Arenas
Iraq	Constitutional Union Socialist Nation Most independents	Monarch	Istiqlal National Democrats Communists Baath	Streets Army
Iran	Independents	Monarch Army UK U.S.S.R. United States	Tudeh/Communists Iran Party	Streets

Jordan	Community
	Arab
	  Constitutionalists
	Most independents
		Monarch
		Army
			Communists
			Baath
			National Socialists
			Muslim Brotherhood
			Liberation
				Streets
				Saudi Arabia,
				  Egypt
				Army

Egypt	Wafd
	Liberal
	  Constitutionalists
	Sa'dists
	Independent Wafdist
	  Bloc
	Watani
	Ittihad
	Sha'b
		Monarch
		UK
			Muslim Brotherhood
			Young Egypt
			Communists
				Streets
				Political violence
				Army

Syria	National Party People's Party Independents	Army Foreign powers	Communists Arab Socialists Baath	Army Foreign powers

Conservatives reacted quickly to the threat posed by the rise of the challenger parties. Challenger parties typically were calling for land reform, nationalization of industry, and other redistributive schemes that threatened conservatives' interests. Their increasing mobilizational capacity meant that if competitive elections continued to take place, they might well eventually gain the power necessary to implement their policy visions. Conservatives were unwilling to let this occur. Instead, they defected from democratic rules, rigging elections, suppressing challenger parties, and turning to monarchs, armies, and foreign powers for political support. Faced with these defections, challenger parties also defected, typically taking to the streets and turning to the army in pursuit of power. A vicious cycle unfolded that destroyed nascent democratic arenas, paving the way for the establishment of authoritarianism. The following discussion of the Egyptian case illustrates these dynamics in more detail.

At independence, Egypt's party system contained two types of parties. Several conservative parties emerged whose interests and activities revolved around defending the status quo. In general this meant pursuing only diplomatic channels to rid Egypt of lingering United Kingdom (UK) influence while supporting the socioeconomic status quo and a secular public sphere. With the exception of the Wafd, these parties were not ideological (they did not articulate specific policy visions for Egypt) and did not have organized mass followings; they were little more than elite groupings whose political support at election time rested on patron-client ties (Botman 1991; Terry 1982).

The Wafd at first represented a mixture of two types of parties. It was a conservative party in that it was a group of large landowners and wealthy urban professionals who defended the economic status quo (Mitchell 1993: 38) and mobilized a rural following through patron-client links (Botman 1991: 56). It was a mass-mobilizing, ideological party in that it recruited urban mass support through policy appeals centered on its nationalist, anti-UK stance. Yet over time the Wafd changed in ways that made its profile more consistent with that of a conservative party. In the 1940s and 1950s it lost its mass following—particularly in urban areas. During and after World War II, difficult economic circumstances hurt Egypt's poor and middle classes. Neither the "core" conservative parties nor the Wafd offered solutions to these classes; none were willing to consider land, agricultural, and labor reforms. The Wafd's failure to meet the masses' needs alienated much of its mass support (Terry 1982: 262), rendering it more and more a patron-client party.

The Wafd lost this following to three mass-mobilizing, ideological challenger parties that earned the allegiance of urban youth, workers, the middle class, and substantial numbers of rural Egyptians. The Muslim Brothers sought to make Islam the organizing principle in society, economy, and politics. Their branch organization grew rapidly through the 1940s, by which time they boasted a membership of between three hundred thousand and six hundred thousand along with another half million sympathizers—a good many taken from Wafdist strongholds (Mitchell 1993: 309, 328). By the late 1940s the Young Egypt/Socialist Party was calling for radical land reform, nationalization of industry, and extensive social welfare programs (Vatikiotis 1978: 75–77). By 1951 the party operated sixty-five local branches, and its newspapers—which regularly condemned conservatives—circulated to between one hundred thousand and two hundred thousand readers per week. The Communist Party was also showing signs of strength, organizing a strike of some twenty-seven thousand workers in Cairo in 1947 and possessing a card-carrying membership estimated at five thousand by 1952 (Agwani 1969: 48).

From the 1920s through the early 1950s the Wafd was electorally the majority party. However, it typically was prevented from governing. Responsibility for this antidemocratic outcome was shared by the British (who still retained troops in Egypt), the king (who had the constitutional right to dismiss cabinets and parliaments), and the core conservative parties (who, wishing to access power despite their electoral inferiority to the Wafd, regularly enabled the UK and the king by either backing or serving in undemocratically constructed cabinets). The core conservative parties—along with the UK and the king—were the first to defect from competitive electoral norms. The Wafd soon followed suit. In the 1940s and early 1950s the Wafd appeased and even protected the king's and the UK's interests in return for being allowed to govern.

In the meantime, conservatives took note and were alarmed as the challenger parties emerged and grew. Not only did the challengers represent radically different policy preferences from theirs, but the former also were increasingly well organized and were building mass followings. They represented a long-term threat to conservatives, whose political support depended increasingly on patron-client links only. Conservatives responded with repression. In the 1920s conservative governments thwarted communist organizing by arresting leaders, dismantling unions, and closing down the party. In the 1930s governments rejected Young Egypt's demands that the minimum age for parliamentary candidates be lowered so that its members could run; in 1941 Young Egypt was suppressed for three years. Conservatives pressured the Muslim Brotherhood to withdraw its candidates from parliamentary elections in 1942, rigged the results of the 1945 elections such that the Brothers were defeated in ostensibly safe constituencies (Mitchell 1993: 33), and dissolved and suppressed the Brotherhood in 1948.

Barred from functioning freely and participating in elections, the challenger parties, too, became disloyal to nascent competitive norms. They turned to alternative arenas in the pursuit of power, taking to the streets, leading strikes, marches, and demonstrations that often turned violent. They engaged also in acts of political violence, including assassination campaigns and bomb attacks on UK targets. The Muslim Brothers developed paramilitary formations as well as significant contacts with disenchanted army officers. A vicious cycle of events stemming in part from party-system characteristics had hollowed out Egypt's would-be democratic arena.[13] By the early 1950s, public order had broken down altogether. This situation both motivated and facilitated a July 1952 coup that led to the establishment of stable authoritarianism.

Secrets of Turkey's Success: Depolarization and Mobilizational Symmetry

Turkey commenced its postindependence transitional period with a party system that closely resembled those of the breakdown cases. The primary drama unfolded along binary lines between those defending the status quo and those challenging it—and the two sides were terribly polarized. The status quo party in power at the beginning of this period was Mustafa Kemal Atatürk's Republican People's Party (RPP). Somewhat paradoxically, defending the status quo meant a commitment to sustained radical reforms. In 1923 and 1924 this party had legislated away the dynastic, Islamic Ottoman Empire and founded the secular Turkish Republic. The RPP pushed to strengthen and centralize the state and increase its role in economic and social affairs. In 1924 an opposition party, the Progressive Republican Party (PRP), arose to challenge the RPP. It sought a *de*centralized state and minimal state say in economic and social affairs. Most important, the RPP believed that the PRP did not support either republicanism or secularism—both of which were core RPP values (Zürcher 1991: 156; Dodd 1991: 32).

Not only did the PRP represent a threat to the RPP's core values, it also stood to be mobilizationally superior to the RPP. As soon as the PRP was founded, it rapidly began to organize (Sezgin and Şaylan 1983: 2048; Yeşil 1992: 244; and Usta 1994: 27–31). Within months it had established branches in dozens of major cities and towns. In several provinces the PRP built a presence not only in the provincial capital but also in all county seats and many district seats—an indicator that the party would quickly create a significant grassroots capacity for itself.

In the 1920s the RPP could not have competed with the PRP in terms of grassroots electoral mobilization. The RPP was a party of state centralizers, and for centuries the Turkish center had not possessed a strong or well-elaborated presence among the masses in the provinces. The RPP's elite hailed largely from the army and the bureaucracies and professional schools of the capital; it had to build its party apparatus in top-down fashion. RPP organization extended to most but not all provinces and county seats but did not in most cases extend to the district level.[14] Primarily a party of urban elites, the RPP did not command the loyalty of small landowners and peasants in the countryside (Payaslıoğlu 1964: 428). In general these sided with provincial elites who historically had opposed efforts at state centralization and reform. Finally, the Westernizing and secularizing reforms implemented by the RPP perplexed and alienated many rural citizens, further reducing its potential for successful grassroots mobilization.

Confronted by a challenger that opposed its highest values and stood to develop superior mobilizational capacity, the RPP defected from democratic norms and banned the PRP in 1925. It also used independence tribunals created by a 1925 law to target many of Atatürk's political enemies. More than seventy-five hundred people were arrested under the umbrage of this law; 660 were executed, including six former PRP deputies.

In the breakdown cases, when status-quo parties defected from democratic norms, challenger parties *also* defected, turning to alternative arenas in the pursuit of power. This did not occur in Turkey; the political elites and social forces that had been the motor behind the PRP laid low instead. Why? First, the draconian measures taken by the RPP to silence its opposition had the intended effect. Second, many alternative arenas used by challenger parties in the breakdown cases were simply not available in Turkey. There was, for instance, no monarch to turn to; Atatürk had eradicated the sultanate when he abolished the Ottoman Empire. The RPP also kept close watch over the army, denying opponents the ability to politicize it. These differences were crucial because they bought Turkey time during which nascent democratic institutions could be salvaged.

Yet the absence of a challenger party defection did not *guarantee* that a competitive founding regime would evolve. Instead, key developments in the ensuing years facilitated this outcome. Between 1925 and 1950, the Turkish party system became less polarized and more mobilizationally symmetrical. Two additional opposition parties arose in sequence to challenge the RPP: the Free Republican Party (FRP) in 1930 and the Democrat Party (DP) in 1946. FRP leaders convinced the RPP that they supported republicanism and secularism, but the RPP believed that many who were joining the party's provincial organization opposed both (Tunaya 1952: 628; Weiker 1973: 86). Again the RPP repressed the opposition, closing the FRP after only four months. In 1946, however, DP elites worked hard to convince the RPP that neither they nor their followers opposed secularism or republicanism (Prather 1978: 50). They succeeded, and the RPP agreed to compete with the DP in free, fair elections in 1950. The DP won these elections and the RPP stepped down from power, inaugurating Turkey's turn to a sustained competitive electoral regime.

The RPP's willingness to compete in 1950 did not hinge only on depolarization, however. Like the PRP, the FRP and DP demonstrated impressive mobilizational capacity.[15] A second key development of the 1923–1950 period was improvements in the RPP's *own* such capacity. By the late 1930s the RPP regime had finally pacified the rebellious Kurdish-inhabited southeast and begun to establish a solid party presence there. Throughout the 1930s and 1940s the party worked to elaborate its organization across Turkey. It also built numerous community centers (called "People's Houses and Rooms") in an effort to augment the party's contact with and popularity among the masses. These hosted cultural and sports events and offered self-improvement classes and social assistance to citizens. By 1950, 478 houses and 4,322 rooms had been opened. These developments reduced the mobilizational asymmetry in Turkey's party system.

Between 1923 and 1950, depolarization and increasing mobilizational symmetry facilitated the establishment of competitive electoral politics as a largely stable regime type in Turkey. During these years the RPP saw its opponents de-radicalize while it substantially improved its own mobilizational abilities. These changes rendered it confident that in 1950—unlike in earlier years—it would be able to defend its interests in a democratic arena. This is a key reason why the RPP allowed free, competitive elections to go forward in 1950.

We may now consider in more detail the first of two rival explanations for Turkish pluralization, its shortcomings, and how the present analysis augments our understanding of this important outcome. Specialists will note that depolarization and increased mobilizational symmetry in Turkey's party system were not the only factors rendering the 1950 poll free and fair. International factors also influenced events. In the late 1940s, Turkey was fielding expansionist threats from the Soviet Union and wished to align itself with the West in the emerging Cold War scenario. Many argue that RPP leaders presided over political pluralization in the belief that doing so would help Turkey acquire moral and material support from the Western alliance.[16]

International context did facilitate pluralization, but it does not furnish a complete account of events. Increased mobilizational symmetry in the party system dramatically reduced the threat competitive elections posed to the RPP. Also, international factors fail to sufficiently explain the RPP's willingness to step down from power when it lost the election. The international argument implies that the RPP would have yielded to its opposition regardless of the latter's ideological stripes. Yet the RPP had spent two decades implementing Atatürk's Westernizing, secularizing agenda—one it cared fiercely about defending.[17] Had the DP not been led by elites with credible secular credentials who assured the RPP that that agenda would be secure in the event of a DP victory, the transition very well might not have gone forward. Depolarization in the party system arguably was at least as pivotal to the transfer of power as were international circumstances.

The Relevance and Origins of Turkish Bipartism

As with the other multiparty cases, Turkey developed more than one important political party because no imperial power occupied its territory and because, prior to the onset of the interim transitional period, an influential parliament functioned that was peopled by indigenous elites. One key trait distinguished Turkey's multiparty system from those of the breakdown cases, however. While the latter saw four or more parties occupying the political stage, Turkey developed a two-party system. This bipartism likely contributed to political depolarization in Turkey.

A substantial literature attempts to link the number of parties to polarization levels.[18] Yet this literature also has its critics,[19] and the Turkish case—wherein a two-party system manifested dramatically different polarization levels—cautions against the assertion of a mechanical relationship between the variables. This chapter instead asserts that, in polarized systems, relative to a two-party scenario, a large number of parties may hinder prospects for *de*polarization.

Elite choices and behavior should constitute intervening variables between potentially polarizing contextual factors (socioeconomic, ideological, etc.) and actual levels of polarization.[20] Prospects for depolarization therefore should depend on elite actions, and the number of party players may affect party leaders' willingness and/or ability to participate in a depolarizing dynamic. In Turkey, three challengers confronted the RPP *in sequence*. The RPP suppressed the first two, each time sending signals about the parameters within which it would tolerate competition. The opposition came to understand that it would not be given the chance to compete until it conformed to these strictures. The fewer parties there are in a polarized system, the smaller the number of party leaders who must take appropriate decisions in order for depolarization to take place. By contrast, in the breakdown cases where two or more challenger parties existed simultaneously, *multiple* party leaderships, each beholden to specific constituencies and in competition with one another for popular support, would have had to adjust their behavior for depolarization to have occurred—a much taller order.

Turkey's divergence from the other multiparty cases as a two-party system therefore requires explanation. Gary Cox (1997) offers a synthesis of the institutionalist and sociological approaches to explaining the number of parties.[21] Electoral laws influence how social cleavages translate into the number of viable competitors for office at the district level. Social structure and electoral structure then combine at the national level to determine how district-level candidacies are linked together to form national party systems.[22] Explaining the emergence of numerous parties in the breakdown cases is straightforward. According to Cox, "systems should have many parties only when there are many cleavages combined with a permissive electoral system" (1997: 274). Electoral systems in most of these cases were permissive, particularly with regard to district magnitude, a crucial variable influencing the formation of parties (Ordeshook and Shvetsova 1994: 105).[23] At the same time, most of these countries are extremely socially heterogeneous, encompassing ethnic, regional, sectarian, and/or linguistic cleavages.[24]

Cox also explains why—despite the existence of majoritarian electoral rules commonly associated with two-party systems—explaining the emergence of Turkey's two-party system requires some substantial effort. Theoretically, majoritarian rules should produce bipartism at the district level. How many *national* parties aggregate from district-level contests will depend on a country's stock of social groups (religious, ethnic, etc.) that possess the organizational cohesiveness necessary to solve the coordination problems inherent in building national parties.

In the late 1940s as political liberalization began in Turkey, dissenting elites had strong incentives to launch national parties. The RPP had been in power for two decades and was organized in nearly every province. Given majoritarian electoral rules, to win enough parliamentary seats to be the majority party and control policy, any new party would have to organize broadly and deeply across the country and best the RPP in a majority of districts. Yet the incentives do not assure the outcome. Cox discusses the very real possibility of coordination failure, noting that "differences in the ability of political forces to coordinate often contribute to the maintenance of dominant-party systems" (1997: 249).

The RPP's opponents were able to build formidable national parties as a result of two things: long-standing center-periphery conflict and a social structure in the periphery that facilitated political coordination (Angrist 2000: 111–155). For a century and a half, Turkish politics had pitted military and bureaucratic elites tied to the capital against local provincial actors hailing from commercial, agricultural, and religious backgrounds. They argued about taxation, how much power to concentrate in the central state, what role the center would play in society and the economy, and the role religion would play in politics. These questions consistently split the community into the same two camps, and no other significant cross-cutting cleavages existed. The PRP, FRP, and DP mobilized the Turkish periphery, and their sequential challenges to the RPP represented the continuing political salience of the center-periphery cleavage.

These challengers succeeded in launching national parties because they tapped into powerful networks of provincial elites who had long opposed unchecked central government power. Key institutional by-products of center-periphery conflict had created important social capital and a capacity for collective action among these provincial elites. During the nineteenth century, a tiered, territory-wide system of provincial administrative councils emerged, capped by a parliamentary body in the capital. These institutions fostered dense elite networks in the countryside that enabled provincial leaders to act collectively in their battles with the Turkish center. These elite networks extended to the lowest administrative levels, were vibrant, and encompassed all of Turkish territory. Provincial elite networks helped the PRP, FRP, and DP solve collective action problems as they set out to build national organizations capable of humbling the RPP.

The second rival hypothesis regarding Turkish pluralization can now be scrutinized. This hypothesis focuses on the preferences and activism of a rising private commercial and industrial middle class.[25] It posits that by the late 1940s, this class was unhappy with the RPP's interventionist economic policies and arbitrary governing tendencies. It reacted by forming the DP and driving democratization in order to defend its interests. Two problems render this approach incomplete. First, it cannot account for the fact that the DP was a *multiclass* coalition, supported by the private middle class as well as Islamists, large and medium landowners, and peasants. Understanding the DP as a reflection of center-periphery conflict helps illuminate this aspect because the various groups that constituted the DP also constituted the periphery. Second, the class argument cannot explain how the DP overcame collective action dilemmas inherent to party-building endeavors. The argument advanced here fills this gap by asserting that DP collective action was facilitated by elite networks in the countryside, which had been generated by institutions established to manage center-periphery conflict.

Conclusion

This chapter sheds new light on the emergence of competitive politics in Turkey and the establishment of authoritarian regimes in much of the rest of the Middle East. The discussion of the Turkish case highlights the ways in which a focus on party system characteristics fills in the lacunae of rival arguments about political pluralization there. Overall, the analysis suggests additional lessons regarding the broader comparative enterprise of theorizing macro-historical regime-formation processes. This concluding section articulates the advantages of a parties approach to this enterprise relative to three primary rival approaches—political culture, modernization theory, and class structure.

The political culture school operates on the assumption that beliefs and belief-driven behaviors fit certain types of regimes better than others and that an elective affinity will tend to manifest between culture and regime type.[26] Modernization theory understands regime types to be related to countries' achievements in terms of industrialization, urbanization, educational attainment, and the like.[27] Both share the liability that they are correlational constructs. Neither can specify the relevant actors whose decisions and behavior produce regime configurations. Yet the material presented here shows regime configurations to be the product of struggles among purposive political actors over the rules of the game. As neither political culture nor modernization approaches can speak systematically to the question of agency, they are not the most useful analytical points of departure for investigations of regime formation.

By contrast, class approaches do specify and theorize about agents. They identify social classes, their relative strengths, and the coalitions they form as the pivotal factors that shape political systems.[28] Perhaps it is in part because they speak satisfyingly to agency issues that the works of Barrington Moore (1966) and Dietrich Rueschemeyer, Evelyne Huber Stephens, and John D. Stephens' (hereafter RSS) (1992) are important and enduring. Indeed, the class approach is the most potent rival to the focus on party system characteristics evident in this chapter. Nonetheless, for world-historical time periods where parties exist, focusing on party system characteristics rather than class has several analytical advantages.

This claim is substantiated in part by noting important parallels between this chapter's insights and those revealed by the debate about whether class structure or party system characteristics better explain why most newly democratic regimes in interwar Europe survived that turbulent time, while a handful broke down into authoritarian rule. RSS argue that working classes by and large were responsible for democratic breakthroughs. Democratic breakdown occurred where state/large land-lord/bourgeois alliances prevented the working class from recruiting enough allies to do its democratizing work.

Yet RSS admit that, in actuality, a *wide array* of class configurations brought democracy into being. RSS also indicate the causal centrality of party system characteristics to outcomes. They note the crucial role of parties as mediators between class interests and political outcomes and argue that, where polarization existed, "democracy could be consolidated only where there were two or more strong competing political parties at least one of which effectively protected dominant class interests" (1992: 9). Thomas Ertman, too, shows that democracy survived only in countries that possessed capable status-quo parties. Democracy broke down when conservative parties were nonexistent, weak, or fragmented, supporting authoritarian initiatives when threatened by the emergence of strong leftist parties (1998: 476–477).[29]

Both RSS and Ertman find that party system characteristics were crucial to regime trajectories in interwar Europe. They suggest that polarization threatens the survival of nascent competitive politics, as does this chapter. They also flag the centrality of conservative parties' perceived ability to defend their interests in elections and parliaments to the viability of new democratic arrangements. In much the same vein, this chapter demonstrates that nascent competitive politics could not be consolidated in countries where status-quo parties felt they might be outpolled by challenger parties. In the Middle East and interwar Europe, then, party system characteristics seem to furnish a more robust and parsimonious account of regime trajectories than do class-based analyses. Why should this be the case?

One of the class analysis school's most compelling claims is that people's political behavior is motivated in large part by material interest. It would seem particularly valid to assert that economic interest will drive politicking during critical junctures when a community is reformulating the rules of the political game. As such rules strongly influence who gets what, when, and how—for the long term—material concerns should be at the forefront of actors' behavior in a regime-founding context. Indeed, the empirics of the cases summarized here support this assertion. In the multiparty breakdown cases, a key aspect of the clash between conservative and challenger parties was diametrically opposed economic policy agendas. In the Turkish case, center-periphery conflict turned in large part on divergent preferences vis-à-vis taxation and the state's role in the economy.

The stuff of politics, then, may well be in large part a struggle over material wealth. It does not follow, however, that class actors necessarily should be the agents that are privileged in investigations of regime-formation processes. After all, classes often are divided (Downing 1992: 7; Przeworski and Sprague 1986: 8; Vitalis 1995), rendering problematic the notion that one or another social class will act in concert for a given political objective due to shared material circumstances. In addition, the existence of a given social class does not necessarily result in collective action by that class (Katznelson 1986: 7, 19). The fact that classes cannot be counted on to organize successfully for the pursuit of common goals further complicates efforts to theorize regime formation primarily from a class perspective.

A third problem with anchoring regime-formation theorizing to class variables is that, while parties function as classes' "representatives," there seems to exist no systematic cross-national relationship between class structure and party system structure. Empirically, similar class structures have translated into varying party system structures (Burton, Gunther, and Higley 1991). This chapter has shown that several nonclass variables affect party system structures. These include electoral rules; social cleavages other than class (region, ethnicity, language, etc.); choices made by outsiders (e.g., the actions taken by imperial powers that structured party-building incentives); and a society's stock of social capital that is available for party-building initiatives.

If parties are classes' representatives, and if similar class structures can yield *varying* party system structures, then an important intervening step in regime-building processes is left untheorized if party system characteristics and their determinants are not considered. This is particularly the case in settings where parliaments and elections structure at least a portion of the emerging rules of the game, as these institutions will frame parties' incentives, opportunities, and constraints in ways that may have little to do with class structure or class concerns. Because parties are the vehicles through which actors must pursue parliamentary power, party system characteristics strongly influence actors' calculations as to how they can best defend their interests. This chapter has demonstrated that if key actors conclude that a given party system configuration threatens their core values and interests, they are likely to defect from democratic norms and throw their weight behind antidemocratic actors, institutions, and initiatives. Competitive politics emerges only when no key actor reaches such a conclusion.

Notes

1. It is critical to note that three military coups interrupted civilian rule in that time period. Considered together with the military's ongoing political role and with limitations on certain civil liberties, these interventions mean that "democratic" is not yet a fully apt adjective for Turkish politics. Still, as governing parties and/or coalitions have been voted in and out of power for more than a half-century now, Turkish politics is by orders of magnitude more competitive than that of any other Muslim state in the region.

2. In most cases, transitional periods began at independence. I identify 1923 as the beginning of Turkey's transitional period because the Ottoman Empire experienced its terminal collapse in that year when Turkish political-military leaders defeated the armies that invaded following World War I, declared Turkey a republic, and began fighting over its future political structure. For Iran, I identify 1941 as the beginning of a roughly analytically equivalent transitional period because in that year a new, weak king assumed the throne, inaugurating a pivotal period during which Iran's political parties jousted with one another and with the king over the contours of Iran's post–World War II political regime.

3. The qualifier "Muslim majority" excludes Israel. The circumstances surrounding Israel's regime-formation saga (e.g., the role played by tens of thousands of migrants fleeing persecution in Europe) diverge so greatly from those conditioning developments in the rest of the region that Israel is not easily comparable to its neighbors. Libya, North Yemen, and the Gulf States are excluded because parties either did not exist at all or played extremely marginal roles in regime-formation processes after independence. Lebanon is excluded because electoral law design meant that the parties that existed simply were not the primary actors in postindependence parliamentary politics. Between independence (1943) and the start of civil war (1975), parties never won more than a third of the seats in parliament; the vast majority of parliamentarians were independents (Harik 1975; Baaklini, Denoeux, and Springborg 1999).

4. These were not the *only* parties present in these countries; each faced would-be rivals for power. The latter, however, either were elite organizations only and/or were rural only, urban only, or regional parties. The preponderant parties' territorial breadth and social depth rendered their rivals irrelevant to regime-formation processes.

5. Egypt is the one multiparty case where foreign occupation began early and lasted nearly as long as in Tunisia, for although it formally became independent in 1936, a significant British political-military presence remained until 1952. Still, the UK appeared relatively less intransigent in the face of indigenous pleas for independence than did the French in Tunisia. Whereas the French showed no willingness to retreat for more than three decades after the first Tunisian calls for independence emerged in 1920, Britain's arrival and departure as an occupying power in Egypt took place in a sufficiently step-wise manner that domestic elites never concluded that creating a single mass party would be necessary to push Britain out. Britain did not declare Egypt a protectorate until 1914. In 1922 in response to nationalist agitation, Britain terminated the protectorate. Then, the 1936 Anglo-Egyptian Treaty granted Egypt a fuller independence and seat at the League of Nations.

6. It should be noted that the French supported Bourguiba in such endeavors, in particular as he used his considerable party apparatus and Tunisia's police forces to crack down on Salah Ben Youssef's challenge to his authority in 1955–1956.

7. For more on the Tunisian case, see Rudebeck (1967); Ling (1967); and Moore (1965).

8. The Turks were never colonized and indeed fought off the prospect of foreign control in the wake of World War I. Though Iran never experienced explicit colonial control, the UK and Russia exercised significant, sovereignty-reducing influence there from the late nineteenth century through the years analyzed here. And while Iraq, Jordan, Egypt, and Syria officially became independent in the 1930s and 1940s, in most cases their former rulers remained interested and influential parties in domestic politics. The lingering shadow of the colonial powers in these cases and in Iran is important because, as will be discussed later, in conjunction with party system characteristics, it tended to facilitate authoritarian rather than democratic regime outcomes.

9. For details on this struggle, see Waterbury (1970); Clement H. Moore (1966); and Zartman (1973).

10. It should be acknowledged that the cases discussed here evinced serious problems where prospects for democracy were concerned (e.g., rigged elections and the activism of antidemocratic actors like kings and armies). Historically, however, very few states saw problem-free democracy born full-blown; instead, most were host to struggles to reform imperfect systems.

11. Key works in this school include Rustow (1970) and Przeworski (1988, 1991).

12. Challengers were not yet capable of winning electoral majorities, and conservatives in many cases still had the power to deliver the all-important countryside. The claim made here is that conservatives, understanding that challengers were developing organizational and ideological advantages where electoral mobilization was concerned, worried about the long-term costs of tolerating these challengers—especially given the rural-to-urban migration that was occurring at this time.

13. In advancing a party-centered argument, this chapter does not mean to suggest that other actors were irrelevant to regime outcomes. The role of outsiders is especially noteworthy. The French supported Bourguiba in his authoritarian ambitions. In Egypt, UK behavior warped competitive institutions. The UK and the Soviet Union leant support to Iran's conservatives when the latter defected from competitive norms. By contrast, what follows will show that international influences pushed Turkey in a democratizing direction. Still, the impact of outsider influence depended in part on party elites' choices (themselves shaped by party system characteristics) and thus was not independently determinative of outcomes. In Egypt and Iran, for example, conservative parties enabled and/or invited—rather than shunned—the interference of outsiders, arguably due to insecurities bred by the threat they faced from challenger parties.

14. For details on the organizational structure of the RPP and other Turkish parties, see Kabasakal (1991).

15. For the FRP, see Kabasakal (1991: 122) and Çavdar (1983: 2055). The point is substantiated for the DP case by Prather (1978: 88) and Rustow (1960: 409).

16. Yılmaz reviews these arguments and offers his own formulation (1996).

17. Many correctly view these massive transformations wrought by Atatürk on the Turkish political community as central to its eventual achievement of political pluralism. This chapter proposes that that outcome also crucially depended on the emergence of a unified, substantial, and organized opposition that rose up repeatedly to counter the hegemony of Atatürk's party. Absent such pressure from a formidable opponent, it is not unimaginable that the RPP might have ruled Turkey well beyond 1950 in Westernizing, secular, *authoritarian* fashion, much as occurred in Habib Bourguiba's Tunisia.

18. See, for example, Duverger (1954); Downs (1957); Sartori (1976); and Mainwaring and Scully (1995).

19. See Sani and Sartori (1983) and Linz (1978b).

20. This assumption is supported by Heper's analysis of depolarization in contemporary Turkey, which he attributes in significant part to actions taken by party chiefs. His analysis also cautions us that depolarization is not *impossible* in the context of a large number of parties—that is, the situation in Turkey today (2002: 142–146).

21. Duverger's work (1954) reflects the institutionalist approach, whereas the classic sociological statement is Lipset and Rokkan (1967).

22. "Social structure" refers to the existence of groups (labor, religious, ethnic) with the organizational cohesiveness to solve the coordination problems involved in building national parties; "electoral structure" includes rules for the selection of presidents and prime ministers as well as for the distribution of upper-tier seats and campaign finance.

23. Syria's 1949 electoral law provided for multimember districts and mandated quotas for the election of non-Muslim deputies. Iraq's 1924 and 1946 electoral laws also provided for multimember districts; in a few districts, quotas for Christian and Jewish deputies were mandated. Jordan's 1949 electoral law provided for sixteen electoral districts. Five were represented by a single deputy, but eleven elected between two and five deputies. In each the law dictated how many deputies were to be Muslim and how many were to be Christian. These laws can be found in Davis (1947) and/or (Browne 1910).

24. Egypt is comparatively homogeneous and it conducted majoritarian elections with single-member districts. Party number in this case may be explained by the fact that, as parliamentary politics became perverted, even parties with tiny parliamentary blocs could secure cabinet representation. This gave rival elites incentives to build additional parties. This explanation is consistent with Cox's argument that electoral structures such as rules for the selection of prime ministers will affect how district-level outcomes aggregate into national party systems.

25. Key works that embody this approach are Keyder (1987) and Ahmad (1993).

26. Examples of this approach for Middle East cases include Waterbury (1970); Sharabi (1988); and Hammoudi (1997).

27. Two Middle East modernization classics are Issawi (1956) and Lerner (1958).

28. For the Middle East, see Gerber (1987) and Bellin (2000).

29. I wish to acknowledge here the strong influence that Thomas Ertman's work—particularly, his attention to the organizational bases upon which parties are built—has had on my thinking and on the arguments presented here.

7

Opposition and Economic Crises in Jordan and Morocco

ELLEN LUST-OKAR

Using Morocco and Jordan as examples, this chapter examines government-opposition relations during periods of economic crisis, which many scholars have argued can trigger movements for democratic political reforms. The chapter shows how governments can influence the nature of opposition decisionmaking by offering political reward—in particular the right to contest legislative elections—to some groups but not others. In situations where opposition groups are either uniformly included in, or excluded from, electoral participation, political demands will increase as popular discontent grows. However, where the opposition is divided into included and excluded groups, the former will be unlikely to jeopardize their position by uniting with the latter, thereby weakening the movement for political reform.

The notion that prolonged economic crises lead to increased political unrest is prevalent in the literature on economic adjustment and political liberalization. Increased popular discontent accompanying declining standards of living may make it easier for political opponents to mobilize popular discontent and press political demands. Economic reforms also create new winners and losers among political elites. New coalitions of political opponents can form, thus mobilizing popular frustration to demand political change. Not surprisingly, then, scholars and policymakers assume that, with all other factors remaining the same, prolonged economic crises increase the likelihood of political instability and institutional reform.[1]

Yet a look at the cases of Morocco and Jordan challenges this assumption. Since the early 1980s, both countries experienced economic decline and increased discontent. In Jordan, opponents responded to this as expected: as the crisis continued, opponents increasingly challenged the king. In Morocco, however, the opposition's movements seem enigmatic: the opposition did not continue to mobilize the masses, demanding political reform, as the crisis continued. Indeed, the same opponents who took advantage of increased discontent to challenge the king became unwilling to do so, even as the masses became more frustrated. Furthermore, the explanations found in the literature on political reform do not provide reasons for this divergence.

To explain this phenomenon we must examine how the structure of government-opposition relationships affects whether political elites will use economic grievances to mobilize popular opposition. When incumbent elites have not created divisions between opposition groups, opposition elites are more likely to mobilize political unrest as economic crises continue. However, when incumbent elites have effectively divided political opposition into loyalist and radical camps, opponents are less likely to mobilize unrest as the crisis continues.

This chapter examines how state-created institutions influence the dynamics of government-opposition relations during prolonged economic crises. It begins by showing why the cases of Morocco and Jordan are instructive and why traditional explanations fail to explain the different levels of opposition unrest in the two cases. It then considers how the distinction between divided and unified structures of contestation (SoCs) helps to explain the problem at hand. Finally, it concludes by considering how the typology extends beyond cases of monarchies.

Economic Crises, Political Opportunities? The Cases of Morocco and Jordan

Before proceeding, it is important to recognize why a study of Morocco and Jordan is particularly instructive. Both are monarchies in which political power is centered in the palace. The king controls the distribution of resources and, most important for this analysis, determines the rules of the political game. He decides who may formally participate in politics and sets the boundaries within which they may do so.[2] Monarchs are not alone in creating rules governing political participation; indeed, all authoritarian (and other) elites manipulate their environments. However, a study of monarchies is useful because these rulers manage their oppositions quite openly.

Both Morocco and Jordan have also faced prolonged economic crises. Morocco's crisis began after 1975, as phosphate earnings declined and oil prices rose (Berrada and Saadi 1992: 325–391; El Malki 1989; Larbi and Sbihi 1986; Leymarie and Tripier 1992; Payne 1993: 139–167; Benazzou 1986; Khrouz 1988; Benazzou and Mouline 1993; Morrisson 1991). Subsequently, it turned to the International Monetary Fund (IMF) for support, implementing structural adjustment programs. Real wages declined and unemployment rose throughout the 1980s.[3] The economic crisis in Jordan began by 1983, when Jordan found itself subsidizing Iraq's war against Iran. In 1988 the internal debt increased 47.6 percent over the previous year, and in October Jordan accepted an IMF structural adjustment program. Real wages declined and unemployment rates reached approximately 20 percent in 1992 (Malki 1992: 1).

Finally, these cases are instructive because traditional explanations do not explain the different patterns of political unrest. For instance, scholars have suggested that where crises are short-lived or minor, or reform policies are piecemeal, political opposition is less likely to mobilize during economic crises (Heydemann 1993; Perthes 1994: 44–71). However, in both cases, reforms have led to an increase in mass discontent. Others may suggest that differences in civil society explain the divergent experiences; if Jordan's civil society is more developed than Morocco's, it would explain why the Jordanian opposition put sustained pressure on the regime (Harbeson, Rothchild, and Chazan 1994; Norton 1995, 1996).[4] Yet Jordan has a much weaker civil society than Morocco.[5] Similarly, one could argue that the divergences exist because unions, which were an important part of the support for Moroccan opposition parties, become less capable of mobilizing during economic crises (Nelson 1995: 45–58; Geddes 1994: 104–118). However, this explains why opponents become less *capable* of pressing demands, not why they become less *willing* to do so, and there is strong evidence that Morocco's opposition parties were capable of mobilizing the masses but unwilling to do so. Finally, one could argue that Morocco's opposition elites were simply more satisfied with their political gains than their Jordanian counterparts. Again, though, the parties' demands and the level of state repression did not change significantly. In short, according to conventional wisdom, we should have expected the oppositions in both Morocco and Jordan to remain mobilized until either they obtained their political demands or were soundly repressed. Yet this was simply not the case.

Mobilization in Divided and Unified SoCs

The key to understanding why political opponents may become less willing to mobilize, even though they are capable of doing so, is found in the institutional arrangements that structure political opposition. As Arang Keshavarzian rightly notes in Chapter 4 of this book, institutional arrangements can influence relations between actors within the state as well as those standing in the opposition, and both have an important impact on regime stability. However, here I focus on institutions that govern oppositions and, specifically, the distinction between divided and unified SoCs. As noted previously, authoritarian elites determine which opponents may participate in the formal political system and which opponents may not. This variation yields three ideal types of SoCs. In the unified, exclusive SoC, no political opponents are allowed to participate in the formal political sphere. In the unified, inclusive environment, all political opponents participate in the formal system. Finally, the third type is the divided SoC, where incumbents allow some political opponents to participate in the political system while excluding others.[6]

SoCs shape the incentives that different opposition groups face when deciding whether to demand political change. The inclusion of some opponents and exclusion of others yields two types of groups: included and excluded (or illegal) opposition. At the same time, opponents are divided according to their ideological demands, yielding moderate and radical groups. Because incumbents pay lower costs to compromise with moderate than radical groups, certeris paribus, in the divided SoC included groups are moderate and excluded groups are radical.

In divided SoCs, legal and illegal opponents have divergent interests. As part of their role in expressing and relieving popular dissatisfaction, incumbents allow included opponents to challenge the regime. Thus, their mobilization costs are smaller than those of illegal opponents. However, in return for this privilege, they agree to help maintain the system; thus, they pay a high price if they create an opening that illegal opponents may exploit, thereby destabilizing the system. In contrast, illegal opponents can capitalize on the increasing discontent and radicalization to mobilize popular unrest. These groups face higher costs for mobilizing popular protest than their loyalist counterparts. However, unlike loyalists, illegal groups are not penalized more for destabilizing the system. Hence, they pay smaller mobilization costs if they join an ongoing conflict than they do if they mobilize independently.

Furthermore, divided and unified SoCs create different dynamics of protest as crises continue. In the divided SoC, included opponents who previously mobilized popular movements may become unwilling to challenge incumbents as crises continue, even if these demands have not been met. Because they have the organizational structures and legal status that lower the costs of mobilizing an isolated protest, they are often able to exploit the early stages of crises to demand reforms. However, as the crisis continues, radicals gain strength, as do all opponents. Initially, this makes excluded radicals more likely to join in ongoing demonstrations, even if they are unwilling to mobilize independently. Therefore, to avoid the possibility that radicals exploit unrest to demand radical reforms, moderates choose not to mobilize. The very same elites who previously exploited economic discontent to demand political change now remain silent, while radicals who may take to the streets if the moderates chose to mobilize are unwilling to do so alone.[7] Thus,

> *Hypothesis 1:* In the divided SoC, moderates who previously challenged incumbent elites may choose not to do so when radical groups enter, even if incumbents have not accommodated their own demands.

In contrast, in the unified SoC, opponents remain willing to mobilize as crises continue. Unlike their counterparts in the divided case, loyalists do not fear the inclusion of radicals in their unrest. As the probability of successfully opposing the government increases, the expected utility of conflict increases. When there is only one opposition group, it should be obvious that once the opposition is willing to mobilize, it remains willing to mobilize as long as its probability of success increases and its demands have not been met. Even when important divisions exist between opposition groups, opponents who have become willing to challenge the regime will continue to do so as economic crises continue. Knowing that another opposition group will challenge does not decrease the willingness of the first to challenge the regime. Thus,

> *Hypothesis 2:* As the probability of success increases in an unified SoC, a moderate group that has previously challenged the government will continue to do so, regardless of the radicals' strategy, until its demands have been fully met.

Economic Crises and Political Opposition: The Cases of Jordan and Morocco

The differences in the SoCs of Jordan and Morocco explain the different dynamics of political unrest during the 1980s. The divergence in the Jordanian and Moroccan attempts to manipulate political opposition began in the early 1970s. Importantly, this divergence was not an inevitable outcome of either differing characteristics of these cases or of their leaders. Prior to 1970, both King Hussein and King Hasan II fostered a unified, exclusive SoC. However, following a series of coup attempts in 1971–1972, King Hasan II reestablished a role for political parties. The king signed a new constitution in 1972 and called for local and national elections in 1976 and 1977, respectively. Although King Hussein also faced Palestinian and then Jordanian military threats in 1970 and 1973, he chose to retain a tight hold on political opposition. He postponed general elections from 1967 until 1989 and closed parliament from 1974 until 1984.

Through their different approaches to political opposition, the monarchs created different SoCs. In Morocco, political party elites were sharply divided from groups left out of the political system. The palace controlled the loyalist oppositions' participation in the political arena and limited their demands. Included opposition elites were required to accept the king's supremacy and support Morocco's bid for the Western Sahara. Within these constraints, however, they acted as the king's "spokesmen of demands" (Zartman 1988: 64), providing an important channel of communication between the masses and the palace and relieving popular frustrations. In return for their loyalty, they enjoyed privileged access to the palace, and party newspapers received government subsidies. Illegal opposition groups remained outside this system (Munson 1993; Leveau 1981: 271–279; Lamchichi 1989; Ben Ali 1991: 61–74). Many of these groups questioned the legitimacy of the king and challenged the entire political system, including the role of the included opposition parties. Despite their potential for anti-regime activity, though, King Hasan II allowed the growth of the Islamic opposition in the early 1980s, attempting to counter his secular opponents. He thus created a divided SoC.

In contrast, King Hussein kept all opposition illegal. He allowed the professional associations and the Muslim Brotherhood a limited political role and promoted divisions among opponents. Most notably, he promoted the Muslim Brotherhood to counter secular opponents and played upon divisions between Palestinian and Jordanian opposition elites to weaken the opposition. However, he did not separate opponents into legal and illegal factions in the formal political system. Jordan had a unified SoC.

Challenge in the Divided SoC: The Case of Morocco

The divided SoC in Morocco helps to explain why the loyalists became less willing to challenge King Hasan II as the crisis continued. The king created incentives for legal opponents to refrain from promoting a conflict that the excluded opposition could exploit. As radical, excluded groups became stronger and the likelihood that they would exploit unrest increased, the included elites became less willing to mobilize the masses in order to obtain political reforms.

The Early 1980s:
Challenge in a Nonexplosive Environment

Legal opposition elites exploited the discontent surrounding the 1981 economic crisis to demand both economic and political changes. Although the government made economic concessions, it rejected political demands and refused to engage in dialogue with the opposition-led Democratic Labor Confederation (Confédération Démocratique du Travail, or CDT). Indeed, although it allowed the Moroccan Labor Union (Union Marocaine du Travail, or UMT), Morocco's relatively progovernment union to call a general strike, it prohibited the CDT from also striking. It apparently hoped to defuse popular hostility while containing the CDT.[8]

Despite the repression, the opposition demanded reform, calling a general strike on Saturday, June 20. Not all members agreed to the strike, but the majority saw the crisis as an opportunity to force the government to recognize their economic and political demands.[9] Held on a Saturday and at a national level, it challenged the regime's ability to maintain control. An energized, angry populace supported "their strike," and in Casablanca and Mohamedia unemployed youths rioted. The armed forces responded, and by the end of June 22, there were a large number dead,[10] thousands arrested, and party newspapers were suspended.[11] On June 23, parliamentary opposition called for an inquiry into the government's response (Jibril 1981: 28–31; *Africa Diary,* October 1–7, 1981: 10684–10685; Maghreb arabe presse, June 25, 1981; *Maroc soir,* June 27, 1981: 1). The palace responded with economic concessions but also increased security. On July 9, the king denounced the instigators of the riots and, blaming the CDT, announced the division of Casablanca into five administrative districts that would strengthen local control (*Le temps,* July 10, 1981: 1) As the 1983 elections approached, the king also dangled the hope of greater political inclusion in front of the opposition, leading party members to expect future concessions if they withheld from repeating the 1981 strikes.

Importantly, political contestation in the early 1980s remained primarily between the king and the parties. The masses had exploited the national strike to express their frustration. However, no other political opponents mobilized in concert with the strikes. No other opposition groups were strong enough to press additional demands. Within a nonexplosive environment, the opposition took advantage of the lower mobilization costs accompanying the economic crisis to demand reform, just as the conventional wisdom would predict.

The Mid-1980s:
The Strengthening of Radical Opposition Groups

As the crisis continued, more radical opponents gained popular support,[12] while legal opponents appeared weak. Included opponents did not want to repeat their experience in the 1981 general strike. They also joined in the government in preparation for new elections, with party leader 'Abd al-Rahim Bu'abid appointed minister of state (*Africa Diary*, October 9–15, 1983: 11621). This put them in a difficult position: They wanted to mobilize the masses against price increases, and yet they were afraid to sacrifice the chance for gains in the upcoming elections by confronting the king. Thus, they spoke against the adjustment policy and denounced rising prices, but they did not mobilize a general strike.[13]

Nevertheless, in January 1984 violent demonstrations spread throughout the country. In response to increased prices and rumors of impending tuition increases, students took to the streets.[14] With nearly half of the security forces located around Casablanca, where the Islamic summit conference had convened, security forces responded slowly. Demonstrations mounted, with individuals from a wide range of social groups in approximately fifty cities joining the students (Munson 1993: 156; Younger 1985: 205–211; Majid 1987).[15] After nearly three weeks, security forces restored order. Hasan II then appeared on television, promising not to raise prices on staple goods such as bread, cooking oil and sugar, something that only weeks earlier he had argued was inevitable (*Washington Post,* January 23, 1984). By January 23, all was quiet. Approximately one hundred persons had been killed and a large number of Socialist Union of Popular Forces (Union Socialiste des Forces Populaires, or USFP) party members were prosecuted, but the party did not respond.

Although the 1984 riots resembled the 1981 strikes, they were far more significant. These demonstrations began without negotiations between the unions and the government. Furthermore, while the opposition parties' statements had fueled public frustration, the parties had not called a strike. The 1984 rioting lacked a clearly defined leadership in officially recognized channels. This was evident in the throne speech on July 7. The king, waving a picture of Ayatollah Ruhollah Khomeini and tracts from the illegal opposition group Ila al-Amam, blamed Communists, Marxists, Leninists, and Islamists for the unrest (*Africa Diary,*

July 1–7, 1984: 11944; Seddon 1986: 179–197). Popular frustration had strengthened social forces outside the official channels of power, and radical opponents could now challenge the government when the costs of mobilization were low, as they had been during the Islamic conference in January 1984.

Opposition-Palace Interaction in an Explosive Environment

After 1984, both the opposition and the palace recognized that radical opponents could exploit public dissatisfaction, making demands that neither liked. Consequently, the king sought to bring the included opposition more closely into the role of political control. Fearing both the high costs of repression and, for many, the demands of the radicals, the legal opposition therefore became less willing to mobilize the masses in order to challenge the palace.

Following the rioting, the king strengthened his control over various social sectors. In a campaign to foster his religious legitimacy, he appointed a new minister of Islamic affairs (Younger 1985: 205–211). In 1988, he also strengthened nonreligious associations in the larger cities,[16] using them to give individuals an alternative venue for political participation. Most important, however, the palace reinforced the role of the legal political parties. As William Zartman noted, after the 1981 and 1984 riots, the king required all candidates in the September 1984 elections to be members of a party. Henceforth, opposition was to be organized and organizations were to be responsible, thereby enlisting them in the government's job of control. With a common interest in avoiding anomie, government and unions bargain over demands in support of the polity (Zartman 1988: 81).

The opposition hoped the partnership could expand its power. Yet they were disappointed. During the 1984 elections, the nationalist parties, including the Istiqlal Party, lost parliamentary seats to the pro-monarchy, Constitutional Union (Union Constitutionnelle, or UC).[17] In addition, the parties suffered from internal weaknesses. In part, this was because the socialist USFP lost support after the fall of the Berlin wall. This was also because of strong internal debates over the extent to which they would benefit from cooperating with or challenging the king. By the late 1980s, some party leaders argued that unless they put pressure on the king, they would remain in an unacceptably stifling political situation. In 1989 the king asked the opposition parties to support a postponement of the elections for two years, giving time for the situation in the Western Sahara to improve. Although relations between the USFP and Prime Minister Azzedine Laraki were tense, the USFP agreed—but only after intense internal debate and the palace promised political concessions. When early 1990 failed to bring these political and economic changes, CDT and USFP leaders began to rally for a general strike.

With Morocco suffering from drought and a deteriorating economy, the opposition demanded reforms. By April 1990, the CDT called for a general strike, but other opposition parties refused to join.[18] Consequently, the union leaders postponed the strike. A stalemate lasted until December, during which time debates within the parties and discussions between the CDT and the General Union of Workers in Morocco (Union Générale des Travailleurs au Maroc, or UGTM).

The UGTM led them to call a jointly sponsored strike on December 14, 1990. The government warned public servants against participating, and security was tightened in Casablanca and Rabat. Nonetheless, while all remained under control in the large coastal cities, parts of Fes went up in flames.

The violence in Fes mirrored the earlier riots. People from the shantytowns rioted; police responded fiercely; death and arrest counts were high; and in the end the government and the unions blamed each other for the devastation (Hizb al-Istiqlal 1995; Lijnat al-Tansiq al-Watani wal-Dawli 1993; Radcliffe 1990). The lesson for the palace, however, was that it could no longer contain nationwide popular strikes. Unlike 1981, when the level of discontent may have surprised both sides, or 1984, when the government was caught off guard with its security forces concentrated in Casablanca, the danger of the 1990 strike was understood. The palace had ample time to prepare for the strike, and both opposition and government officials had expected it would remain under control.[19] Nevertheless, even with advanced warning, the palace failed to control all parts of Morocco at once.

The palace and included opposition elites modified their positions to avoid a confrontation that radicals might exploit. The king formalized social pact negotiations with the major unions (the UMT, the UGTM, and the CDT) and established advisory councils including opposition members (e.g., the National Council on Youth and the Future, headed by USFP leader Habib El Malki). It also allowed the opposition to express its discontent with the Gulf War through a well-organized, segmented demonstration in Rabat, and in 1992 the king announced plans to revise the constitution.

The opposition parties tried to exploit this opening. They formed the "Bloc," or Kutla, composed of the Istiqlal, the USFP, the Party of Progress and Socialism (Parti du Progrès et du Socialisme, or PPS), and a union for teachers, the Organization for Democratic and Popular Action (Organisation de l'Action Démocratique et Populaire, or OADP). This was intended to increase the opposition's bargaining power in the negotiations over constitutional revisions. By presenting a single candidate in each district of the elections, it was also able to improve election results. Coordination faded, however, and only the Istiqlal and USFP parties presented a joint slate.

The opposition's demands were far from met. In campaigning for the upcoming elections, the parties continued to demand political reforms (FBIS [Foreign Broadcast Information Service], September 17, 1993). Furthermore, while the direct elections were a success for the opposition parties, the indirect elections were disappointing. After the USFP, OADP, PPS, and Istiqlal parties won 100 of the 222 seats in the direct elections, the minister of interior allegedly stepped in to reverse this success. In the indirect elections, the nationalist parties and their associated unions won only 22 of 111 seats. The nationalist parties called "foul" (FBIS, September 21, 1993; Munson 1998: 37–39; Munson 1999: 259–281; Bayer 1993), but they remained the parliamentary minority.[20]

Although the king offered the opposition parties a limited role in the cabinet (which they refused),[21] he would not allow them to mobilize the streets to press their demands. The postponed general strike of 1994 demonstrates this. In February 1994, the CDT called for a general strike, but the UGTM, the UMT, and the opposition parties were unwilling to agree. A UGTM leader explained, "We could smell trouble in the air." The prolonged economic crisis raised levels of frustration, and combined with Ramadan fasting, they feared a general strike would become uncontrollable.[22] The king also announced that a general strike would be illegal.[23] If the CDT persisted in mobilizing, the penalties would be high. Within twenty-four hours of the deadline, the CDT delayed the strike. Consequently, the king responded publicly and directly to the union's demands in his throne speech of March 3 and resumed social dialogue.[24]

By the mid-1990s, the opposition parties were unwilling to mobilize the masses to push their demands. In part, this was due to internal difficulties.[25] More important, many opponents feared the demands and inertia of dissatisfaction among the masses themselves. This was evident during the train strike of 1995. Shortly before 'Id al-Adha, the "Feast of Sacrifice" and a major Muslim holiday, train workers called a nationwide strike. Their dissatisfaction had been mounting, and at last the three major unions (the UMT, CDT, and UGTM) announced an indefinite strike. Union leaders expected the work stoppage to be relatively short, three to four days at most. Union members were prepared for a much longer, harsher struggle. For nearly one month CDT leader Nubir Amaoui worked to end the strike. He was concerned, in part, that a prolonged struggle would lead to violence and that it could possibly spread to, and be exploited by, other groups. Undoubtedly, this could result in repression of the union and the party. Within the party, it could also exacerbate already high tensions. Despite his concerns and his popularity as a union and party leader, the strike continued for twenty-eight days, ending on June 6, 1995.[26] The strike participants won some of their demands,[27] but the strike also demonstrated the extent to which the legal opposition fears an uncontrollable mass movement.

The opposition ended the strikes despite their continued demands. The opposition parties recently had experienced difficult negotiations with the government. Hoping to entice the opposition parties to join the government, the king had offered them portfolios after the 1994 elections, but the parties refused, demanding the removal of the minister of interior, Driss Basri.[28] The king responded that removing the heavy-handed interior minister would "dangerously affect the good running of the sacred institutions" (FBIS, January 12, 1995: 15, 16; FBIS, January 17, 1995: 129), and negotiations broke down. After nearly one month, Prime Minister 'Abdallatif Filali formed a cabinet of traditional loyalists,[29] and opposition demands remained unmet (FBIS, March 29, 1995: 37; FBIS, December 12, 1995: 22).

The union's decision to thwart the strikes also came despite fewer threats from the government. In contrast to the discussion of a general strike in 1994, when the palace prohibited mobilization, the palace took a less threatening tone. It argued that the strikes would hurt the economy, but it did not repress the opposition.[30] It did not need to do so. Rather, the legal opposition's underlying fear that Islamist opposition could use disorder as a springboard for mounting a struggle checked their activities. Islamists in Morocco remained fragmented, but they were getting stronger.[31] Through the economic crisis, Islamists strengthened their ties with the people by providing social support services the masses desperately needed. In contrast, the opposition parties proved unable to improve the economic situation and focused on political debates in which the majority of Moroccans had little interest. Islamist activity on the campuses, and confrontations between Islamists and secularists, became more common. Islamists rioted at the University of Fes in February 1994, leaving five seriously injured (*Foreign Report,* February 24, 1994: 1–2). In addition, Islamist groups had access to potentially dangerous resources, as the discovery of arms caches in and around Fes in the summer of 1994 evidenced. Party leaders made some efforts to diffuse competition with the Islamists by drawing them into the party structure.[32] However, the chasm between the two camps was wide. Many Islamists viewed the party system as conservative and ineffective, and they rallied for a more radical departure from the status quo. Similarly, most opposition party elites considered the Islamists' agendas to be worse than the current system. The Islamists' increasing strength, at the parties' expense, worried party elites.[33] Hence, they declined to promote popular unrest, which they feared Islamic elites would harness to demand radical change.

The parties also feared increased repression. Since 1990, the government granted some concessions. The revision of the constitution, public acknowledgment of the union's demands following the proposed general strike in 1994, the removal of Prime Minister Muhammad Karim Lamrani, a long-time opponent of the unions, and the resumption of social dialogue were all steps toward negotiation with the legal opposition. However, the palace also made it clear that opposition attempts to press demands through popular mobilization would not be tolerated. Loyalists knew that if they promoted unrest, they would pay very high costs. Party elites, who remember the repression of the 1960s and the early 1970s under the current minister of interior, feared a return to the "Days of Basri."

The opposition parties were thus squeezed between two major threats: explosion from the bottom and repression from the top. Together, these narrowed the legal opposition's political space, limiting its willingness to use the prolonged economic crisis to demand political concessions. Loyalists thus preferred to back down rather than to escalate conflicts with the palace.[34] As one Moroccan intellectual put it in 1995, "We look at Iraq, Algeria and Iran and know that we are much better off."[35]

Opposition-Government Interactions in a Unified Environment: Jordan

Unlike Morocco, Jordan's SoC was unified. In this environment, opponents should continue to demand reforms until their demands are met, regardless of minor concessions made over the course of the crisis. They are also more likely to form coalitions across ideological divides.

Palace Interactions with Excluded Opponents

At the beginning of the economic crisis, Jordan had a unified, exclusive SoC. Nevertheless, political opponents used the professional associations, informal organizations, and underground parties and publications to demand reform.[36] In 1982, responding to increasing pressure, the king enlarged the number of appointments to the National Consultative Council (NCC).[37] The next year, the minister of interior allowed the formation of an illegal political party, the Democratic Unionist Association.[38] Finally, in 1984 the king reopened parliament by holding elections for empty seats in 1985.[39]

However, none of these changes met opponents' demands. As the economic situation worsened, opponents from secularist and Islamists tendencies as well as Transjordanian and Palestinian origins called for reforms. Most notably, the relationship between Islamists and the king, which was traditionally cooperative, deteriorated by the mid-1980s. This was largely because of their increased strength. Islamists in Jordan capitalized on the Iranian revolution, the increased economic discontent after 1983, and their access to governmental institutions (and particularly in the ministries of education and religious endowments) to gain popular support. By 1985, 'Abdallah Akaylah, a Muslim Brotherhood representative, estimated that 10 percent of the population supported the Brotherhood (Kawar 1985: A21). The Brotherhood was the single strongest, organized political force in the country.

As Islamists gained strength, they demanded reforms. Many based in secondary schools and universities argued that the Jordanian monarchy was not "wholly Islamic" and that legislation should be based upon the principles of Islam. The king responded to the increasing discontent by recalling parliament in January 1984, but he was unwilling to compromise on the Islamists' fundamental demands. By 1985, in part as an attempt to reconcile his relationship with Syria, Hussein publicly attacked the Brotherhood.[40] The *mukhabarat* (intelligence services) then moved against some of its most prominent figures,[41] and the government passed the Law on Sermons and Guidance in Mosques, giving the government the right to censor sermons and ban preachers.

In part, the rift between the Brotherhood and the palace was due to the king's foreign policies. His engagement with Yasir Arafat in the peace process raised considerable opposition, which he hoped to circumvent by repressing opposition forces (Kawar 1985: A21; Alougili 1992). Furthermore, as the economic situation worsened, he turned away from his alliance with Iraq and toward restoring relations with Syria (Brand 1994). Distancing himself from the Muslim Brotherhood could help in this, too, as Syria had long claimed that Jordan had supported its own Muslim Brotherhood opposition.

Yet to attribute the increased tension between the king and the opposition to the change in foreign policy misses an important point:

the Islamists in the unified SoC were not deterred from confronting the king. As the Brotherhood gained strength, it became less likely to compromise with the king. Islamists did not fear the threat of other groups joining in the fray but rather used popular discontent to demand political reforms.

The first popular unrest occurred in 1986 at Yarmouk University. On May 11 students demonstrated, demanding the revocation of increased fees, the Arabization of the university's curriculum, an end to the rigid control over students' political and social lives, student representation on university committees, and the release of detained colleagues. After authorities responded with arrests, the protests grew to nearly fifteen hundred people and became increasingly political. They continued to express their economic concerns but also demanded political reforms until riot police stormed the campus. The unrest left at least three dead, many injured, and nearly eight hundred students arrested. Hussein angrily blamed the Communist Party and Muslim Brotherhood for the unrest (*The Middle East,* July 1986: 12), recognizing that the opposition spanned the ideological spectrum and had the potential to coalesce, using economic grievances to demand political change.

Throughout the end of the 1980s, popular dissatisfaction increased, centering on charges of corruption, limited freedom of speech, the under-representation of the urban majority in the NCC, and the failure of national legislation to conform to Islam. Although the government allowed demonstrations in support of the intifada and, in May 1988, King Hussein relinquished control over the West Bank, tensions mounted. The government reportedly detained dozens of left-wing opponents (Moffett 1988: 9). The regime also dissolved the editorial boards of Jordan's major newspapers and replaced them with hand-picked members. The editor of *al-Ra'i* then wrote, on behalf of the regime, that the professional associations had surpassed their role. As the associations boycotted the paper, the government threatened to shut the associations down, and most believed increased repression was inevitable.[42]

However, the economic decline reached a crisis, forcing Jordan to accept IMF-directed adjustment plans. On April 17, 1989, Jordanians awoke to dramatic price increases on basic goods, an unacceptable increase for a population that had seen its average annual per capita income decline by 50 percent in six years.[43] Nearly immediately, rioting started in the south and spread to Amman. The violence escalated into what some opponents have called the "Jordanian intifada," lasting three days and leaving at least seven killed and thirty-four injured (Andoni 1989a: A22; *Washington Post,* April 24, 1989: A11).

Although the parties did not start the rioting,[44] they used it to demand reforms. Underground parties with links to the outlying areas promoted the unrest and pressed their agendas,[45] leading authorities to detain approximately 150 members of the Communist Party. A broad spectrum of civic organizations issued communiqués demanding reforms: personal freedoms, the lifting of martial law, relegalization of political parties, and the resumption of parliamentary life. They also charged the government with nepotism, corruption, and fiscal mismanagement, calling for the resignation of Prime Minister Zayd al-Rifa'i (Andoni 1989b: A1, 20).

King Hussein returned from the United States to confront the unrest. Notably, the Palestinians, often considered the king's greatest political threat, had refrained from rioting. The violence occurred in the king's traditional stronghold, among the Transjordanians in the south. This demonstrated not only the level of discontent but also the limitations of a system based upon the co-optation of tribal elites. Furthermore, after the riots, Jordanians of both East Bank and Palestinian origins voiced similar demands. As a senior government official explained, "the real issue was a popular rejection of a whole government system that does not allow for the minimum required level for political expression of participation."[46] Another argued, "the barrier of fear [had] collapsed. People [were] much more aware of their power to make change. They [were] saying, 'enough is enough.'"[47]

The king responded with reform. Prime Minister Zayd al-Rifa'i resigned on April 24, and the king's cousin, Zayd Bin Shakir, took his place. Hussein also called the first general elections since 1966 (Jaber and Fathi 1990: 67–86; Mufti 1999: 100–129; Robinson 1998: 387–410); granted political prisoners amnesty; allowed reasonable criticism in the press; and although martial law remained in effect, allowed political parties to reorganize publicly.[48] Finally, the palace and the opposition set about negotiating the rules by which the opposition could formally enter the political arena. By June 1991, the National Charter (al-Mithaq al-Watani) was ratified at a conference of two thousand leading Jordanians. As in Morocco, legal political parties in Jordan agreed to accept the legitimacy of the monarchy and also to operate without foreign funding or influence.

The political liberalization resulted from the economic decline and increased popular discontent that strengthened the opposition.[49] In response to economic difficulties, Palestinians and Transjordanians demanded reform. In a formally unified SoC, all groups were excluded from the system and thus expected to gain from the confrontation. Hence, as the crisis came to a head in 1989, Islamists and secularists, Transjordanians and Palestinians, joined in demanding reform.

Toward a Unified, Inclusive System

The changes after 1989 were dramatic, but they did mean a reduction in the king's control. As one observer noted:

> What's happening here [in Jordan], then, is new and different—a fundamental, perhaps generational, transition that is both less threatening and more promising than the crisis-mongers would have you believe. Husayn is not so much losing his grip as he is loosening it in a calculated effort to tighten the hold of his Hashemite dynasty. (Geyelin 1989: A25)

Although the press freedom increased, newspapers remained subject to close censorship (Hawatmeh 1998: 9). Similarly, the courts remained under the palace's control, with little incentive to challenge the government. King Hussein changed the rules of the game but not the distribution of power (al-Zouby 1992: 92–121).

More important, Hussein maintained a unified SoC.[50] Moderates, such as Ibrahim 'Izz al-Din, argued for this strategy, stating: "You cannot deny people the right to organize as they wish. The best thing is to give every group the chance to operate publicly. If you try to suppress any opinion or trend, you will have problems such as we have witnessed in many parts of the world" (*Jordan Times,* July 27, 1993: 1). Islamist and secular parties, as well as those connected to Transjordanian and Palestinian origins, entered the formal political system.

Palace Interactions with the Legal Opposition

Although liberalization initially reduced opponents' challenges, their demands increased over time. Opposition elites expected that the government would become more accountable and that corruption would decline. This seemed warranted, given the king's decision to remain neutral during the Gulf War, rather than siding with his Saudi and U.S. sponsors and elites' statements that democracy was necessary for economic reform.

However, the expectations went unfulfilled. In part, this was because Hussein sought peace with the Israelis, hoping to rejoin the international community and ease his economic problems. An active, influential opposition could be a stumbling block to a peace agreement, and thus the palace took early measures to check the Islamist forces. The king appointed only one Islamist, Ishaq Farhan, to the forty-member senate, leaving it dominated by Transjordanian loyalists (Jaber 1990: 61–83). Furthermore, Prime Minister Mudar Badran offered the Muslim

Brotherhood only one seat in his first cabinet, which the Brotherhood chose to reject. Although the palace would subsequently allow the Brotherhood to enter the government as the tensions before the Gulf War mounted (Milton-Edwards 1991: 88–108), it dismissed the government soon after the Gulf War, in June 1991. Throughout 1991 and 1992, the ministry of interior banned large public meetings held by the Islamists, and in the Political Parties Law of 1992, the government officially barred political parties (broadly interpreted to include the Muslim Brotherhood) from using schools and religious institutions for political activities. Finally, while it accepted the election results, the palace downplayed the strength of the Muslim Brotherhood, noting that only 10 percent of the 1.6 million eligible voters, and only 25 percent of all voters, cast ballots for Islamic fundamentalists (Andoni 1989d: 4).

A more significant reversal in liberalization took place after the signing of the Oslo agreement in 1993. King Hussein saw the agreement as removing the major obstacle to forging a separate Jordanian-Israeli peace agreement. Consequently, seeking a Jordanian-Israeli agreement, he tightened control over policymaking. Revisions in the electoral law issued on August 13, 1993, just months before the November 1993 elections, disadvantaged leftist and Islamic opponents.[51] In addition, the palace limited the roles of both parliament and the cabinet, most notably failing to inform either of the details of the Washington agreement signed in July 1994 or the peace treaty of October 1994 prior to their signing.[52]

Nevertheless, the treaty exacerbated the political tensions. Armed with increased popular discontent over the peace accords and a deteriorating economy, and united in a common demand for political power, a broad political coalition formed to oppose Hussein's policies. By early 1995, Islamists and leftists formed an Anti-Normalization Committee, directing their attacks at the king's most fundamental policies and threatening his legitimacy. These attacks not only made the continuation of the peace process more difficult,[53] but they demanded that the king go beyond relatively "easy" political changes that had already taken place. Demands for more freedoms and a larger policymaking role were asking for significant concessions from the palace.

The palace responded with repression. Continued criticism of the peace treaty was disruptive and unacceptable, and those willing to step across these lines would be punished. In November 1995, Prime Minister Zayd Bin Shakir warned, "'Any denial of [Jordan's] achievements is tantamount to treason,"[54] and he took steps to tighten the Press Law in order to "safeguard a 'responsible' press" (Zayd 1995: 1). One month later, King Hussein repeated that he was prepared for "a show-down with the opponents of his policies towards Israel and in the region generally."[55]

In part, he was reacting angrily to Jordanian opposition to the peace treaty, which had only intensified after Jordanians watched King Hussein and Queen Noor grieve the assassination of Israeli Prime Minister Yitzhak Rabin.[56] Yet, even when the peace treaty became a fait accompli, the escalation continued.

In a unified SoC during a prolonged economic crisis, the opposition front remained united. In 1996, the economic situation deteriorated, leading the government to announce that it would once again raise bread prices (i.e., lower subsidies) by 300 percent. Despite King Hussein's personal appeal on July 12 to the Jordanians to support the government's decision, opposition escalated. On July 21, activists broke into the parliament on the first day of the extraordinary session. In addition, parliamentary opposition members from the leftists to the Islamists spoke strongly against the rising prices. Petitioners presented thirty thousand signatures, including those of forty-one MPs, to parliament asking the government not to increase prices, and the parliamentary opposition warned that the government could face a no-confidence vote (Kamal 1996: 11). However, on August 16, the government raised bread prices while King Hussein closed the parliamentary session. Widespread public rioting shook Jordan for a second time in less than a decade, and the palace called in army units and imposed a curfew (Ryan 1998: 54–66).

The palace clamped down. Ignoring the opposition, it sponsored the 1997 Press and Publication Law, providing more restrictions on publications and more severe penalties for infractions (Lucas, 2005). It also refused to engage in serious dialogue with the opposition about revising the 1993 Electoral Law. As a result, ten opposition parties boycotted the upcoming elections by August 1997. The national turnout rate was a low 54.5 percent, and in urban areas where political parties are strong, it plummeted as low as 20 percent (Omar 1997: 12–13). Once again, the opposition coalition spanned ideological tendencies and the Palestinian-Transjordanian divide,[57] and it was willing to put pressure on the king.

As popular support for Hussein reached a nadir, the opposition called for public demonstrations in support of Iraq. This was particularly important because the government banned the demonstrations, in marked contrast to the demonstrations during the 1991 Gulf War. Furthermore, it demonstrated that the opposition was willing to risk crossing the line, mobilizing the demonstrations despite the prohibition. On February 13, more than two thousand opponents protested after Friday prayers at a mosque in Amman. The following week, demonstrators marched in the typically loyalist, southern town of Ma'an, ending in a three-day confrontation that left one killed and the town under curfew.

Nevertheless, the opposition front remained united. By June 13, 1998, these members, now including the nine political parties, the Muslim Brotherhood, the lawyers' syndicate, and eleven prominent individuals, came together formally to form the Conference for National Reform. Despite continued threats of repression, they held their first National Congress on July 25, 1998.[58]

The importance of this broad coalition should not be understated. There is little love lost between the various opposition groups. Secularist-Islamist tensions are high, and the Palestinian-Transjordanian divide is deep. Indeed, in 1989 some Islamists accused a prominent female, secularist candidate, Toujan Faysal, of "apostasy," declaring her incompetent, dissolving her marriage, and promising immunity to anyone who would "shed her blood" (Moffett 1989: 4). Furthermore, even after King Hussein's relinquishment of the West Bank alleviated tensions, there are important differences between Transjordanian and Palestinian views. Finally, power struggles between the coalition partners constantly threatened to tear them apart.[59] Yet, despite this, the coalitions continued to challenge the king.

In the unified SoC, we expect such spiraling conflict between the king and the opposition. As the economic situation deteriorates, the probability that the opposition can succeed in mobilizing unrest increases. Because no political opponents will be disadvantaged in an exploited conflict, they are willing to coalesce to press their demands. The king's only hope of controlling the situation is to co-opt greater portions of the political field while increasing the costs of mobilization through greater repression. Not surprisingly, by 1998 most activists and observers agreed that the system had returned nearly full circle to the dark years of 1988.[60]

However, while opposition groups feared the King's retribution, they did not fear each other. Indeed, repression only united them further. Indeed, political pluralism, and a jointly fought struggle to obtain it, can benefit all. As the Muslim Brotherhood leader Khalil al-Shubaki explained with regard to the Brotherhood's cooperation with leftist parties: "It is coordination over a common cause. It does not mean that we recognize the legitimacy of their thoughts. We believe in political pluralism as long as it is within the general Islamic framework. What we want for ourselves, we want it for others too" (Lust-Okar 2004)."[61]

Conclusion

The dynamics of political unrest during periods of economic crises should vary systematically, depending on SoCs. In the unified SOC, political demands increase as popular discontent increases. During prolonged economic crises, political opponents become more likely to demand political change. The coalitions they form also widen as the crises continue. In the divided SoC, included opponents become less likely to press for political change as economic crises continue. During prolonged crises, excluded political contenders expand their popular support. This opposition becomes an increasing threat to both the government and the loyalist opposition, and it nearly paralyzes the latter. Included elites, fearing that radical forces may exploit political instability to press their own demands, become unwilling to mobilize the masses against incumbents.

In short, extending the analysis of government-opposition relations to include how incumbents structure the relations between competing opposition groups is theoretically fruitful. Indeed, SoCs are not limited to monarchies. A brief look at Egypt suggests that the divided SoC after Hosni Mubarak has helped to keep the loyalist opposition in check, particularly in the early to mid-1990s. Similarly, in Iran the shah's decision to eliminate competing opposition parties in the mid-1970s essentially removed any last vestiges of legitimacy from the party system. The result was an unified SoC in which a broad coalition of opposition forces united to overthrow the shah.

Despite the importance of SoCs, a large number of questions remain unanswered. The most difficult issue is to discover why incumbents promote the institutional arrangements that they do. Why do incumbents choose to admit a wider or narrower portion of political constituencies to participate in the formal system? Understanding this is much more difficult than examining how these institutions affect political behavior, but it is extremely important. The second question that remains is how well incumbents in these institutional arrangements withstand severe political challenges. When does a degree of political liberalization limit opponents' demands, and when does it provide fuel for greater mobilization? Preliminary work suggests that a weak security system, in which opposition groups can exploit some level of political unrest, may actually help reduce opposition in the divided SoC but not in the unified one. To fully understand the prospects for political reform in authoritarian states, we first must understand more fully how incumbents promote and preserve different relations among their political opponents.

Notes

1. Discussions of how opposition elites exploit economic crises to demand political change were particularly prevalent in the early 1990s. See Widner

(1994); Eckstein (1989); Stokes (1996: 544–565); and Buendia (1996: 566–591). A large literature also rests on the assumption that economic crises stimulate political instability, including Harik and Sullivan (1992); Salamé (1994); Barkey (1992); and Bienen and Herbst (1996: 23–42).

2. On the regimes, see Massad (2001); Brand (1994, 1998); Satloff (1994); Jureidini and McLaurin (1984); Fathi (1994); Mutawi (1987); Sehimi (1992); Zartman (1988); Ben Ali (1989: 51–72); and Waterbury (1970).

3. The unemployment rate among those with secondary education grew from 27.6 percent in 1984 to 43.4 percent in 1990 (Direction de la Statistique 1990, 1993).

4. Similar hypotheses are drawn from the mobilization literature. See Tilly (1978).

5. In Jordan, all political parties were driven underground in 1957, and the trade unions were effectively depoliticized in the early 1970s. The divide between Palestinians and Transjordanians also weakened civil society. In Morocco political parties have been allowed to operate openly from the early 1970s, and the two main opposition parties, the Socialist Union of Popular Forces (USFP) and Istiqlal, have close ties with two of the three large umbrella unions, the Democratic Labor Confederation, which is tied to the USFP, and the General Union of Workers in Morocco, which is tied to the Istiqlal.

6. This typology overlaps in part with those of Dahl (1971) and Tilly (1978, ch. 3), but neither examines the effects of divisions in the formal system on the oppositions' willingness to mobilize.

7. For a more formal presentation of this argument, see Lust-Okar (2005).

8. On demands, see *Ittihad Ishtiraki,* June 12, 1981: 2. The UMT leadership argued, however: "18 juin 1981: succes total de la greve generale a Casablanca et Mohammadia dans l'ordre, la determination, l'enthousiasme et la responsabilite" (June 18, 1981: Total success of the general strike in Casablanca and Mohammadia in order, determination, enthusiasm and responsibility) (*L'avant garde,* June 18, 1981: 1).

9. Personal interviews with party leaders and members, as well as Moroccan observers.

10. The minister of interior recorded sixty-six deaths and eleven injuries; opposition parties, the Association of Moroccans in France, and a Canadian member of the International Commission of Jurists argue that six hundred to one thousand demonstrators died (*Le monde,* July 1, 1981: 6; *Africa Diary,* November 19–25, 1981: 10747–10748).

11. The USFP and CDT claimed that 162 of their members were arrested (*Maroc soir,* June 28, 1981; *Al bayane,* July 16, 1981).

12. Prices of sugar, oil, and flour increased 30 percent, 52 percent, and 87 percent, respectively, between 1982 and 1985 (Santucci 1986: 904–932).

13. See, in particular, my interview with 'Abd al-Majid Bouzouba (adjoint secretary-general and secretary of information of the CDT, council member of USFP); (Bouzouba 1995). Other party members and observers confirmed this insight.

14. As a result, prices increased by 67 percent on butter, 33 percent on cooking oil, and 16 percent on lump sugar.

15. The most serious demonstrations took place in al-Hoceima, Nador, and Tetouan in the north (Clément 1993: 392–406).

16. These associations, supported by palace grants, were formed in Marakesh, Sale, Fes, Oujda, Figuig, Taza, and Tangier. Their leaders have included El Hadj

Mediouri (head of Royal Security), Muhammad Awad (palace adviser), Muhammad Kebbaj (minister of finance), Ahmad Osman (king's brother-in-law and former prime minister), and Maati Bouabid (former prime minister).

17. The Constitutional Union, formed one week before the elections, got 24.79 percent of the votes and eighty-three seats. The USFP won 12.39 percent of the votes and thirty-nine seats; Istiqlal won 15.33 percent of the votes and forty-three seats (*Lamalif,* October 1984: 4–5; Eickelman 1987: 177–204; Claisse 1985, 631–668).

18. Interviews with Mustapha Terrab (adviser to King Hasan II), July 12, 1995; 'Abd al-Majid Bouzoubaa, July 14 1995; and 'Ali Yata (secretary-general of the PPS, MP). See also, *Économie et Socialisme,* January 1992: 87–114.

19. Interviews with Muhammad El Merghadi (USFP member), Nubir Amaoui (secretary-general of the CDT, member of USFP Central Committee), May 1995; and 'Abd al-Majid Bouzoubaa, July 14, 1995.

20. Election results gave the MP fifty-four seats, the UC sixty-six seats, and the National Democratic Party (Parti National Démocrate, or PND) twenty-two seats. The democratic bloc obtained fifty-three seats for the USFP, forty-nine seats for the Istiqlal, fifteen seats for the PPS, two seats for the OADP, four seats for the CDT, and two seats for the UGTM. Loyalist parties got thirty-three seats for the National Assembly of Independents (Rassemblement National des Indépendants, or RNI), twenty-five for the National Popular Movement (Mouvement National Populaire, or MNP), three for the Party of Democracy and Independence (Parti Démocratique et de l'Independence, or PDI), three for the UMT, and two for independents.

21. The opposition argued that no real political change was possible as long as Driss Basri, the long-serving, heavy-handed minister of interior, remained in office. Some were also concerned that limited inclusion in the government would weaken the parties (*Middle East,* November 1993: 12). Interviews with 'Abd al-Majid Bouzoubaa, Nubir Amaoui, Brahim Rachidi (member of the USFP, vice president of Maarif commune and member of parliament), Casablanca, June 1, 1995. See also *Le Matin du Sahara,* October 9, 1993; Agnouche, unpublished manuscript; and Waltz (1999: 282–305).

22. Interview with M. Chirat (member of the UGTM leadership and Istiqlal Political Bureau), July 20, 1995, Casablanca. Party and union members from both the Istiqlal/UGTM and USFP/CDT confirmed this account.

23. The argument was based on Article 14 of the constitution, which states that a (yet-undrafted) law will outline when strikes are legal. In the law's absence, the king argued, the palace had the right to declare the planned strike illegal.

24. Most notably, the king dismissed Prime Minister Lamrani, who was hostile to trade unions, and appointed Prime Minister Filali.

25. The cooperation between the Kutla parties deteriorated, and there were major changes in the OADP leadership, explosions within the USFP, and, for a first time, a fervently divisive congress for the PPS. See interviews with party members and *La vie économique,* July 28, 1995: 3–4; *Maroc hebdo,* July 28–September 7, 1995: 6–7; Barraoui (1995: 3–4); and Mansour (1995: 24–25).

26. That union and party leaders shared these concerns was widely rumored and noted in interviews with party members. A Western diplomat also confirmed this in an interview, Rabat, Morocco, June 27, 1995.

27. The unions gained reimbursement of half the salary for the strike period, a yearly bonus of 1,350 dirhams per worker and the formation of a new, national advisory council (*Ittihad Ishtiraki,* June 3, 1995: 1).

28. Driss Basri was dismissed only when King Muhammad VI assumed the throne after his father's death. On the debate, see FBIS, January 11, 1995: 19.

29. The cabinet included the MP, UC, and PND, while Ahmed Osman's RNI and Mahjoubi Ahardan's MNP remained outside government due to a dispute over their choice of ministers and portfolios (FBIS, March 22, 1995: 23).

30. This was first noted in my interview with El Merghadi, Fes, May 16, 1995, and confirmed by other party and nonparty members.

31. USFP internal memorandum cited in Soudan (1995: 16–17). Politically involved Moroccans voiced concerns of increasing Islamist strength, and the related threat of military intervention, including Najeeb Akesbi (USFP member, professor of economics, Agricultural Institute, Rabat, July 13, 1995); Abdelhay Moudden (professor of political science), Rabat, July 6, 1995; Abdallah Saaf (professor of political science, Mohamad V University), Rabat, July 24, 1995; and Aissa Elouardighi (member of the Central Committee of the OADP), Rabat, June 26, 1995. This was noted as well by a U.S. economic officer in Casablanca, March 8, 1995.

32. Examples include a Friday Islamic supplement in the Istiqlal Party newspaper and the USFP appeal to Islamists through the return of Mohammad Basri (Marks 1993: 24–25).

33. As Clement Henry Moore noted, "time may be running out for the parties" (Moore 1993: 42–67). Similar concerns were expressed in a meeting of PPS youth before the 1995 National Congress, Centre d'Etude et de Recherche Aziz Bellal, Rabat, July 8, 1995, and in an interview with Hafez Amiri (USFP member and former youth recruiter), Rabat, July 7, 1995. The U.S. political officer in Casablanca estimated that among youth, Islamists outnumbered leftists by ten to one (interview, Casablanca, March 8, 1995).

34. Party members noted "now was not the time" to mobilize the masses, but students argued that the parties had become unwilling to challenge the palace (economic students, group interviews, April 30, 1995). Western diplomats also noted this reluctance in interviews (Rabat, 1995).

35. Interview with Abdelhay Moudden (professor of political science), July 6, 1995, Rabat, Morocco. Other party members and the previously cited U.S. political officer concurred (Rabat 1995).

36. In March 1982, a notable family published *al-Ufuq Al-Iqtisadi* (Economic Horizons) to campaign for democratic freedoms. The government stopped it after twenty weeks.

37. The National Consultative Council was established in 1978 as an appointed, advisory council to the government. The council had no power to set or reject legislation, and served primarily to "co-opt intellectuals and businessmen, to appease the traditional sectors of society and to mobilize support for the regime" (Khouri 1981:435–447).

38. Interview with Jamal Sha'ir, April 27, 1997.

39. Some suggest that opening parliament also was intended to help prepare the kingdom to engage in Palestinian-Israeli-Jordanian peace talks (Khouri 1984: A10). However, popular pressure played a role as well (Fathi 1994: 103).

40. Letter from King Hussein to Prime Minister Zayd al-Rifa'i, published in the *Jordan Times,* November 11, 1985: 1.

41. Most prominent among these was Akaylah, forced to resign from his position in the ministry of education and barred from returning to the University of Jordan. In total, the government "retired" seven Muslim Brothers from their positions in the education ministry.

42. First noted in interview with Muhammad Masri (researcher, Center for Strategic Studies), Amman, November 10, 1995; other Jordanians and Western observers concurred.

43. Economic studies showed a decline from $1,800 per capita in 1982 to $900 in 1988 (Andoni 1989c: 4).

44. Interviews with Radwan 'Abdallah (professor of political science, Jordan University), November 1995; 'Isa Madanat (founding member of the Jordanian Communist Party), November 20, 1995; also Andoni (1989b: A1, 20); Tyler (1989b: A23).

45. First noted to me in an interview with 'Isa Madanat, Amman, Jordan, November 20, 1995.

46. Anonymous former senior official, cited in Andoni (1989c: 4).

47. Jordanian journalist, cited in Moffett (1993: 3). Similarly, Tyler (1989a: A21).

48. Twenty-two Muslim Brotherhood adherents, fifteen Islamists with other affiliations, and ten secular antigovernment candidates were elected. Mudar Badran was appointed prime minister because of his better ties with Islamists.

49. Thus, public opinion is based upon how well the economic grievances were met, not the political demands (Center for Strategic Studies 1993: 3).

50. Two small radical groups remain on the fringe: Islamic Jihad al-Bait al-Muqaddas and Hizb al-Tahrir (Milton-Edwards 1991: 88–108; Taji-Farouki 1996).

51. The previous voting scheme allowed voters to cast ballots for as many candidates as there were seats in the multimember districts. The opposition argues that removing the option of casting multiple votes led voters to choose their candidates according to tribal loyalties and patronage ties and that gerrymandering favored traditional, rural districts over the cities and Palestinian refugee camps (al-Urdun al-Jadid Research Center, 1995).

52. The palace dominated the executive branch after liberalization. Noted by Radwan 'Abdallah, November 19, 1995, and confirmed by other Jordanian activists, nonactivists, and Western observers.

53. A study conducted in 1994 found that 80 percent of Jordanians opposed the peace treaty (EIU 1994: 8).

54. Zayd (1995: 1) and my notes from Abdul Karim Kabariti (minister of foreign affairs), opening remarks at a seminar on democracy and the rule of law, Amman, November 19, 1995.

55. Andoni (1995: 16–17). Most notable was the arrest of Islamist Layth Shubaylat on December 9, 1995. The public perceived his arrest as a signal to opponents of normalization.

56. Prime Minister Yitzhak Rabin, who had been King Hussein's partner in the signing the Jordanian-Israeli peace treaty and with Yasir Arafat on the Oslo accords, was assassinated by a young Israeli on November 4, 1995. I witnessed Jordanians watching as the official television station carried a live broadcast of clearly distraught King Hussein and Queen Noor as they attended the Israeli prime minister's funeral. Jordanians, many of whom sympathized more with the Islamist paper's headline, "Death of a Murderer," than they did with what they perceived as the king's view of Rabin, were shocked.

57. Boycotting parties included the Islamist Muslim Brotherhood; the Islamic Action Front; the secularist-leftist Jordanian People's Unity Party and HASHD; the Constitutional Front Party; the Jordanian Arab Partisans Party;

and the Nationalist Action Party (al-Haqq). Former minister of interior Sulayman 'Arar, leading the Mustaqbal Party, and former prime ministers Taher al-
Masri and Ahmed 'Ubaydat, also joined the boycott.

58. The conference was timed to coincide with the seventieth anniversary
of the First National Congress (al-Mu'tamar al-Watani), in which nationalist
opposition forces issued a "National Pact" (al-Mithaq al-Watani), expressing
their grievances to Amir 'Abdallah.

59. Divisions within parties are also problematic. Interviews with Radwan
'Abdallah, November 15, 1995; Sa'eda Kilani (journalist for *Jordan Times*),
December 1, 1995; and 'Isa Madanat, November 20, 1995. See also Shahin
(1992: 1, 5).

60. Interviews with party elites and observers in 1998.

61. See also Robinson (1997: 373–387).

8

Princes, Parliaments, and the Prospects for Democracy in the Gulf

MICHAEL HERB

This chapter compares Arab monarchies with monarchies else-where in the world. It considers whether the path to democracy followed by contemporary European constitutional monarchies can be replicated in the Middle East, particularly in the several monarchies that have elected parliaments but cannot meet today's standards of democracy because these legislatures are very weak vis-à-vis the monarch. Where parliamentary elections are already reasonably free and fair, correcting this con-stitutional imbalance of power between the legislative and executive branches emerges as the crucial step toward achiev-ing democracy, but the comparison reveals numerous barriers to constitutional reform in the Arab monarchies.

The Arab world lacks any democracies, yet we find elected parliaments in several Arab monarchies. Elections to these parliaments are often rea-sonably fair: if the elected parliaments had more power over the execu-tive, these countries would be democratic or close to it. What are we to make of these political systems, which are authoritarian by the standard measures but also incorporate major democratic elements? In the 1990s, those who study the Middle East looked for signs that the Arab world would join the third wave of democratization. These hopes were dashed—monarchies and republics alike remain authoritarian. More recently, some have suggested that the hints of liberalization seen in recent years have amounted to very little or, in fact, have strengthened the existing authoritarian regimes. Daniel Brumberg, for example, finds in the Arab monarchies (and other liberalizing Arab autocracies) a "gradualism whose small steps trace the sad contours of an unvirtuous circle," which does not offer "a real path forward" (Brumberg 2002: 66–67).[1]

In this chapter, I compare the experiences of the existing parliaments in Arab monarchies with the experiences of monarchies with parliaments in other parts of the world. Some of these experiences were successful, in that weak parliaments became strong and their countries became democracies. Elsewhere these parliamentary experiences ended in a transition only to a different type of authoritarianism. These comparisons help us to identify some of the proximate barriers to the achievement of rule by parliamentary parties in the Arab monarchies and bring crucial evidence to bear on whether, and how, these parliaments offer a way toward a more democratic future.

The discussion of constitutional monarchies offers an insight into a process of democratization that has received little attention in the transitions literature. This literature addresses the clear-cut and relatively sudden transitions of the type found in the third wave in southern Europe and Latin America, where elections presaged an imminent transition to democracy (Carothers 2002). This is the sort of transition that many looked for in the Arab world in the 1990s, and I argue here that there is little reason to think that elections will lead quickly to democracy in any of the Arab monarchies. The comparisons with monarchies outside the region also advances our understanding of these somewhat distinctive, even peculiar, authoritarian regimes. It is true that my analysis here is framed in terms of democratization—it verges on what Jason Brownlee calls "democracy forecasting" (Brownlee 2002a: 478). However, an examination of the role of parliaments in these regimes, and the ways in which they do and do not constrain the executives, helps us to understand how these authoritarian regimes work.[2] Parliaments are centrally important political institutions in these authoritarian regimes, defining the character of the regimes and shaping their relations with citizens.

From Constitutional Monarchy to Parliamentarism

The historical literature also provides us with a standard term—parliamentarism—to describe a monarchy in which political parties in the parliament determine the composition of the government, with the monarch having little voice. If the suffrage is universal, and the monarch (or an unelected second house) lacks substantial residual powers, such a system is a standard democracy. In this chapter, I am specifically interested in how and under what conditions parliamentarism is achieved.

In a comparative context, the Arab monarchies with parliaments are constitutional monarchies. This usage has wide acceptance in the historical literature to denote a monarchy with an elected parliament that has not wholly usurped the monarch's power to determine the composition of the ministry. Unfortunately, the term "constitutional monarchy" also commonly denotes a democracy decorated by a monarchy; this is true in Arabic as well as in English. Terminological confusion ensues, but coining a new term—always to be done with hesitation—is unlikely to make matters clearer. Thus, I will follow the historical literature and use the term to denote systems in which monarchs retain substantial powers.

Like any regime type, though perhaps more clearly, constitutional monarchy is bound to a specific historical context. Its origins are in a nineteenth-century attempt to systematize a version of the British model of government suitable for adoption elsewhere in Europe. The model was not the British system of the mid–nineteenth century, when parliament ruled, but instead the British system of the eighteenth century, when the monarchy retained real powers. This model was exported—much as electoral democracy is today—to other parts of the world: the new Balkan states, with their Belgian constitutions and German monarchs, are particularly suggestive examples. Outside Europe, in the period up to World War I, many thought that the secret to European power lay in constitutions, and this led to the creation—in form, at least—of constitutional monarchies in the Ottoman Empire, Iran, and (somewhat more successfully) Japan. Today constitutional monarchism is found only in the non-Western world. Although it no longer enjoys the international respect it commanded in the nineteenth century, it persists because it provides a useful solution to a problem faced by most monarchs of the modern age: how to allow limited liberalization while retaining substantial powers for the throne.

There is little explicitly comparative work that attempts to understand the process by which parliamentarism is achieved in constitutional monarchies. Political scientists who have explored the process of transition in earlier democratizers tend to assume parliamentarism and identify democratization with the enfranchisement of the male working class. Robert Dahl, for example, in *Polyarchy* (1971), hardly mentions kings or monarchies in his discussion of the earliest democracies. In fact, political scientists seem to have something of a blind spot for the issue of how parliamentarism is won. This hobbles our understanding of the Arab constitutional monarchies, where democratization is about control of the cabinet more than about the franchise.

Among scholars of Middle Eastern politics, there has been some work on the specific attributes of monarchism in recent years.[3] Several scholars have argued that monarchism facilitates democratization in the Arab world; these arguments tend to center on the ability of monarchs to create a system of mutual security that reduces the risks associated with moves toward democracy (Dahl 1971: 16, 47; Herb 1999: 262–263; Korany, Brynen, and Noble 1998: 275–276).[4] Yet there is also much skepticism of the idea that the future of the Arab monarchies holds anything but revolution. In particular, constitutional monarchies mix two principles of political legitimacy, one monarchical and the other democratic. Some doubt the stability of this mixture in the modern world, because monarchical rule lacks legitimacy (Anderson 2001: 59; Huntington 1968: 166–191).

The logic of a cross-regional comparison of monarchies may give rise to some skepticism, given the substantial differences in time, social and economic context, and region among the various cases. However, there are reasons to think a comparison not only makes sense but is long overdue. Those who wrote the constitutions of the Arab constitutional monarchies clearly found the European experience relevant because they patterned their constitutions after the European tradition of constitutional monarchy: a reading of the constitutions of Kuwait, Morocco, Bahrain, and Jordan reveals this quite clearly.[5] The comparison, moreover, does not require an assumption that the Arab monarchies will recapitulate in every respect the experience of monarchies elsewhere. My argument is simply that profound constitutional similarities make it useful to look at the experiences of monarchies elsewhere when trying to understand the role of parliaments in Arab monarchies.

Lessons from Elsewhere

In seven European countries (Britain, Belgium, the Netherlands, Norway, Sweden, Denmark, and Luxembourg), monarchs surrendered power, over time, to a parliament. This gradual and permanent surrender of monarchical power to parliamentary parties failed in a much larger group of cases found across most regions of the world. One factor stands out clearly in the successful cases. Government manipulation of elections characterized almost all constitutional monarchies that failed to make a transition to parliamentarism. It was rare in the successful cases.[6] The standard political histories of Sweden, Norway, Denmark, Belgium, and the Netherlands make little or no mention of electoral manipulation by governments, even in earlier periods.[7] Almost all constitutional monarchies that failed to make a direct transition to parliamentarism suffered from serious electoral manipulation for much of their histories, including those of Iraq, Egypt, Portugal, Spain, Bulgaria, Romania, Italy, Brazil, and Hungary. The constitutional monarchies of France, Japan, and Greece also suffered from electoral fraud in substantial periods (al-Hasani 1957; Livermore 1976: 97, 288, 314; Carr 1982: 213–214, 357; Herr 1971: 115; Hitchins 1994: 21, 379; Seton-Watson 1967: 17, 45, 91, 151–154, 246–247; Campbell and Sherrard 1968: 100; Scalapino 1953).

In Egypt and Iraq we find a form of politics generally comparable to the experience of constitutional monarchies in places as varied as Brazil, Bulgaria, Spain, Portugal, Italy, and Romania (though European powers had a larger role in the Middle Eastern cases). In these countries kings ruled through political parties, in systems that look, on the surface, to be parliamentary. In the Brazilian constitutional monarchy, when the cabinet became troublesome the king would "name a new, more acceptable ministry, and grant it a dissolution of the Chamber of Deputies." Elections followed, and "any cabinet presiding over elections to the Chamber of Deputies had to be supremely incompetent if it failed to secure a large majority of seats" (Barman 1999: 169). Students of Iraqi politics in the monarchical period will recognize this dynamic, which is also found elsewhere. In Bulgaria, for instance, at the turn of the century, elections were held "to provide a newly appointed cabinet with a dependable majority in the assembly" (Crampton 1997: 124). In Italy "it was the government which made the election, not elections the government" (Mack Smith 1997: 180). Iraq and Egypt differ in one respect from many of the other cases, in that the British played an active role in politics along with the palace and the parliament. Typically the British sought to extend their influence through the monarchy, and this tended to weaken the parliament. It also had a further delegitimizing effect on the political system because political outcomes were determined not only by the elected parliament and the monarchy but by a third external force that, on occasion, imposed its will on the other two political actors.

Electoral manipulation of the sort found in these constitutional monarchies did not necessarily prevent the emergence, or survival, of parties with some real electoral appeal. But government electoral manipulation had a corrosive effect on parties, and it tended to throw the legitimacy of the entire system in doubt. The Egyptian Wafd, for example, stands out in the history of Arab political parties for its early vitality and grassroots organization. By the end of the parliamentary monarchy in Egypt, however, it was perceived to be as corrupt as the rest of the political establishment and was swept away by the Free Officers.[8] Where elections had some measure of honesty, political actors remained within the system, even though they might strongly protest limitations on the franchise or continued royal power (as was the case in the nineteenth-century constitutional monarchies of northwestern Europe). Where governments stole elections, the answer did not so clearly lie in parliamentary parties and leaders, themselves corrupted by the system.

Once a tradition of electoral manipulation was in place, it was hard to overcome: free elections were held on occasion in some of these cases (and many of these constitutional monarchies lasted for decades), but none managed a durable transition to parliamentarism. In the end, some of these constitutional monarchies fell to coups, others reverted to undiluted absolutism, and still others were destroyed by war. While electoral manipulation no doubt sprang from deeper causes, these deeper causes of the failure of parliamentarism seem to have been manifested in electoral manipulation: the correlation between electoral manipulation and the failure of constitutional monarchies is striking.[9]

Achieving Parliamentarism

In the successful cases, the achievement of parliamentarism occurred slowly. Typically an extended period of negative parliamentary control over the cabinet preceded parliamentarism—the monarchy retained the initiative in appointing the ministers but had to do so with an eye to the desires of the parliament. Moving from this stage to parliamentarism did not require changing the constitution, so long as it gave the parliament one of two powers: the power to remove ministers or (more commonly) the power to block legislation, particularly the budget.[10] These constitutional powers were negative—the parliament could paralyze government, but the king retained the nominal power to appoint the cabinet. Parliamentarism was achieved when kings realized that any cabinet without parliamentary support could not govern and that there was little option but to allow parties to appoint the government.[11]

Sometimes, though, monarchs simply ignored the constitution. Of course, this held risks: the opposition could call strikes, lead demonstrations, form rifle clubs (in Norway and Denmark), and even threaten revolution. Nonetheless, the threat by kings to circumvent the constitution could moderate the demands of parliamentary deputies.

In other cases, however, the moderation of parliamentary deputies seems to have reflected the lack of enthusiasm for parliamentarism in the electorate. We can attribute this, in part, to limitations on suffrage, which typically existed throughout the period in which parliamentarism was achieved (except in Denmark). This raises the possibility that the sort of sustained balance between the monarch and the parliament that occurs in constitutional monarchies cannot be maintained in the presence of full suffrage. That is, with full suffrage, monarchies must either be fully absolutist or fully democratic. In modern monarchies, where universal suffrage is the norm, this would close off the sort of gradual emergence of parliamentarism seen in the historical cases.

Parliamentarism also required parties. A parliament of constantly shifting factions, or a collection of independents, could defeat a government on specific issues or vote ministers out of office, but it could not formulate a program or form a government itself. Only parties could make parliament's preferences durable, and give parliament the ability to dictate the composition of the ministry to the monarch. Finally, the king had to delegate his powers to the ministry, in reality as well as formally. He could not run a parallel government from the court (Verney 1957: 234). In practice, it appears that kings often delayed surrendering effective control over the ministries of foreign affairs and the military.

Princes and Parliaments in the Arab Monarchies

There are six constitutional monarchies in the Arab world today: Jordan, Kuwait, Morocco, Bahrain, Qatar, and Oman. Two monarchies remain absolutist: the UAE and Saudi Arabia. Local elections have been promised in Dubai, and there has been much talk of reform in Saudi Arabia.[12] The discussion above suggests some of the major barriers to parliamentarism that may—or may not—be present in the Arab constitutional monarchies today:

- governments that steal elections
- constitutions that provide insufficient powers to the parliament
- an electorate that does not desire parliamentarism (and thus the election of parliamentary deputies who do not press for it)
- monarchs who violate the constitution by either closing the parliament or by refusing to recognize its powers
- an absence of political parties or parliamentary blocs
- distortions in the electoral system that lead to an underrepresentation of the opposition in the parliament

In the following sections, I will examine these barriers to parliamentarism in each of the Gulf Cooperation Council (GCC) states with parliaments. I also comment on the situation of the two Arab monarchies outside the Gulf—Jordan and Morocco—as well as on Saudi Arabia.

Kuwait

The constitution does not pose a barrier to parliamentarism in Kuwait. A majority of the elected deputies in the unicameral *majlis al-umma* can remove confidence in individual ministers (following an interpellation, or *istijwab*). A majority can also declare that it cannot work with the prime minister. In the latter case the emir chooses whether to dismiss the government or the parliament; if the parliament again votes against the prime minister, he loses his job.[13] The government does not steal the elections. They are reasonably fair (though with a certain amount of vote buying), and the parliament reflects the state of public opinion— among men—in Kuwait.[14] The way in which electoral districts are drawn tends to favor pro-government candidates, but not overwhelmingly so.[15] Expansion of the suffrage to women, while a necessary step, will not likely result in more pressure for parliamentarism.

The *majlis al-umma* exercises a strong negative constraint over the government and its composition. Since 1992 the Kuwaiti parliament has used its powers to force ministers from office and to influence the choice of new ministers. In 1998, to avoid the imminent removal of confidence in a minister from the ruling family, the government re-signed (*al-Hayat,* March 16, 1998). Earlier, in 1994, the ministers of interior and defense (both shaikhs of the ruling family) swapped posts when one ran into serious trouble with the *majlis al-umma* (*al-Watan* [Kuwait], April 14 and 15, 1994; *Mideast Mirror,* April 14, 1994). In the cabinet shuffle following the 1999 elections, another shaikh left the cab-inet, also under the threat of interpellation (*al-Quds al-Arabi,* May 5, 1999). The prime ministers formulate the composition of the cabinet so as to include important groups in hopes of inoculating the cabinet against interpellations. However, while there is no reason to trivialize the substantial influence the *majlis al-umma* has over the Kuwaiti cabi-net, neither does the parliament determine who will hold cabinet posts.

In part this may be because deputies make a strategic choice to avoid challenging the ruling family. In 1986 the various blocs in parlia-ment demonstrated an unusual unity and set out to remove confidence in the minister of justice, who was a shaikh of the ruling family. The vote was not taken; the minister resigned, and the emir then closed the parliament (al-Mudayris 1999: 41–42). But in recent years the threat of an unconstitutional suspension of parliament seems to have receded. Certainly the ruling family appears to be willing to tolerate the status quo, in which the *majlis al-umma* imposes a strong set of constraints on government actions and ministerial appointments but does not rule. In March 2004 the *majlis al-umma* appeared to have mustered the votes to remove the minister of finance from office, and the prime minister responded by saying that this was a "natural" part of Kuwaiti political life (*al-Rai al-Am,* March 9, 2004). Suspending parliamentary life could have serious costs for the ruling family in a society in which political elites from all sections of society have an investment in parliamentary life and in which there are no ideological, sectarian, or tribal groups providing a reliable reservoir of support for absolutism.[16]

The threat of suspension is not the only factor holding deputies in check. Only a minority in the *majlis al-umma* explicitly wants parliamentarism. The parliament is divided into a number of blocs. The largest, the Islamist bloc, has around fourteen members. Other blocs include the populist Popular Bloc, the liberals, the independents (typically fairly close to the government), and deputies of the Awazim tribe. Of these blocs, only the Popular Bloc is primarily concerned with challenging the ruling family, whereas the liberals and Islamists display more desire to do combat with each other than with the monarchy. Hence, the government can typically draw on the support of one or another of the opposition groups, in addition to the pro-government deputies, in defending ministers subjected to a vote of confidence. Thus, the liberals—long the bulwark of the Kuwaiti opposition—came to the rescue of ministers in 2000 and 2002, voting with the government.[17] Even if the opposition were united, it is not clear that a majority of deputies would support a real push for parliamentarism. The opposition, in its various flavors, has won only around half of the seats in recent elections. The remainder goes to deputies inclined to support the government to one degree or another. The electoral system encourages this but is not a sufficient explanation. If Kuwaitis felt strongly about it, they could vote for parties and for opposition candidates. They in fact do not. This strongly suggests that, at least in Kuwait, the twin principles of monarchical and popular legitimacy can coexist, despite virtually full manhood suffrage.

In Kuwait, as in the other Gulf monarchies, members of the ruling family hold the portfolios of defense, foreign affairs, interior, as well as the post of prime minister. These posts do not appear, today, beyond the risk of interpellation. Yet parliamentarism cannot be achieved without removing the dynasty from these posts, and this is not a trivial issue: the balance of power within the ruling family depends on the allocation of these posts to its members (Herb 1999). A concerted parliamentary effort to strip these posts from the family would likely run into serious resistance. However, today it is not clear where the ruling family would draw a line because the opposition in parliament is neither united enough or strong enough to push the ruling family to its limit. This is not so much because the parliament fears the reaction from the ruling family as that the opposition cannot consistently muster the votes to find these limits.

Bahrain

In Bahrain, the constitution is itself an obstacle to parliamentarism. The new 2002 constitution specifies that the elected lower house (the *majlis al-nuwwab*) can remove a minister (or declare its inability to work with the prime minister) only with a two-thirds majority. The elected lower house cannot block legislation, except unanimously. The constitution provides for an appointive upper house of equal numeric strength (forty members) and disputes between the two houses are decided by a joint vote. These constitutional provisions are powerful obstacles to progress toward democracy in Bahrain; the previous constitution, of 1973, was modeled after Kuwait's, and the current one is a step backward. On a more positive note, the government does not manipulate the process of counting ballots (*al-Hayat,* May 10, 12, and 18, October 25 and 26, 2002).

The most serious barrier to parliamentarism in Bahrain is sectarian. Bahrain has a Shiite majority, while the ruling family is Sunni (its rule originated in the eighteenth century conquest of Bahrain). The 1990s saw widespread disturbances among the Shiite population, and violent repression by the ruling family. The violence, and related moves such as naturalizing Sunnis from outside the country, exacerbated the sectarian divide in Bahrain. Clearly this poses a major barrier to any future democratization, which requires not only a devolution of power by the ruling family but also the granting of substantial political power to the Shiite majority. Even more clearly than in the other cases, any determined effort by the parliament to demand parliamentarism would result in a suspension of the parliament. The ruling family has firm control of the instruments of state coercion and proved its ability to survive a popular uprising in the 1990s. The leading Shiite opposition group, the Jam'iya al-Wifaq al-Watani al-Islami, has a good understanding of the limits of the situation. It has demanded a return to the 1973 constitution but has also made it clear that it accepts the Al Khalifa monarchy and seeks change through peaceful reform.[18]

Bahrain has had two experiences with parliaments, the first from 1972 to 1975 and the second from 2002 to the present. Both parliaments have challenged the government, though not primarily on sectarian lines. Of the thirty elected members of the 1972 body, sixteen were Shia (Peterson 1988: 74). The ruling family suspended the parliament when it refused to approve a restrictive state security law, but both Sunnis and

Shia (in the nationalist opposition) led the fight against the law, and it did not become a sectarian issue (Musa 1987: 116–132; Nakhleh 1980: 169–170; Khuri 1980: 230–232).

Of the forty elected members of the 2002 *majlis al-nuwwab*, a mere twelve are Shia, as a result of a boycott by al-Wifaq in protest of the weakening of parliamentary powers in the 2002 constitution (Louër 2004). Despite its constitutional weaknesses and the absence of the Shiite opposition, the current *majlis al-nuwwab* has proven more obstreperous than anticipated. In 2003 the *majlis al-nuwwab* conducted a major inquiry into losses in the government's retirement funds. In early 2004, seventeen deputies demanded to interpellate three ministers. These deputies included members of the two largest political blocs, the Sunni Islamist Muslim Brotherhood and the Salafis (*al-Wasat,* January 21, 2004; *Akhbar al-Khaleej,* March 9, 2004). The *majlis al-nuwwab* interpellated the minister of finance in late April, but by the end of May the three interpellations had fizzled out. The Sunni Islamists blocs did not support a formal vote of confidence in the minister of finance or a second minister. The third got off on a technicality, but one that the deputies should have known about; in Bahrain, as elsewhere, a minister can be interpellated only on matters concerning the cabinet post he currently holds (*al-Ayyam* [Bahrain], May 26, 2004; *al-Wasat,* January 21, April 21, 22, 25, and 26, 2004; *Akhbar al-Khalij,* March 9, April 21 and 22, 2004).

The sectarian divide in Bahrain makes parliamentarism an especially distant possibility. Shiite moderation lessens the risks of a parliamentary opening, but it is a long way from a parliamentary opening to parliamentarism. Democracy is hard to achieve when it involves the surrender of power by a minority in the context of sectarian polarization. However, given the intractable nature of the sectarian divide that exists in Bahrain, an elected parliament offers perhaps the most promising avenue for giving the Shiite majority a voice in government and, in the long term, reducing the salience of the sectarian divide in Bahraini politics.

Qatar

In June of 2004, Qatar's emir finally issued the country's new constitution, which Qatar's citizens had overwhelmingly approved in a referendum in April 2003. The constitution, however, will not come into effect until it is published in the official gazette. The emir, citing the need to prepare, said that this would require a full year (*al-Raya* [Qatar], June 9, 2004). Under the new constitution, Qataris will elect the unicameral *majlis al-shura,* but it will enjoy few powers compared to the parliaments of Kuwait, Jordan, or Morocco. The new parliament will be able to re-move confidence in ministers but only with the assent of two-thirds of its members. Because the emir will appoint fifteen of the forty-five deputies, removing confidence in a minister will require unanimity among the elected deputies, short of a revolt among the appointed members.[19] Elected members have a slightly better chance of rejecting legislation, which requires a simple majority of all members present. Even then, the constitution gives the emir wide powers to issue laws when the parliament is not in session, and these can be rejected by the *majlis al-shura* only with a two-thirds majority.[20] In short, this is a parliament of a very different sort compared to that found in Kuwait. One thing can be said in favor of the Qatari experience: the government avoided interference in the municipal elections of 1999 and 2003 and probably will continue this tradition in the upcoming parliamentary elections, if only because the deputies will have little power to constrain the monarchy beyond using the parliament as a soapbox.

Oman

Oman's *majlis al-shura* is truly advisory, with no powers whatsoever specified in the Basic Law. Oman held its first elections with universal suffrage in October 2003—previous elections had been held with a limited electorate. While there were no accusations of manipulation of the balloting, the government sharply restricted the ability of candidates to hold meetings and announce platforms: it was viewed as a sign of progress that the government allowed candidates to distribute their biographies to voters (*al-Hayat,* October 4 and 5, 2003; *Ash-sharq al-Awsat,* October 4, 2003). An election in such circumstances does not allow for the real expression of the electorate's opinion. While Oman, like Qatar, has a history of incremental steps forward, a substantial number of steps will be needed even to reach the point where Kuwait is today. Candidates must be able to campaign freely in elections, and the parliament must be given substantial constitutional powers.

Comparisons Outside the GCC

Jordan

In Jordan, as in Kuwait, the parliament has substantial powers. An absolute majority of the deputies in the elected lower house—the *majlis al-nuwwab*—can remove confidence in a ministry, forcing it from office.

New governments must secure a positive vote of confidence.[21] In recent elections, the government has not directly manipulated the results of balloting. Jordan has experienced two periods of relative political opening: one in the 1950s and 1960s and another since 1989. Elections in the 1950s and 1960s ranged from reasonably fair (1956) to outright stolen by the government (1963) (Hourani 1989; Madi and Musa 1988 [1959]: 603, 36–37; Aruri 1972: 179–180). The four elections since 1989 (the most recent in 2003) have been "relatively free and fair," without the sort of pervasive manipulation seen in many of the constitutional monarchies that failed to make a direct transition to parliamentarism (Wiktorowicz 1999: 607; International Crisis Group 2003: 16). The real problem with the electoral system is instead malapportionment (Posusney, Chapter 5, in this book). A majority of Jordanians are of Palestinian origin and live in urban areas such as Amman, Zerqa, and Irbid. These areas elect few deputies in proportion to the number of eligible voters living in them. In 2003, districts with approximately 27 percent of the eligible voters elected half of the deputies.[22] This malapportionment saps the legitimacy of the parliament. Disparities in voter turnout suggest the size of the problem: although turnout in eight of thirteen governorates exceeded 77 percent, turnout of eligible voters amounted to a far more modest 43 percent in Amman and 48 percent in Zerqa.[23]

Despite the limitations of the electoral system, since 1989 the *majlis al-nuwwab* exerts a measure of influence over the composition of the cabinet.[24] This has included parliamentary attacks on prime ministers, although this is easier in Jordan than in Kuwait because Jordanian prime ministers usually do not belong to the ruling family (Herb 1999: 232). In 1991 parliament brought down a government—but not by directly using its power to withdraw confidence (Brown 2002: 117-118; Brand 1998: 108). Even the parliament elected in the 1997 elections (boycotted by the main Islamist party) did not lack vitality; it too brought down a government, also indirectly, in 2000. In that episode, a parliamentary majority signed a petition demanding a special session of parliament (not then in session) to remove confidence in the government. The deputies also threatened to prevent a quorum for a special session of parliament needed to pass pressing economic legislation. The king responded by dismissing the government and appointing a leader of the rebellious deputies to form a new one. Nonetheless, this was not quite as vigorous an exercise of parliamentary power as it may appear at first blush. The prime minister had lost popularity not only in *majlis al-nuwwab* but also apparently in the court (*al-Hayat*, April 28, May 12, and June 22, 2000). A cabinet crisis in 1994 revealed a similar dynamic, in which opposition elements in the court and in the lower house united against a ministry (*al-Hayat,* May 24, 1994). The *majlis al-nuwwab* has enough power to oblige the king to find prime ministers who can manage the parliament, but there is little apparent demand for parliamentarism.[25]

More recently, in 2003, two separate governments won votes of confidence in the *majlis al-nuwwab* with overwhelming majorities (84 and 85 votes, respectively, of 110) (*al-Hayat,* August 15, 2003, December 24, 2003). Yet while the *majlis al-nuwwab* has passed recent votes of confidence by large margins, it has been less accommodating in passing legislation. Most notably, it refused to raise the penalties for honor killings and has balked in approving other royal decrees issued in the absence of parliament (*al-Hayat,* August 12 and 13, 2003). This has placed a substantial barrier in the way of reform, but the lower house has not used its power to block legislation to demand a greater voice in the formation of the cabinet.

Jordan's parties are weak, partly as a result of this malapportionment. In the 2003 elections the largest party—that of the Muslim Brotherhood—won only seventeen of 110 seats. By some counts, all other formal parties failed to win seats (*al-Hayat,* June 19, 2003).[26] The government has also designed an electoral system that weakens parties and produces deputies more beholden to tribal, family, and clan groupings. This could only have had the desired effects, of course, if such primordial loyalties were strong in the electorate, as they are—though especially so in areas where Jordanians of East Bank descent live. Once in parliament, however, deputies have organized themselves into blocs, and this has become markedly more prominent recently. These blocs have had an important role in selecting the parliamentary leadership, in staking out positions on votes of confidence in the government, and in legislation (*al-Dustur* [Amman], July 26, December 1 and 10, 2003).

The threat of suspension provides a powerful check to the ability of the Jordanian parliament to challenge the monarchy. The most recent unconstitutional suspension of the parliament ended only in 2003. The king dissolved parliament in 2001, then he delayed elections on the grounds that districting reforms had to be implemented and because the regional situation (unsettled, to be sure) militated against elections. While the Jordanian monarchy prefers to have a parliament, the power of the monarchy is permanent and that of the parliament contingent.

Morocco

In several formal respects, the Moroccan experience appears a good deal more advanced than those in Jordan and Kuwait. The parliament enjoys powers comparable to those of its Jordanian counterpart: a majority of the elected deputies can remove confidence in a ministry, and new governments must secure a positive vote of confidence.[27] The party system is the most developed among the monarchies. Party lists were used in the 2002 elections, discouraging the independents found in other Arab monarchies and strengthening parties.[28] Even more impressive, the king called on the opposition parties to form a government in 1998, and the leader of the opposition USFP held the post of prime minister until 2002.

In the end, though, the Moroccan experience is more reminiscent of that of the constitutional monarchies that failed to make a direct transition to parliamentarism than it is to those monarchies that achieved parliamentarism. Morocco stands out among the existing Arab monarchies for the prevalence of fraud in its parliamentary elections. Election results, especially in the past, have owed as much to the machinations of the interior ministry as to the will of the electorate. Voter turnout has suffered accordingly (see Posusney, Chapter 5, in this book; Maghraoui 2001a: 80; Eickelman 1986). This had led to serious corrosion of the party system and has thrown into doubt the legitimacy of the parliament. Nonetheless, the trend is positive. King Muhammad VI (who came to power in 1999) staked some of his credibility on the fairness of the 2002 elections, which met a higher standard than previous efforts. Yet the Islamist party, which did very well in the elections, decided beforehand to run candidates in only fifty-six of the ninety-one electoral districts, thus reducing the threat it posed to the monarchy and the existing elite but also minimizing the degree to which the elections clearly represented popular opinion (*al-Hayat,* September 26, 2002; *Le Monde,* September 27 and 29, 2002). In the 2003 municipal elections the government "prevailed on" the Islamist party to run candidates in only 15 percent of the twenty-four thousand constituencies (Agence France-Press, September 10, 2003). A more radical Islamist party, which might have garnered significant votes, did not participate in the 2002 parliamentary elections.

The experience with the opposition government also looks less impressive when we consider the limits on the prime minister's power. In practice, the king wields many powers directly, particularly over the ministries of sovereignty. This is at the expense of the prime minister. When Muhammad VI removed Driss Basri (his father's strongman interior minister) and named a replacement, the prime minister learned of the event only after the fact (Maghraoui 2001b; Ben Mlih 2001: 7). The king, in a 2001 interview, found it necessary to deny that there were two governments, one inside the palace and one outside, all the while asserting that the king had "special responsibilities" for foreign affairs, defense, the interior, religious affairs, and justice (*al-Sharq al-Awsat,*

July 24, 2001). Moroccan kings have long held the defense portfolio personally.

The political parties' connections to the electorate often seems tenuous, and by appointing an "opposition" government in 1998 the king did as much to co-opt the opposition as he did to turn over power to it.[29] The aftermath of the 2002 elections put the limitations of the system in sharp perspective. The elections resulted in a fractured lower house with the four largest parties each controlling between 41 and 50 of the 325 seats.[30] The parties began building coalitions in earnest, and two major and fairly evenly balanced blocs emerged, with the Islamist party a key part of the right-leaning bloc (*al-Hayat,* October 11, 2002). Had this process continued, Morocco might have found itself with a relatively clearly defined governing coalition and a distinct opposition. Yet the king ended the process of coalition formation by asking a technocrat to appoint a cabinet. The blocs dissolved as parties rushed to join the government. Of the larger parties, only the Islamist party remained in the opposition. The result tended to confirm the skeptics' view of the entire political elite— with the possible exception of the Islamists—as creatures of the regime.[31] The system strikingly resembles the nominal parliamentarism of the failed constitutional monarchies, although efforts to clean up Morocco's elections suggest some grounds for limited optimism.

Saudi Arabia

Saudi Arabia has not held nationwide elections. The king appoints all members of Saudi Arabia's national assembly, the *majlis al-shura,* and the body lacks any real powers to constrain the monarchy. In the spring of 2004, it was regarded as progress that journalists would be allowed to attend its sessions and that two hours of its weekly deliberations would be broadcast (*al-Hayat,* March 16 and 20, 2004). Since early 2003, however, talk of reform in Saudi Arabia has substantially increased. Petitions have circulated calling for elections and one for a "constitutional monarchy."[32] The crown prince has called for elections for half the seats on regional advisory councils, although he has also complained that the bureaucracy (and other members of his family) have blocked movement on this reform. The ruling family seems to have split on the issue, with one group, led by Crown Prince Abdullah Ibn Abdul Aziz Al Saud, favoring reform, while another group, associated with the minister of interior Prince Naif bin Abdulaziz, opposed it (Doran 2004; *Shu'un sa'udiya* no. 13, 2004: 6–7). The incapacity of the king prevents the resolution of the conflict, and the advanced age of all the major players makes it difficult to make predictions concerning how it will in the end be resolved. Should Abdullah assume the kingship in good health, however, reforms will likely move forward.

The experiences of the other monarchies offers some things to look for in any future Saudi experience with parliamentary reforms. First, the constitution matters. A parliament with the powers of that in Kuwait offers much more promise for movement forward than one in the Qatari mold. Second, while we can anticipate that elections will follow the Gulf model of procedural fairness, any electoral exercise is useful only if candidates can campaign and take public positions on the issues (as is not the case, for example, in Oman). Third, even should a parliament receive substantial powers on the Kuwaiti or Jordanian models, parliamentarism will not likely ensue. The threat of suspension will limit the ambitions of deputies. Some parts of the electorate will have limited enthusiasm for a quick transition to the rule of parliamentary parties. And political parties—or non-party blocs of the sorts found elsewhere in the Gulf—are not likely to win a majority of the seats. Tribal, sectarian, clan, and provincial loyalties are as strong in Saudi Arabia as they are in Jordan or Kuwait, and it would be odd indeed if the ruling family did not design an electoral system that would emphasize these loyalties and discourage electoral blocs.

Conclusion

A comparison of the currently existing Arab monarchies with those in other parts of the world does not allow us to predict whether or not the Arab monarchies will become democratic. It does, however, provide us with some insights into the democratic potential of these parliaments, and it can help us to better understand the role of elected parliaments in these authoritarian regimes.

Table 8.1 sums up several of the more important barriers to parliamentarism in the Arab monarchies. In Kuwait, Jordan, and Morocco, the constitutions themselves pose few barriers to parliamentarism. The elected houses of parliament can remove ministers and block the business of government. These are the powers used in other constitutional monarchies to achieve parliamentarism. That they are not used to this end in these three Arab monarchies must be traced back to political practice. The constitutions of Qatar, Bahrain, and Oman much more sharply restrict the authority of their parliaments, and any substantial progress toward parliamentarism in these monarchies must include constitutional changes—as the Bahraini opposition, at least, fully recognizes.

Table 8.1 Barriers to Parliamentarism in the Arab Monarchies

	Kuwait	Jordan	Morocco	Bahrain	Qatar	Oman	Saudi Arabia	United Arab Emirates
Parliamentary powers	Strong parliament	Strong parliament	Strong parliament	Weak parliament	Weak parliament	Very weak parliament	No elected parliament	No elected parliament
Government election fraud	Minor government manipulation	Some government manipulation	Serious government manipulation	Minor government manipulation	Minor government manipulation (municipal elections)	Sharp limits on campaigning; no known manipulation	No elections	No elections
Electoral malapportionment	Malapportionment is not a barrier to parliamentarism	Substantial mal-apportionment against Palestinian-Jordanians	Not an issue	Probable malapportionment against Shia	None known	None known	No elections	No elections
Threat of parliamentary suspension by the monarchy	Comparatively small threat of suspension since 1992	Most recent suspension from 2001 to 2003; substantial threat of further suspensions	No recent suspensions; election fraud more likely than suspension	Parliament suspended from 1975 to 2002; substantial threat of further suspensions	Parliament has not yet met	Parliament weak; no need to suspend	Parliament weak; no need to suspend	Parliament weak; no need to suspend
Support of the electorate for parliamentarism	Approximately half of the deputies support the government	Most deputies support the government, partly due to malapportionment	Many pro-government deputies; Islamists partly excluded	Most deputies support the government, but this is due to Shia boycott of the elections	Not clear	Not clear	No elections	No elections
Parliamentary parties	Independents predominate; electoral system discourages parties; parliamentary blocs are active	Independents predominate; electoral system discourages parties; parliamentary blocs are active	Electoral system encourages parties; few to no independents	Independents predominate; electoral system discourages parties; parliamentary blocs are active	No parties in municipal elections	No parties in municipal elections	No parties	No parties

Note: Roughly speaking, countries to the left have made more progress toward parliamentarism, those to the right less.

The absence of direct government manipulation of elections in the Arab monarchies (except Morocco) offers a good deal of encouragement, and there can be little hope for the eventual achievement of parliamentarism if this tradition is not maintained. In other constitutional monarchies honest elections have kept the political opposition engaged in the parliamentary process even while the monarch retains control of the executive. In Jordan, however, bias in electoral districts against Jordanians of Palestinian origin impeaches the legitimacy of the parliament and the entire political process. In one light, it might be possible to draw an analogy between this and the lack of full suffrage in some earlier constitutional monarchies. Yet in the earlier cases, the reaction of excluded classes tended to focus on gaining access to the parliament, while in Jordan malapportionment tends to alienate many Jordanians from parliamentary life as a whole. Bahrain, too, appears to have difficulties with malapportionment, in this case directed against the majority Shiite population.

Instead of stealing the elections, Arab monarchies have more often suspended their parliaments. The mere threat of a suspension dampens the ambitions of parliamentary deputies, and this threat remains very present in Jordan and Bahrain. Oman's *majlis al-shura* poses such a modest threat to the monarchy that even the threat of suspension appears unnecessary. The Moroccan monarchy has typically stolen the elections rather than suspended the parliament. It is in Kuwait that the elections have remained relatively free and where the threat of suspension has receded somewhat: this gives us good reason to view Kuwait's progress toward real parliamentary power as more advanced than that of the other Arab monarchies.

We would be wrong to suppose that monarchism survives in the Arab world only through repression. Parliaments represent their electorates, and not all voters in the Arab monarchies want parliamentarism. In fact, many explicitly do not, preferring instead that most political power remain in the hands of their monarchs. This poses a substantial barrier to parliamentarism for the plain reason that the deputies elected by these voters, while they sometimes use the parliament to defeat the government on specific issues, do not seek structural change that would give parliamentary parties the power to appoint the ministers. We see this most clearly in Kuwait, where pro-government deputies occupy about half of the elected seats in the parliament. The electoral system encourages this, but these deputies also represent a substantial body of opinion in the Kuwaiti body politic. In the other monarchies the desires of the electorate can be harder to read—full representation for Palestinian-Jordanians might change the generally pro-government composition of

Jordan's elected lower house, as might elections in Bahrain with fairly drawn districts and full participation of the Shia. So, too, in Morocco the partial exclusion of Islamists from the elections, and the partial co-optation of the existing opposition parties, weakens the opposition in its parliament.

Finally, all of the parliaments, except the Moroccan, lack a strong party system. Parliaments without parties can exercise an occasional veto over the government but cannot hope to wrest control over the appointment of ministers. Yet there is a certain amount of progress in this regard; even where independents dominate, in Kuwait and in Jordan, deputies increasingly find it useful to coalesce into blocs in the parliament. Were some of the other barriers to parliamentarism in the monarchies to ease, these blocs provide a solid basis for the further development of parties.

Of all the Arab world's monarchies, which has made the most progress toward parliamentarism? Saudi Arabia and the UAE, of course, are the farthest away, lacking even elected parliaments. Oman's parliament has no powers specified in the constitution, and Qatar's parliament will labor under a constitution that gives it very few powers—nor is it clear that the ruling family will allow free campaigning or the emergence of an opposition bloc in the parliament. Bahrain's parliament does have opposition blocs, and the country has an active political life. But the constitution sharply limits the power of the elected *majlis al-nuwwab*. This leaves Jordan, Morocco, and Kuwait. Of these, Morocco, while giving the formal appearance of being much farther ahead of the other cases, resembles many constitutional monarchies in the Arab world and elsewhere—systems in which monarchs allowed the form of parliamentarism but deprived it of its substance by interference in the elections and by denying the prime minister the authority to rule.

Jordan's parliamentary experience suffers from widespread apathy and a lack of legitimacy among many Jordanians, particularly (though hardly exclusively) those of Palestinian descent. Yet some of this also grows out of Jordan's very difficult regional situation and the worsening of the Arab-Israeli conflict in recent years. These factors pose real barriers to any expansion of parliamentary powers or further inclusion of Islamists or Palestinian-Jordanians. However, neither can it be assumed that were some of these other problems to fade that the Jordanian monarchy would flatly refuse to allow the power of the parliament to grow at the expense of the monarchy.

Kuwait in particular stands out from the other monarchies. The parliament enjoys a substantial degree of legitimacy among the citizen population. Those who are excluded—notably women—have focused their efforts on gaining admission, not on attacking the institution. Yet the legitimacy of the parliament does not come at the expense of the legitimacy of the role of the ruling family in politics—there is little appetite in much of the electorate for parliamentary dominance of Kuwaiti politics. Of the Arab dynasties, however, Kuwait's seems the most comfortable with a politically powerful parliament. Although there is nothing inevitable about further progress toward parliamentarism in Kuwait, it is perhaps here, among the Arab monarchies, where such progress would be least surprising.

The parliaments of the Arab monarchies are not mere façades. While we cannot predict the eventual achievement of parliamentarism, neither can we rule it out. If the tradition of free elections is maintained, and with constitutional improvements in some of the monarchies, the parliaments hold out promise for the transformation of these political systems in a more democratic direction.

Notes

I am indebted to Jason Brownlee, Amaney Jamal, Ellen Lust-Okar, Jennifer McCoy, Rashid Naim, Michele Penner Angrist, Marsha Pripstein Posusney, and Mark Tessler for their helpful comments.

1. Brumberg is less pessimistic in his 2003 Carnegie Endowment working paper.

2. This bears some comparison with the analysis of authoritarian regimes with democratic elements in other parts of the world. See, for instance, Levitsky and Way (2002).

3. For a work that looks specifically at constitutions and raises some of the issues I examine here, see Brown (2002).

4. Posusney, in Chapter 5 herein, does not distinguish monarchies as a specific regime type but cites evidence that "democratic transitions can emerge from prolonged periods of controlled contestation" that allow opposition groups to "ultimately negotiate democratization with reluctant incumbent authoritarians."

5. English versions of the constitutions of most Arab monarchies can be found at the International Constitutional Law Project, www.oefre.unibe.ch/law/icl/index.html and at www.gsu.edu/~polmfh/constitutions.htm.

6. A distinction must be drawn between fraud organized from the center and the undue influence of local notables: the latter did not destroy the independence of the parliament against the government.

7. Patronage allowed British cabinets to control a sizable number of seats in parliament in the eighteenth century, though in the smaller constituencies mostly. Electoral manipulation generated much less mention from the 1832 reforms forward. See Holmes and Szechi (1993: 37); McCord (1991).

8. For an explanation of the underlying causes of the "slide to authoritarianism" in Egypt see Angrist, Chapter 6, in this book; see also al-Bishri (1987).

9. There are a few exceptions. Elections in Imperial Germany were quite free, with universal male suffrage. The monarchy was destroyed by World War

I and was followed by a fragile democracy. See Hewitson (2001); Suval (1985). Elections in the Austrian half of the dual monarchy, while flawed, were not regularly stolen by the government. Conflict between nationalities blocked the formation of a coherent party government (Jenks 1974).

10. See also Brown (2002: 10). In Norway and the Netherlands, parliaments acting on their own could remove confidence in ministers: Storing (1963: 51–52, 150–152); Newton (1978: 66, 71).

11. For details on the achievement of parliamentarism in Belgium, see Kossmann (1978: 201, 208–368); Hislaire (1945: 97); in Denmark, Jones (1970: 75–87); in Sweden, Verney (1957: 103, 32–33); in the Netherlands, Newton (1978: 73–74); Kossmann (1978: 285–288); in Norway, Storing (1963: 52–53); Derry (1957: 179–180).

12. On Dubai, see *al-Hayat,* April 3, 2003. A year later, Dubai's rulers had made no further announcements on the subject.

13. Articles 101 and 102. Ministers who sit in parliament even if they are not elected members cannot vote on motions of confidence.

14. *Al-Hayat,* July 5, 1999; interviews with prominent defeated incumbents in *al-Qabas,* July 10, 11, and 12, 2003; see also Tétreault (2000). The government did steal the elections in some constituencies in 1967 (al-Najjar 2000: 86–92).

15. Kuwaiti voters cast two votes in two-member constituencies with no runoff. The system encourages voting according to tribe, clans, and sect, while discouraging ideological parties: it also makes vote buying easier. See al-Harbi (2003: 28–33).

16. The last unconstitutional closing generated a determined protest movement in 1989 and 1990. See al-Mudayris (2002).

17. For a detailed accounting of the political orientations of members of the Kuwaiti parliament since 1962, see my Kuwait politics database at www. gsu.edu/~polmfh/database/database.htm. On the Awazim, see *al-Rai al-Am,* March 7, 10, and 12, 2004.

18. See, for example, the interview with Ali Salman, the head of the Wifaq, in *al-Hayat,* October 23, 2002, and his comments reported in *al-Wasat,* May 22, 2004.

19. Articles 77 and 111.

20. Articles 70 and 100. Issuing laws when parliament is not in session is a favored tactic of Arab monarchs and has been an issue in Kuwait and Jordan.

21. Articles 53 and 54.

22. Calculations are based on election data from the website www.electionsjo.com (accessed April 20, 2004). The calculation omits the six seats reserved for women, which were allocated in a way that mirrored the malapportionment in the other 104 seats.

23. Jordanian Ministry of the Interior website, http://www.moi.gov.jo/election_details.php?id_e=8 (accessed April 22, 2004).

24. On the Jordanian opposition, see also Lust-Okar, Chapter 7, in this book.

25. The Islamic Action Front, which constitutes the main opposition in the parliament, with seventeen members, demanded parliamentarism in February 2004, earning some attention but with few prospects for success (*al-Hayat,* February 24, 2004).

26. For the similar results of previous elections, see Lust-Okar (2001: 550–551).

27. Articles 60, 75, 76. See also Denoeux and Maghraoui (1998: 108–114).

28. On Arab electoral systems, see Lust-Okar and Jamal (2002).

29. On the Moroccan opposition, see Lust-Okar, Chapter 7 herein; Ben Mlih (2001: 4–13).

30. Moroccan Ministry of Communication website, www.mincom.gov.ma/ french/generalites/orga_eta/elections2002/resultatglobal.htm (accessed August 13, 2003).

31. It hardly helped that when the prime minister selected "younger faces" for the cabinet, he wound up with the sons and daughters of party leaders and former cabinet ministers (*al-Hayat,* November 8, 2002).

32. This petition can be found on various websites. See www.islamonline. net/Arabic/doc/2004/02/article02_20.SHTML (accessed April 20, 2003).

9

Too Much Civil Society, Too Little Politics? Egypt and Other Liberalizing Arab Regimes

VICKIE LANGOHR

*Studies of democratization have generally viewed nongovern-
mental organizations as being completely distinct from parties,
assuming that each type of group plays a different role in
democratization and that each attracts different types of
activists. This chapter, focusing on the role of civil society
groups in several Arab countries, shows that opposition to
authoritarian regimes is much more fluid. The presence or
absence of political and financial opportunities can significantly
influence the organizational form that opposition takes. In several Arab liberalizers, limitations on party formation and activity have generally been stricter than those that regulated NGOs,
and NGOs have been able to raise money much more easily.
These factors have helped to make advocacy NGOs, not parties,
the most vocal secular opposition in these Arab liberalizers, but
this development has been detrimental to chances for long-term
democratization.*

In his provocative article "The End of the Transition Paradigm," Thomas
Carothers offered a corrective to common ways of thinking about liberalizing authoritarian regimes. At the height of a worldwide wave of liberalizations in the early 1990s, he noted that optimistic assumptions that
any liberalizing regime was in transition to democracy led observers to
count as many as one hundred countries that were expected to become
democratic. By 2002, no more than twenty had moved beyond tentative
liberalizations to institute meaningful political competition. The other
four-fifths—including countries in Central America, Africa, and the former Soviet Union—"have not achieved relatively well-functioning

democracy or do not seem to be deepening or advancing whatever democratic progress they have made" (Carothers 2002: 9).

Carothers' argument is important not only for democratization studies but also as an invitation to rethink the role of Arab liberalizations within them. Discussions of the global "waves" of democratization routinely single out the Arab world as impervious to democratization, and Arab cases are generally ignored in scholarly research. It is often forgotten that in or before the optimistic early 1990s cited by Carothers, several Arab regimes—like their counterparts in Eastern Europe, Africa, and Asia—engaged in important liberalizing efforts. That these efforts have not led to meaningful democratization does not make the Arab world a democratic "outlier"; rather, it is part of a larger trend in which most recent moves away from authoritarianism have faltered. The Arab world may have specific conditions, ranging from the role of Islam in politics to exceedingly high levels of exogenous rents, which have particularly hampered its democratization progress. However, the fact that most transitions worldwide in this period have faltered suggests that more generalizable factors, such as the weakness of opposition parties and specific electoral arrangements, may also be at work. One such factor that has impeded democratization in several liberalizing Arab regimes has been the rise of advocacy NGOs such as human rights and women's groups, rather than parties, to the position of the key secular opposition in the country.

Scholarship on the role of civil society and NGOs in democratization has generally treated NGOs as entities completely distinct from parties,[1] attributing different functional roles in transitions to the two types of groups and assuming that they attract different types of activists. The experiences of several Arab countries suggest that it would be more useful to see both NGOs and parties as part of a larger topography of opposition. In this approach, opposition is perceived as being somewhat free-floating, with the presence or absence of political and financial opportunities significantly influencing what organizational form opposition takes. If, for example, it is very difficult to achieve legal recognition for political parties but relatively easy to establish NGOs, or if parties are poverty stricken while foreign funds for NGOs are readily available, it may be rational for activists who in other circumstances would organize themselves through parties to operate through NGOs. In several Arab liberalizers, most particularly Egypt and Tunisia, insufficient or reversed liberalization measures have kept opposition parties weak and relatively powerless. In the Palestine Authority, another key reason for opposition party weakness was the decision of most Palestine Liberation Organization (PLO) factions to boycott the 1996 elections for the Palestine Legislative Council. At the same time, liberalization created the conditions for Arab participation in a larger trend in the global South: the proliferation of human rights, women's, and environmental groups.[2] With effective opposition parties rare in most Arab liberalizers, advocacy NGOs in several Arab countries have become the most vocal secular opposition. They have also assumed roles, from defending the economic interests of workers and farmers to calling for the replacement of incumbent regimes, that typically are played by opposition parties. This chapter contends that an important reason for this development is that limitations on party formation and activity have generally been stricter than those regulating NGOs and that in many countries parties are financially precarious while NGOs have been able to raise money internationally.

While it may not be surprising that in these conditions advocacy NGOs have become increasingly prominent opposition actors, this development harms the chances for sustainable democratization. Advocacy NGOs generally advocate the interests of a specific group or the importance of a particular principle, such as respect for human rights, making them ill-equipped to mobilize a much broader set of constituencies around the larger goal of regime change. Equally important, as groups almost entirely dependent on foreign funding, these NGOs often have strong support abroad but shallow roots at home, allowing them to be more easily discredited by hostile governments than parties would be. The structural weaknesses that severely hinder NGO efforts to foster democratization are best demonstrated by an examination of a large campaign by Egyptian NGOs in 1999 to oppose laws limiting NGO activities. In many ways this campaign operated within a context more propitious to NGO success than that found in most other Arab liberalizers. Egypt has one of the longest histories in the Arab world of formally organized voluntary associational activity, beginning in the first decades of the twentieth century. Although this activity was severely curtailed in the 1950s and 1960s, Egypt's liberalization began in the late 1970s, a full decade earlier than that of most other Arab liberalizers, which has given both old and new NGOs a relatively longer period to build their organizations. Finally, the 1999 campaign had high-profile support from Western donors and governments, which has been missing in many other Arab liberalizers. As Margaret Keck and Kathryn Sikkink (1998) have argued, such support can be crucial in maintaining the freedom of NGOs to operate in authoritarian contexts. Despite these propitious conditions, Egyptian NGOs' attempts to mobilize for associational freedom and to expand their campaign to encompass more fundamental regime change failed, powerfully demonstrating the limits on what Arab advocacy NGOs can be expected to achieve in the battle for democratization.

Advocacy NGOs as Opposition:
Tunisia, the PA, and Egypt

Blessed with two attributes commonly cited as key facilitators of democracy—high literacy rates and a large middle class[3]—Tunisia appeared poised to successfully democratize when interior minister Zine El-Abidine Ben Ali overthrew president Habib Bourguiba in 1987 and announced plans for a more democratic Tunisia. Amnesties of political prisoners and abolition of the lifetime presidency soon followed (Alexander 1997: 35). Opposition parties, which began to break away from the ruling party in the late 1970s but had not been allowed seats in the parliament, became more prominent as new parties emerged and were offered government subsidies to defray campaign costs (Bellin 1995: 133–134). At Ben Ali's invitation the government, representatives of the eight recognized opposition parties, and national labor, human rights, and women's organizations engaged in spirited negotiations on, and eventually signed, a "National Pact" outlining a consensus on the general content of Tunisia's national identity and a commitment to democracy (Anderson 1991).

That commitment has not become a reality. As the first elections under the new regime neared, the Islamist Tendency Movement (MTI) as denied recognition as a party. When members ran as independents, they polled 14.5 percent of the vote—more than three times as much as the next largest opposition party—but the ruling RCD was awarded 100 percent of the seats (Dillman 2000: 216). The MTI was subsequently forbidden to contest elections, and its members have been subjected to continued police repression.[4] With the MTI out of the way, the RCD chose to ensure a minimum of opposition party representation by not contesting a certain number of seats in the 1994 and 1999 elections. The tightly controlled nature of these contests was demonstrated by the fact that in both elections the opposition parties won the exact number of seats left uncontested, giving the RCD 88 percent and 81 percent of the seats, respectively (Dillman 2000: 216–217).

While political parties were rendered all but irrelevant to the conduct of opposition politics, human rights groups became some of the loudest opposition voices. The Tunisian League for the Defense of Human Rights (Ligue Tunisienne des Droits de l'Homme, or LTDH), founded in 1977, was the first human rights group in the Arab world. When the regime jailed and tried Islamist activists in military tribunals in 1991 and 1992, LTDH was its most outspoken critic. The regime attempted to silence LTDH by forbidding associations to have party leaders on their boards—which LTDH did—and mandating that they accept all interested parties as members, which LTDH feared would lead the government to weaken its message by flooding it with ruling party supporters (Bellin 1995: 138).

LTDH assumed a lower profile until October 2000, when it elected a much more outspoken leadership, including a board of directors without a single member of the ruling party and a secretary-general fresh from several years' imprisonment on political charges. The new, more oppositional LTDH joined the National Council on Liberties in Tunisia (Conseil National pour les Libertés en Tunisie, or CNLT), founded in 1998 by LTDH defectors dissatisfied with its earlier conciliatory approach, in speaking out against violations of the rights of nonviolent Islamists, particularly the MTI. The regime responded with a court ruling suspending LTDH's newly elected board, the ransacking of the office of a CNLT founder, and denial of permission to travel abroad to several CNLT members.[5]

Like Tunisia, the PA since its inception in 1994 has been characterized by ineffective secular opposition parties and nongovernmental organizations that have assumed the mantle of the main secular opposition to the late Yasir Arafat's regime.[6] In the PA, however, it was the decision of several secular opposition factions in the PLO to boycott the 1996 legislative elections, combined with these factions' long experience in operating voluntary associations, which led secular opposition to be channeled through NGOs rather than parties. The Israeli occupation of the West Bank and Gaza in 1967 fostered intense associational activity. Associations were created to resist the occupation and compensate for Israeli neglect of social services, first by leftist PLO factions such as the Popular Front for the Liberation of Palestine (PFLP), the Democratic Front for the Liberation of Palestine (DFLP), and the Palestinian Communist Party (Brynen 2000). Fatah, the largest PLO faction, followed suit after the PLO's defeat in Lebanon in 1982. The close link between voluntary associations and PLO factions led to a semicorporatist form of associational organization in which almost every West Bank and Gaza grassroots organization was affiliated with a PLO faction, and each faction had its own women's, labor, and other federations. This dense network of associations gained great domestic legitimacy by providing for Palestinian society during the first intifada, which began in December 1987.

The 1993 signing of the Oslo accords and the creation of the PA in 1994 created a dramatically new political environment. Associations that had assumed many state functions in a stateless environment would now operate within the context of an emerging state run by an elected president and the PLC. Given the distinct ideological platforms of each of the factions, the high degrees of factional identification among Palestinians, and the ease with which faction-identified voluntary associations could have been used to mobilize voters, each of the main factions was in an ideal position to transform itself into a political party and contest legislative elections in 1996. The Popular and Democratic Fronts for Palestine and Hamas, however, boycotted these elections on the grounds that they legitimated the Oslo accords.[7] Election-day polls suggest that the boycotting factions could have made a respectable showing in the parliament had they run; because PFLP members largely ignored the boycott call, the party could have won at least their votes had it participated (Shikaki 1996: 18). The result of the boycott was a legislature in which Fatah and its members who rejoined the party after running as independents won 75 percent of the seats, while Islamist-identified candidates won seven seats and independents, including two affiliated with the PFLP, won eleven (Shikaki 1996: 20).

Although secular left factions opted out of the legislative process, many of their activists chose to use NGOs to oppose the Fatah-dominated PA. One long-time feminist activist critical of this trend observed that

> nongovernmental organizations provided in the past, and can provide in the future, useful complements to [left] movements. However, the Left is not mobilizing in and around nongovernmental organizations simply to defend the potential of these institutions to complement political parties. Instead, nongovernmental organizations have become the last bastion of a Left which no longer seems willing or capable of reforming itself to address the political world, as a political movement in the changed realities that Oslo has brought to light. (Hammami 1995: 62)

By the mid-1990s, several leftist intellectuals and activists were criticizing the belief that nongovernmental organizations, not parties, were the best vehicle for forcing democracy on the PA. Muwatin, the Palestinian Institute for the Study of Democracy, a key forum for left intellectuals and academics founded in 1992, made its feelings clear when it chose "Pluralism and Democracy: The Crisis of the Palestinian Political Party" as the topic of its first annual conference in 1995. Muwatin director George Giacaman "reject[ed] nongovernmental organizations' claims that they are in the front line of preserving civil society and thus a democratic culture . . . [and] posited the absence of strong oppositional parties as the real Achilles heel of Palestinian political culture" (Hammami 1995: 62). In 1998 the feminist activist quoted above noted that three years earlier few leftist activists believed that nongovernmental organizations were no substitute for political parties. By 1998, however, this had become the majority position. It is now obvious that nongovernmental organizations have not been able to organize a challenge to the continued "Arafatization" of Palestinian political life. . . . The crisis is now viewed fundamentally as one of political democratization and the absence of the independent political movements necessary to achieve it. (Hammami 2000: 27)

The liberalization process in Egypt has been much more prolonged than those in Tunisia and Palestine, and in its early years it was marked by an efflorescence of opposition parties, which suggested timely movement toward democratization. Twenty-four years of single-party rule ended in the late 1970s with the creation of a handful of opposition parties. Despite significant obstacles to party formation, a more pluralist political framework began to emerge, as parties denied legal recognition successfully challenged their denials in court and the Muslim Brothers, forbidden to form their own party, ran as independents. In the 1980s opposition coalitions based on the Brotherhood won increasing numbers of seats and had a growing impact on lawmaking; in 1984 a Brotherhood-Wafd coalition with 13 percent of the seats proposed 22 percent of all parliamentary bills. In 1987 the opposition almost doubled its votes, dealing the ruling National Democratic Party its worst showing since 1950 (Baaklini, Denoeux, and Springborg 1999: 230). Had several independents not subsequently joined the ruling party, it would not have retained the two-thirds majority necessary to nominate the presidential candidate, who (until the 2005 elections) then ran unchallenged in a plebiscite, or to alter the constitution.[8]

Hopes that the 1980s improvements might lead to a more competitive political system faded in the 1990s. From the late 1980s until the mid-1990s a violent Islamist insurgency saw radical Islamist groups become the de facto government in many parts of the south, assassinating political and cultural figures and decimating a tourist industry whose revenues are central to the Egyptian economy. Further instability was caused by the quickening pace of the government's implementation of an IMF structural adjustment program begun in the 1980s. Between 1993 and 1999 all or part of more than one-third of state-owned enterprises were privatized (Posusney 1999: 38), raising the prospect of massive layoffs in an economy with unemployment rates already between 10 and 22 percent (Pfeifer 1999: 26) while the repeal of land reforms instituted during Gamal Abdel Nasser's presidency required that land distributed to peasants in the 1950s and 1960s be returned to its original owners. These policies severely depressed living standards: between

1986 and 1996 the countryside experienced "growing unemployment, falling real wages, [and] higher prices for basic goods and services" (Fletcher 1996: 4, quoted in Mitchell 1999: 32), while the percentage of the population in poverty nationwide doubled from 21 percent in 1990 to 44 percent in 1996 (Handy and staff team, 1998: 42, quoted in Pfeifer 1999: 26).

Rising Islamist violence and potential social instability generated by structural adjustment made the ruling NDP insistent upon maintaining control of at least the two-thirds of the parliament seats necessary to change the constitution or to nominate the president. It turned its attention first to its most potent competitor, the Muslim Brotherhood. Although the Brotherhood had helped the government turn jailed Islamist militants toward nonviolence, in the months leading up to the 1995 elections the NDP imprisoned the most popular Brotherhood candidates and engineered their convictions in military court. In 1995 such high levels of pro-NDP fraud ensued that the Court of Cassation called, unsuccessfully, for the nullification of the election of more than two hundred of a total of 444 deputies (Kienle 1998: 226–227). These and similar strategies have resulted in NDP majorities of at least 85 percent in the last three parliaments, including an unprecedented 94 percent of the seats in 1995.[9]

While moving to limit the power of opposition parties, the government also clamped down on two other historically oppositional sectors of civil society: the professional associations and the trade unions. While the Engineers' Syndicate had unsuccessfully fought Nasser's Aswan Dam project and the lawyers had battled state-of-emergency laws in the 1980s, the associations reached the peak of their oppositional potential in the late 1980s and 1990s when Muslim Brothers won the leadership of several associations. Brotherhood leadership councils denounced police torture and defended the legal rights of Islamist prisoners, but their success at more mundane matters like providing cheap consumer goods to their members were equally threatening, as every success seemed to bear out the Brothers' electoral slogan, "Islam is the Solution." Assuming that Brotherhood success in association elections had been the result of low turnout, the government responded with a law requiring that associations be put under government administration if their elections did not achieve unusually high turnout levels. When this failed to halt Brotherhood victories, the syndicates were put under receivership under other pretexts. Trade unions were crippled by amendments to the trade union law depriving the workers most at risk of termination under structural adjustment of the right to vote in union elections while significantly easing the reelection of incumbent leaders who were generally members of the ruling party. Under these conditions, the 1996 union elections easily returned a solid ruling party majority (Kienle 1998: 227).

While parties and other oppositional sites in civil society were silenced, advocacy NGOs increased their numbers and strength. The decimation of voluntary associations under the Nasser regime gave way to a new generation of advocacy organizations in the 1970s and early 1980s. Although feminist groups had long been active in Egypt, new women's groups now appeared, pioneered in 1982 by Nawal al Saadawi's Arab Women's Solidarity Association. In 1983 the Arab Organization of Human Rights, based in Cairo but focused on the entire region, became the first human rights group in Egypt; there are currently more than twenty such groups, including associations specializing in prisoner advocacy and rehabilitation of torture victims. Several environmental groups were also created, including one that has waged several successful and well-publicized battles against government attempts to privatize public space in Alexandria.

The new advocacy NGOs—particularly human rights groups—quickly took on the most sensitive issues of the day. While unambiguously rejecting Islamist militants' use of violence, human rights groups called for due process and an end to torture. They played an equally pronounced role in defending the interests of those hurt by structural adjustment. The National Progressive Unionist Party (NPUP), the closest thing Egypt has to a workers' and peasants' party, proved incapable of offering meaningful resistance to laws reversing land reform, which stipulated that within five years plots distributed to peasants in the 1950s and early 1960s would be returned to their original owners unless that owner agreed to sell or rent to the current owner. Given their miniscule number of seats in parliament, the NPUP and allied parties could not have stopped the law's passage. However, as the *Arab Strategic Report,* an annual report produced by Egypt's most prestigious think tank (the Center for Political and Strategic Studies), points out, the NPUP and others could have used the five-year interim period to seek the law's amendment or to provide direct services to their peasant members. They did neither, and the head of the NPUP peasants' section admitted that the party didn't start work on the question until shortly before the law's final stages were to go into effect.[10] A relatively new NGO, the Land Center for Human Rights, instead provided key services to these peasants, documenting abuses of the law and seeking redress, particularly compensation for permanent structures that peasants had built on the land being returned. This is precisely the type of service that the *Strategic Report* argues that the NPUP could have provided to ameliorate its members' plight.

As nongovernmental associations strove to protect the interests of peasants, other new organizations sought to strengthen the ability of workers to mobilize against structural adjustment policy in a climate of severely weakened trade unions. A leading former trade unionist founded the Center for Trade Union and Workers Services in 1995 to strengthen worker organization, and the following year 135 workers resorted to the Center for Human Rights Legal Aid (CHRLA) when the government prevented them from running in union elections (Kienle 2001: 82). CHRLA has defended entire classes of workers who contend they were illegally fired from their jobs.[11] On at least two levels, this type of work brought human rights groups very close to assuming the role that leftist political parties would normally play. In the programmatic sense, some of this work is designed to bolster workers' attempts to oppose structural adjustment laws. These groups also assume a clientelistic nature through this work, as workers and farmers who might be expected to seek the help of a left or populist party now turn to human rights groups to defend their interests.

Why Are Opposition Parties So Weak?

The weakness of opposition parties in the Arab liberalizers is most pronounced in the cases like those of Egypt, Tunisia, and Palestine, where these parties win miniscule numbers of seats in parliament. However, opposition parties in Jordan, Morocco, Yemen, and Algeria have won at least 30 percent of the seats in parliament in different elections during the 1990s. But they, too, have had little legislative influence. There is no question that electoral fraud and outright repression of viable opposition candidates, as in Tunisia's ban of the MTI, have commonly undermined opposition parties. Limited access to the public compounds the problem: large opposition gatherings are often obtrusively monitored by police, if allowed at all, and most opposition groups receive no television or radio coverage, making party newspapers their only method of communication. Whereas these factors significantly weaken opposition parties, they do not tell the whole story, as at least three other factors systematically undermine opposition strength. The first could be called "incomplete parliamentarization," where significant deviations from general parliamentary procedure such as allowing unelected upper houses to censure governments obstruct elected representatives. Where opposition parties have won significant numbers of seats, incomplete parliamentarization has repeatedly undermined their influence. The second problem is the prevalence of independent candidacy among non–ruling party candidates. It is often argued that in Arab liberalizers Islamists win almost all opposition seats while secular parties perform dismally. In fact, what more generally happens is that independents either win the largest number of seats or as many as the largest opposition party—an Islamist party—and secular opposition parties win very few. The prevalence of independent candidacy weakens opposition by preventing the development of party programs that would constitute a clear alternative to ruling parties and win support away from them. A final reason for opposition party weakness is financial fragility.

It is worth first examining why opposition parties in some Arab liberalizers are able to win significant numbers of seats while others are all but shut out of their legislatures. In Egypt, Tunisia, and Palestine ruling parties have won as many as 80 or 90 percent of the seats while opposition parties polled in the single digits. In Morocco, which has no ruling party, the three largest parties received 50, 48, and 42 seats in a 328-seat parliament in the 2002 elections,[12] while in Algeria's latest electoral contest three nonruling parties each won at least 10 percent of the seats.[13] Jordan's Islamic Action Front won 30 percent of the seats in 1989 and 20 percent in 1993, and it boycotted the 1997 elections (Lust-Okar 2001: 550–551). In Yemen's 1993 founding elections three parties each gained significant numbers of seats (Schwedler 2002: 49). Ellen Lust-Okar and Amaney Ahmad Jamal argue that the level of opposition representation in Arab liberalizers is a result of the subtype of authoritarian regime, with liberalizing monarchies more likely than presidential systems to produce significant representation of opposition parties. Because presidents are the products of ruling parties, they contend, their interests are best served by electoral arrangements that favor the emergence of a single large party, including party lists and high thresholds. The legitimacy of monarchs, however, stems in large part from the perception that they are above politics and responsible for the well-being of the nation as a whole, which precludes their formation of a ruling party and leads them to prefer the distribution of seats among a (limited) number of parties whose competition they can then "manage." As a result, liberalizing monarchs tend to adopt mechanisms that favor smaller parties such as small districts and no or low thresholds (Lust-Okar and Jamal 2002).

Lust-Okar and Jamal's argument explains the presence of opposition parties with significant numbers of seats in the monarchies of Morocco and Jordan but not the presidential systems of Yemen and Algeria. Yet significant opposition party representation in these countries may well be the result of unusual constraints that forced presidents to at least temporarily allow a reasonable showing of nonruling parties.

Significant opposition party representation in Algeria was the result of the adoption of proportional representation that, as Marsha Pripstein Posusney notes, is a long-term demand of most Arab oppositions, which is almost never granted (Posusney, Chapter 5, in this book).[14] Algeria's ruling party, however, adopted it to convince opposition parties spooked by the experience of the military shutdown of the electoral process in 1991 to participate in elections. The Yemeni transition was part of the unification of North and South Yemen, during which the leading groups in both countries—the Yemen Socialist Party (YSP) in the south and the General People's Congress (GPC) in the north—reemerged as parties in the unified Yemen. This existence of two parties with significant independent support bases distinguished Yemen from other liberalizing Arab presidential systems from the outset, as the other transitions began with only a single all-powerful party. Yemen's third large party—the Islamist Islah—was founded with GPC support on the understanding that it would serve as a GPC ally. In this situation the 1993 founding elections could produce high numbers of votes for all three parties. Once the YSP was decimated in the 1994 civil war between the north and the south, however, the GPC no longer needed Islah to counterbalance what had been its major opponent, and Yemen came into line with other presidential liberalizers as the ruling GPC and aligned independents captured 75 percent of the seats (Schwedler 2002: 51).

With Algeria the only presidential system in which opposition parties are currently well represented, it seems clear that significant opposition party representation is more common in liberalizing monarchies than in the presidential systems. Even in these monarchies, though, "incomplete parliamentarization," or the adoption of the trappings of parliamentarism with the persistence of practices that run fundamentally counter to common parliamentary procedure, has severely limited opposition power. As Michael Herb notes (in Chapter 8 of this book), incomplete parliamentarization can come in many forms, with a key question being whether or not the constitution itself blocks full parliamentary sovereignty, as in constitutions in which unelected upper houses share equal powers with elected assemblies. While the prime minister is picked by the ruling coalition in Morocco, the king's recourse to a fully empowered upper house elected indirectly through institutions loyal to the king allows him to significantly dilute the expression of voter preferences. The king could thus permit a left opposition government to take power in 1998 while preventing substantive change, as the loyalist upper house significantly diluted the majority that the opposition had achieved in the directly elected lower house, forcing the resulting opposition government into coalition with loyalist parties that weakened its agenda (Sweet 2001: 24–25). This type of outcome not only handicaps the current opposition government; it delegitimizes opposition parties more generally by convincing the public that they are incapable of bringing about change. As Catherine Sweet notes, "rather than blame the regime for engineering the gridlock, most Moroccans fault the . . . government for its impotence" (2001: 25).

A second major reason for opposition party weakness is the prevalence of independent candidacies among non–ruling party candidates.[15] In Jordan, Yemen, and Egypt independents have gotten the largest number of nonruling party seats, or as many as the Islamist party, while secular opposition parties trailed far behind. For example, in 1993 Jordanian independents won 61 percent of the seats, a full 40 percent more seats than the Islamist party (Lust-Okar 2001: 550–551). In Egypt's 2000 elections independents and the largest opposition force—the Muslim Brotherhood—each won seventeen seats, while the four main secular opposition parties won sixteen seats combined (Essam el-Din 2000).[16] The 1997 Yemeni parliament showed almost exactly the same outcome: independents and the largest party tied with fifty-four and fifty-three seats, respectively, while the next largest party won three seats (Langohr 2002: 120).

Independent candidacy is both a cause and a result of opposition party weakness. Some independents are simply popular or wealthy people (or in a country such as Jordan, members of tribes) who want a parliamentary seat and are uninterested in opposition politics. Others are committed opponents of authoritarian regimes who are nonetheless uninspired by the current slate of opposition parties in their country. High barriers to party formation keep these types of candidates in some Arab liberalizers from forming their own parties. Almost all of Egypt's recognized parties were initially denied recognition by the regime's political parties committee and only won recognition through costly court battles, which lead activists who share a common platform to run as independents rather than fight for party recognition. Whatever the case, the prevalence of independent candidacy among non–ruling party candidates weakens the chances for effective opposition to authoritarian regimes by preventing the formation of well-defined alternatives that can win popular support.

A final source of opposition party weakness is the financial fragility of almost all secular opposition parties, and some Islamist parties, many of whom rely on the very governments that they oppose for crucial funds and services. When Egypt's Nasserist Party found itself hundreds of thousands of dollars in the red, members "staged protests imploring the government itself to intervene and save the party from bankruptcy"

(*Egypt Almanac 2003:* 154). When the Egyptian government froze the activities of the Islamist-identified Labour Party, thus closing down its biweekly paper, paper employees went on strike to get the government-funded Supreme Press Council to pay their salaries. The council's refusal, on the grounds that the party should be responsible for the costs of its own newspaper, carried little weight with the striking employees, and "an official party" eventually paid the salaries (Howeidy 2000). An important reason for the financial weakness of opposition parties is the lack of parties representing upper-class interests. Arab business elites have tended to express their interests through sectoral groups such as chambers of commerce rather than parties, largely because authoritarian regimes still control most business opportunities, and the formation of parties that might be perceived as oppositional could jeopardize access to those opportunities.

The poverty of many opposition parties contrasts sharply with the propitious financial environment for Arab NGOs—particularly advocacy organizations—in the 1990s. The conviction in Western policy circles that advocacy NGOs can play central roles in democratization has made associations such as human rights and environmental groups "the single most favored area of U.S. civil society assistance" (Carothers 1997: 115, quoted in Kasfir 1998: 133). European and Canadian governments and nonprofits are also generous funders. The clearest example of the way in which this funding can facilitate NGO proliferation is found in the Palestinian Authority. Although many voluntary associations existed well before the PA's establishment, the trend toward the creation of NGOs was significantly strengthened by a post-Oslo deluge of donor funds. By 1996 the amount of per capita aid for Palestine exceeded that in any other war-to-peace transition, including Bosnia, Rwanda, or El Salvador (Brynen 2000: 79). Aid for democratization efforts—much of which went to NGOs—was particularly popular: donor officials in a 1997 survey argued that democracy and human rights had been comparatively overfunded in contrast to areas such as economic development (Brynen 2000: 162). By 1995 the West Bank and Gaza, with a population of two million, had twelve hundred to fifteen hundred NGOs employing between twenty thousand and thirty thousand people (Brynen 2000: 49), while Egypt, a country of sixty-eight million, has approximately fourteen hundred such organizations.

The political and financial weakness of opposition parties is not the only reason that many activists work through advocacy organizations. Some human rights activists are former members of leftist parties whose persecution by authoritarian regimes convinced them that working to establish the rule of law is more pressing than advancing a party agenda. Similarly, several of the leaders of the new generation of women's advocacy associations are former members of leftist parties who experienced enough sexism within the parties that they decided that women's liberation could best be sought through groups focusing primarily on women's issues (Sadeg al-Ali 2000: 145). The result of these choices, however, has been the location of key battles for democratization in the nongovernmental association sector rather than in political parties. The fact that advocacy NGOs are ill-suited for this job became particularly clear in the campaign in Egypt to prevent the passage of Law 153 of 1998, which not only threatened to severely restrict NGO activity but was seen by advocacy NGOs as particularly designed to hamper their work. As was described earlier, the NGOs went into their anti–Law 153 campaign with some important advantages compared to counterparts in other Arab countries. That Egyptian liberalization began a decade earlier than that of most other Arab liberalizers means Egyptian NGOs are often older and more established than their Arab peers. The possibilities for the success of the campaign were increased by the support of international organizations and the U.S. government for NGOs' efforts. The campaign against Law 153 in fact scored some surprising early successes, prompting a parliament that generally functions as a rubber stamp for the executive to significantly delay passage of the law and to place activists on the law's drafting committee. NGO efforts to forestall the law's passage ultimately failed, however, demonstrating the fundamental inability of advocacy associations even in the most propitious of circumstances to lead campaigns for democratization in the Arab liberalizers.

Egypt: Party Paralysis and Associational Activism

Voluntary associations flourished in Egypt between 1920 and the Free Officer coup in 1952. Under the Nasser regime many associations were either closed, incorporated into regime organizations, or forced underground, and in 1964 the regime formulated Law 32 to regulate those associations that remained. Although the law was a crippling hindrance to many associations, many others were able to function relatively freely, either because they fell into categories relatively privileged under the law or because they were able to escape it entirely by registering their activities under other legal headings.

Law 32 required citizens wishing to form voluntary organizations (subsequently referred to as NGOs) to obtain permission from the Ministry of Social Affairs (MOSA). This permission was often denied on vague grounds, including MOSA determinations that the NGO was not needed or was redundant. Once approved, NGOs had to inform the ministry of all activities, notifying three government offices of the agenda and location of meetings and promptly filing records of meeting proceedings. The law also closely regulated fundraising, allowing only membership dues and offerings given during religious services to be collected without MOSA permission. Permits for any other type of fundraising were frequently denied or significantly delayed, including permission for the receipt of foreign funds so central to advocacy NGOs.

Although Law 32 could seriously hinder NGO work, major sections of the voluntary sector nonetheless managed to function actively. Islamic voluntary associations, by far the largest category of NGOs in Egypt,[17] largely escaped serious MOSA harassment, with the most extensive study of Egyptian NGOs finding they were the least likely of all associations to be dissolved for Law 32 violations (Ben Nafisa and Qandil 1994: 63). The fact that these associations provide desperately needed social services made the government unlikely to seriously hamper their activities, and because many of them were at least partially funded by mosque collections much of their fundraising was exempt from government oversight. Although advocacy associations were precisely the kind of association that Law 32 was designed to stifle, they have also generally been able to function. Business associations, which support the current climate of liberalization and are wealthy enough to self-fund through dues, find their activities unhindered by Law 32. More oppositional advocacy organizations such as human rights groups often avoided Law 32 entirely by registering themselves as civil companies, rendering them liable to taxation but granting them more freedom of operation.

Perhaps the two key categories of nongovernmental associations whose work was most obstructed by Law 32 were the handful of advocacy NGOs that had registered as voluntary associations, including the two leading environmental associations, and nonreligious social service and development associations. Government opposition to the goals of some of these groups may well have accounted for these obstructions. However, one common complaint of NGOs—extremely slow processing of foreign funds due them—may just as well have been a result of an overburdened bureaucracy rather than an intent to hinder the work of any particular group.[18]

The government's decision in early 1998 to replace Law 32 with Law 153 was motivated by a desire to lessen restrictions on "good" (apolitical) NGOs while severely limiting the activities of oppositional advocacy organizations. International donor discourse about the centrality of social service organizations in compensating for government service cutbacks during structural adjustment appealed to the government, and international donors had long called for a less restrictive NGO law. The U.S. Agency for International Development (USAID), which donated $410 million to Egyptian NGOs between 1976 and 2001 (Howeidy 2001) had urged the passage of less restrictive NGO legislation, and in the late 1990s it offered the government several million dollars—which it declined—as technical assistance in revamping the law.[19] Other foreign donors, particularly the Netherlands Organization for International Development Cooperation, were equally outspoken. Law 153 responded to these concerns somewhat by reducing reporting requirements and increasing NGOs' freedom to raise money domestically.

While the government sought to simplify regulation of apolitical NGOs, it also clearly intended to use the new law to stifle oppositional advocacy groups, particularly those which had previously escaped MOSA's purview by registering as civil companies. Law 153 retained many of its predecessor's most regressive aspects, including allowing MOSA to dissolve associations and requiring MOSA permission before accepting foreign funds. It added an article requiring advocacy groups registered as civil companies to register as NGOs or face dissolution. Because Law 153 continued to forbid recognition of NGOs engaged in "political" or syndicate activity, many advocacy NGOs feared they would be denied recognition under the new law and forced to shut down.

Leaders of NGOs became aware in May 1998 of the proposed new law on associations and that the government intended, as it did with many controversial bills, to rush it through parliament before the legislature's summer recess began at the end of June. More than twenty-five organizations signed and distributed an anti-153 statement, soon followed by a second statement presented in the name of sixty-seven associations to the minister of social affairs, Mervat Tellawi. These protests won an early victory, as Tellawi announced that the law would not be passed before the summer recess and committed to meeting NGOs to get their input. Two such meetings were held, the first of which was an invitation-only affair attended by approximately three hundred representatives of eighty NGOs. Before the meeting representatives of about forty left-leaning NGOs gathered to coordinate positions and decided to demand that representatives from NGOs be included in the law's drafting committee. Not expecting the minister to quickly acquiesce, these activists went to the Tellawi meeting without having formulated a list of representatives that they would support and found the rug pulled out from under them when Tellawi immediately agreed. Meeting attendees then responded to Tellawi's agreement by shouting out the names of activists they knew personally as potential representatives; the four with the loudest support won. Two, a doctor and a former attorney general, were respected liberal figures not associated with NGO activism; the third was the head of a high-profile environmental association in Alexandria, and the fourth the director of a Cairo human rights institute who had helped found Egypt's first human rights group in the 1980s.

For the next several months the campaign proceeded quietly. NGOs from twelve of Egypt's twenty-seven governorates came together to form the Civic Forum (CF), which joined the two key groups threatened by the law: apolitical, nonreligious social service and development associations that had suffered from Law 32 and feared 153, and advocacy organizations. Large CF meetings were held to air grievances with 153, and an October 1998 meeting was attended by four members of parliament who promised that open hearings on the law would be held before it was submitted for a vote.[20] The CF and human rights organizations produced several studies detailing the flaws of the new law, which were distributed to lawmakers. In January 1999, a new version of 153 emerged from the drafting committee that the advocacy organization representatives on the committee deemed a real improvement. Further steam was added to the reform campaign when the state council, a judicial body charged with reviewing the bill's constitutionality before it went to parliament, explicitly argued that refusing to register NGOs on the grounds that they were politically active was illegitimate (Rifaat n.d.: ix–x).

For an authoritarian regime in which opposition was strictly controlled, the early successes of the anti-153 campaign were impressive. Delaying submission of the law to parliament to allow more discussion and agreeing to include NGO representatives in the drafting committee were highly unusual concessions. These early successes strongly suggested the existence of a soft-liner–hard-liner split within the government on associational freedom issues. Tellawi had been appointed minister of social affairs shortly before Law 153 was announced, and some advocacy organization advocates saw her appointment as a sign of government flexibility toward NGOs, given her background as an ambassador to Italy and Japan and her extensive previous work with the UN and other international organizations. Further hints of support in some parts of the regime came from the regular appearance in government newspapers of articles critical of Law 153, including several contributions by one of the nongovernmental organization representatives in the drafting committee.

If the hard-liner–soft-liner interpretation was correct, however, then the hard-liners soon made their entrance. Before Law 153 was submitted to the parliament for final passage, most of the changes introduced by the NGOs' delegates in the drafting committee had been deleted, and the state council's rejection of engagement in political activity as grounds for nonrecognition had been ignored. The government paved the way for speedy passage of the new law with a full-scale media barrage designed to discredit NGOs as traitors and thieves out to milk foreign donors. Several months earlier the secretary-general of the Egyptian Organization for Human Rights (EOHR) had been briefly jailed after the organization released a report alleging police brutality against Christians in the village of Kosheh. The government charged at the time that the $25,000 that EOHR had accepted from the British parliament for an entirely unrelated project on women's legal aid was in fact payment for producing the Kosheh report (Pratt 2000). The government has frequently charged that human rights groups take foreign money to produce reports that damage Egypt's international image. As the regime geared up to pass Law 153 government-affiliated publications resumed the offensive with articles depicting the spread of NGOs in the 1990s as a massive scam, including a cartoon in which a poor man suggested to his friend that they form an NGO to increase their income (Kamal 1999). Some opposition party newspapers picked up the charge, referring to human rights organizations as "mercenaries" (Rifaat n.d.).

When the more restrictive version of Law 153 was sent to the parliament on May 14, several advocacy NGOs that had been highly influential in the anti-153 campaign increased the stakes of the battle, reframing it as a question not just of associational freedom but of full-scale regime change. Eight of these groups issued a statement (subsequently referred to as the "Geneva statement") noting that in light of the increasing oppression of human rights groups in Egypt they were studying the idea of opening offices in Geneva, Brussels, and New York. The statement demanded a meeting between human rights groups and President Hosni Mubarak or his representative and a second meeting between human rights groups and UN high commissioner for human rights Mary Robinson, scheduled to visit Egypt in June. It demanded that Robinson institute a moratorium on all UN human rights conferences in Egypt until the government stopped preventing Egyptian human rights groups from holding local and regional human rights conferences in the country. Moving beyond the domain of defense of human rights to more far-reaching democratic reform, the Geneva statement said that its signatories would initiate dialogue with other civil society actors to draw up a plan for political reform in Egypt that they would present to the president. It concluded with the following memorable lines: "The day that the executioners . . . congratulate themselves, imagining that their horrible deeds against the Egyptian citizen have gone unseen, that day will never come." The statement warned that these "executioners" would eventually be held accountable and concluded, "Let them remember well what happened to the executioner Pinochet."[21]

The Geneva statement was not the only initiative taken in the days before the law was passed to increase pressure on the government. Several female human rights activists went on a hunger strike for six days demanding that the NGOs be allowed to present their case to the parliament before its vote (Tadros 1999). Despite these efforts, however, the law was passed, earning a comment from the U.S. State Department that Law 153 "is the wrong direction to go if Egypt wants to energise civil society and promote development" (Tadros 1999).

At this point the endgame of the anti-153 campaign began as human rights groups anticipated the arrival of UN high commissioner for human rights Robinson. During the campaign some advocacy groups had taken the position that should Law 153 be passed, they would not register under it. Others said that if they ultimately failed to quash the law, they would continue fighting it but would be forced to register, lest they be forcibly closed. No decision had to be made immediately on this issue, as the deadline for registration would only come twelve months later. In the days immediately before Robinson's arrival in early June, however, eight women's and human rights NGOs submitted notice of their intent to register to MOSA. When Robinson arrived, she met with Mubarak to express her concern about the "broad language" of the law and promised to continue to closely follow the law's implementation. However, she also noted her satisfaction that NGOs had been "consulted" in the making of the law and that the government had promised to continue such consultation in formulating the law's administrative regulations. Outraged, groups that had not registered charged that the groups that had had played into the government's hands: their agreement to register, it was alleged, was read by Robinson as a sign that the law could not have been all that bad, for the NGOs had not taken a united stand against it. Those that had registered strongly disagreed. As one pointed out, the mere fact of registration did not mean that they could not continue to fight the law.[22] There was also some concern that if some types of organizations did not register, they would be unable to continue their activities. In any case, Robinson's departure signaled that the last card in the human rights groups' hand had been played and that the game had been lost.

What Went Wrong:
Disagreement on the Limits of NGO Opposition

It is not surprising that a government that had silenced political parties, professional syndicates, and trade unions would subsequently attack nongovernmental advocacy organizations, and given the grossly uneven balance of forces in the battle, it is also not surprising that the government would win. However, three main weaknesses that hurt the campaign are worth examining in somewhat greater detail. The first— a lack of democracy and consultation among groups in the campaign— is not specific to advocacy NGOs. Two other problems, though, suggest much more strongly the difficulty with advocacy NGOs trying to lead battles for democratization. Advocacy NGOs in the campaign were sharply divided about the limits of what they could do as NGOs. Some activists in advocacy NGOs saw little alternative but to be as confrontational as possible in their campaign, while others argued that the NGOs were too weak to assume this responsibility. In addition to divisions within the campaign, the almost complete dependence of so many advocacy NGOs on foreign funding made it easy for the government to question their loyalties, severely undermining popular support for the campaign.

The latter phases of the anti–Law 153 campaign were characterized by a pronounced perception on the part of many activists of a lack of democracy and consultation, both within individual human rights groups and among them. Several members of the various organizations alleged undemocratic decisionmaking practices on the part of those who disagreed with them; whatever the truth of any particular allegation, the overall level of distrust clearly hampered attempts to coordinate a unified strategy. Soon after the passage of the law, one of the more active human rights groups permanently split into two separate organizations, in large part due to conflicts over the way its participation in the campaign was handled. One leader of this group (Leader A) argued that the Geneva statement calling for political reform was faxed to his office with instructions that it be signed and returned immediately. He said that when he argued that more time was needed to discuss it, the group's executive director (Leader B) insisted that it had to be endorsed and returned immediately.[23] A few weeks later Leader A was among the group of NGO activists who went to file papers announcing the intent of his NGO to register under the new law. As was previously suggested, the question of whether to register or not, and particularly to register at that time, was a heated one. Leader B contends that he had no idea that the other leader was filing an intent to register the group and that he only became aware of it when a journalist called to alert him. Leader B said that his NGO would probably have eventually registered in any case, as many NGOs were leaning in that direction, but that the real issue for him was that the other leader had registered without consulting the rest of the organization. This, he argued, was why the two groups had split apart.[24]

Members of another advocacy NGO complained that while the anti–Law 153 campaign was supposed to be a joint effort, in fact it had been severely compromised by what two of its leaders described as some activists taking "fateful" decisions without consulting the others. They argued that the women's hunger strike, which they felt was a tactical error to begin with because it was too dramatic a step to take at that juncture in the campaign, was started without other groups in the campaign being consulted.[25]

While the pronounced lack of democracy and consultation within and among human rights groups severely undermined the campaign, the coalition was also sharply divided over the wisdom of advocacy NGOs engaging in high-scale confrontation with the government. One example of this was a statement entitled "We Are Staying," signed by five women's and human rights organizations. "We Are Staying" referred to human rights groups remaining in Egypt rather than opening offices abroad, and it was clearly intended as a direct rebuttal to the Geneva statement. The language of "We Are Staying" also suggested a real desire to play down the intensity of the confrontation with the government. While it minced no words in describing the government's lack of democracy or respect for human rights, it also argued: "We believe that human rights activists in Egypt are not like the Albanians in Kosovo, forced out of their homeland by the murderer Milosevic, and we have not been exposed to the rule of the butcher Pinochet who murdered 170,000 of his citizens." In other words, the situation in Egypt was not nearly so dire that opening human rights offices in Geneva rather than remaining in Egypt was necessary.[26] Two of the organizations that had originally signed the Geneva statement now signed this one, suggesting that some maneuvering had gone on in within their organizations in the interim period.

The question of how confrontational advocacy NGOs should be— and whether they were in fact trying to do a job best left to political parties or opposition movements—was brought up by one longtime human rights leader. This activist argued that human rights groups had not sufficiently realized the structural weakness of their position as they determined how to work for change in regime policies. "NGOs are not political parties," he argued, and they had not even finished building themselves up yet.[27] The question of whether human rights groups were right to frame their opposition to Law 153 in terms of an open confrontation with the regime was raised at an October 2000 workshop designed to analyze the 1999 campaign. A director of a youth and social services group faulted the advocacy NGOs for encouraging more traditional social service and charitable groups to engage in a confrontation with the government for which the latter were wholly unprepared. While advocacy NGOs, he argued, had tried to mobilize their more traditional counterparts to seek political change, encouraging them to participate in demonstrations to press the government to change the law, in essence these charitable and social service NGOs operated "completely outside the framework of the government and politics" and were concerned only with doing what the government required of them so that their funding could be disbursed (Abdullah 2001: 88).

A third and fundamental reason for the weakness of the anti-153 coalition was the almost total dependence of its members on foreign funding. Aside from an early, and quickly aborted, attempt by the EOHR to become a mass-membership organization and fund itself through dues, most advocacy organizations have made little attempt to raise funds locally. Some activists argue that MOSA regulations prevent them from doing so,[28] yet many share the fundamental conviction, expressed in a book issued by the CF during the campaign, that in a society as poor as Egypt's NGOs will never be able to self-fund.[29] Not relying on local funding, however, means that advocacy organizations have no constituency to which they are accountable in Egypt and only a limited number of people there who are personally invested in their success. When the government attempts to shut them down, these advocacy NGOs find few supporters. This problem is compounded by strong public feelings that foreign funding for advocacy organizations is illegitimate, arising partially from a concerted government barrage of arguments that these groups are "selling Egypt out" for personal benefit, a charge that carries weight when many nongovernmental associational leaders have enjoyed a significant improvement in their standard of living through nongovernmental work. In this environment, an anti-153 campaign that focused heavily on limiting MOSA restrictions on foreign funds was guaranteed a narrow audience. As one activist in the campaign admitted, "Most people see that we receive money from abroad and they think that when we oppose government restrictions on this funding we do this because we have something to hide."[30]

Since the defeat of the anti-153 coalition, Egyptian advocacy organizations' freedom of operation remains severely curtailed. A year after its passage, Law 153 was declared unconstitutional, primarily on the technical grounds that it had not been approved by the necessary bodies prior to passage. In 2001 the regime responded with Law 84, which on some levels represented an improvement on 153 by narrowly defining the political activity in which NGOs were forbidden to engage and mandating representation of NGOs on committees arbitrating conflicts between these organizations and MOSA. In many other ways, however,

Law 84 was worse than 153. Access to foreign funding was further restricted; in previous laws NGOs had been allowed to accept money from foreign agencies already in the country without prior MOSA permission, but now all such funding required permission. The new law also continued its predecessors' insistence that MOSA, not the courts, had the right to dissolve NGOs, and it allowed the ministry to freeze the funds of NGOs that joined nongovernmental association networks—including international networks—without MOSA permission.

Law 84 was passed in much the same way as its predecessor, though with much less formal input from the nongovernmental associations. Two brief meetings were held between the new minister of social affairs and associational representatives, but the latter complained that, as with Law 153, all of their suggestions were ignored. The protests of several opposition party members of parliament that the law was unacceptable went unnoticed, and the law was passed over a single weekend.

Conclusion

Many students of politics in the global South have argued that civil society generally, and nongovernmental advocacy organizations in particular, can play central roles in fostering democratization. It is certainly true that these organizations can call attention to, and sometimes limit, the depredations of authoritarian rule by publicizing abuses such as the torture of political prisoners or limitations on free speech. They can also help lay the foundations of a democratic culture by disseminating values essential to democracy, including respect for human rights and the rule of law. Between highlighting, and sometimes limiting, authoritarian abuses on the one hand and laying the foundations for a democratic culture on the other, however, lies the Herculean task of replacing current authoritarian regimes with democratic ones. Groups seeking to challenge authoritarian rule require widespread popular support, and nongovernmental advocacy organizations, which are typically single-issue groups with small local constituencies dependent entirely on foreign largesse, are ill-equipped to lead the charge.

Although most political scientists would find the claim that parties are better suited to challenge authoritarian regimes than NGOs unexceptionable, they have paid little attention to the conditions under which opposition is routed through these organizations rather than through parties. As the Egyptian and Palestinian cases demonstrate particularly clearly, it is often the same people, particularly leftist activists, who move back and forth between party and nongovernmental activity in response to increasing or decreasing constraints on one or the other.

While the effects of the availability of foreign funding on the proliferation of nongovernmental associations have been widely recognized by
scholars and practitioners, the contrast between readily available funds
for associations and the poverty of many parties, and the implications of
this contrast for the forms that opposition takes, have rarely been studied. Similarly, the laws accompanying liberalization processes need to
be scrutinized to determine the relative degrees of freedom that they
afford both NGOs and political parties. Applying general principles of
institutional analysis to the question of opposition weakness by examining the way in which institutions, political and financial, structure
choices to oppose authoritarianism through NGOs or parties would be
an important first step toward understanding the weakness of oppositions in the Arab world and elsewhere.

Notes

1. Schmitter, for example, argues that a central component of civil society
groups is their "absence of an intention to govern the polity" (1997: 240).
Chazan's definition of civil society as "that segment of society that interacts
with the state, influences the state, and yet is distinct from the state" similarly
clearly distinguishes parties from civil society (1992: 281).

2. Human rights organizations began proliferating in Latin America in the
1970s and their number more than doubled between 1981 and 1990 (Keck and
Sikkink 1998: 89–90). Africa experienced similar growth between the early
1980s and early 1990s (Welch 1995: 47).

3. Tunisia's adult literacy rate was 72.1 percent in 2003 (http://hdr.undp.
org/reports/global/2003/indicator/cty_f_TUN.html). The U.S. State Department
reports that "the majority of [Tunisia's] citizens are in the middle class and
fewer than 5 percent fall below the poverty line" (http://www.state.gov/g/
drl/rls/hrrpt/2003/27939.htm).

4. HRW 2000b.

5. Ibid.

6. The Islamist movement Hamas has been and remains the PA's strongest
challenger.

7. Fatah's insistence on adopting a winner-take-all electoral system also
contributed to the factions' decision to boycott.

8. Kienle argues that much of the electoral fraud and increased repression
of Egyptian opposition in the 1990s has been motivated by the regime's desire
to ensure that in each election the number of NDP deputies will easily clear the
two-thirds mark. See Kienle (1998).

9. The numbers are 86 percent in 1990, 94 percent in 1995, and 85.5 percent in 2000. The 1990 and 1995 figures are taken from Langohr (2000) and
Essam el-Din (2000).

10. *The Arab Strategic Report* (in Arabic) (Cairo: al-Ahram Publishers,
1997: 286–288).

11. Interview with CHRLA member, Cairo, April 10, 2001.

12. Online: www.electionworld.org/election/morocco.htm.

13. Online: www.electionworld.org/election/algeria.htm.

14. The rare liberalizer that experimented with proportional representation for the entire electorate was Egypt in 1984 and 1987; it returned to winner-take-all after the constitutional court ruled that the PR system's requirement of party lists discriminated against independent candidacies.

15. Here it is important to distinguish between candidates who ran as independents in the elections only to join ruling parties after the election and candidates who remained independents after the election. In both Egypt and the PA, substantial numbers of ruling party candidates who did not get their party's nomination ran as independents and rejoined the party upon their election; I do not count these people as independents in my discussion here.

16. There were 256 independent candidates in the 2000 elections, but 218 subsequently joined the NDP, leaving thirty-eight members of parliament who remained independents. Seventeen of these were Muslim Brothers who have to run as independents because religious parties are prohibited. By this calculation, there were seventeen "real" independents, exactly as many as the number of successful Muslim Brotherhood candidates.

17. Ben Nafisa and Qandil (1994) note that Islamic NGOs are tied with Community Development Associations (CDAs) as the largest category of NGOs, but that CDAs are not really NGOs, because they are almost entirely state run.

18. When one of the most vocal NGOs in the anti-153 campaign found its foreign checks being delayed, one official from the U.S. Agency for International Development noted that this might be nothing more than the typically slow functioning of the law (interview with USAID official, Cairo, April 11, 2001). The director of a women's literacy and skills training NGO in a poor neighborhood of Cairo, for example, noted that she had been waiting six months for MOSA to process a $400 German grant for a handicraft production machine (interview with NGO director, Cairo, April 3, 2001).

19. Interview with USAID official, Cairo, April 11, 2001.

20. *The Process of Developing Associational Activity and the New Associations Law* (in Arabic), The Civil Forum (Cairo, March 1999), 6.

21. "Human Rights Groups Call for an Immediate Meeting with the President, Begin Consultations on Creating a Political Reform Program, Demand a Meeting with the UN Human Rights Commissioner, Decide to Open an Office in Geneva, and to Place the Situation of Civil Society Before the UN" (in Arabic), statement distributed May 18, 1999.

22. Interview with NGO activist, April 18, 2001.

23. Interview with "Leader A," April 10, 2001.

24. Interview with "Leader B," April 4, 2001.

25. Interview with NGO activist, April 9, 2001.

26. "Announcement by Egyptian Human Rights Groups: We Are Staying" (in Arabic), fax dated June 5, 1999.

27. Interview with human rights activist, April 18, 2001.

28. As one human rights activist told me, "Let the government take off the restrictions on fundraising, not letting us organize raffles or collect donations, and we'll [be happy to] fund ourselves" (interview, Cairo, April 7, 2001).

29. *The Development of Voluntary (Associational) Work and the New Associations Law* (in Arabic) (Cairo: Civic Forum, 1999: 8.

30. Interview with NGO activist, Cairo, April 4, 2001.

Part 3

Conclusion

10

The Outlook for Authoritarians

MICHELE PENNER ANGRIST

The Middle East is a region in upheaval. Given the intractability of the Arab-Israeli conflict, the growing threat of Islamist-inspired terror activity, and the challenges posed by the Iraq war, policymakers, students, and citizens in general require insightful analyses directed at identifying paths toward progress on all of these issues. The prevalence of entrenched authoritarian regimes in the Middle East has been blamed for aggravating the Arab-Israeli conflict and fomenting Islamist violence. The U.S. administration under President George W. Bush defended its decision to unseat Saddam Hussein by arguing that a democratic Iraq would help facilitate democratization elsewhere in the region. The present, therefore, is a world historical juncture in which it is especially appropriate that scholars with expertise in Middle East affairs address the question of democracy's prospects there from a theoretically informed, comparative politics perspective.

That is precisely what this book delivers. Together, the preceding chapters take readers on a sobering but instructive tour of regime dynamics in the Middle East—both in earlier historical periods as well as the contemporary era. Substantively, they emphasize the quality of incumbent-opposition relations in the region, responding to the questions, why are authoritarian rulers so formidable, and why are their opponents seemingly so hamstrung? Theoretically, they highlight institutional arrangements and associated patterns of human agency that contribute to this contemporary state of play. The agenda of this concluding chapter is twofold: it integrates what the authors here have to say vis-à-vis diagnosing the problem of authoritarian rule in the Middle East; it then builds on this analysis in order to suggest what the necessary next steps are for those actors who claim to be committed to democratization.

How Do Dictators Endure?

In Chapter 6, I focus attention on an era of postindependence politics
when pluralization was at least a possibility in many states in the
region. Incumbents held the upper hand in Turkey, Syria, Iraq, Jordan,
Iran, and Egypt—but increasingly substantial opposition parties
mounted serious challenges to their position in the context of semicompetitive elections and movement toward parliamentarism. In the end,
although these dynamics produced pluralism in Turkey, in the latter
cases policy polarization and mobilizational asymmetry drove incumbents to defect from nascent democratic rules. Dictatorships emerged
from the downward spiral of reciprocal defections that followed.

In the ensuing decades, authoritarian rulers in those and other states
across the region got down to the business of consolidating their hold
on power. Their tactics varied, depending in part on whether they
presided over monarchies, single-party states, or other regime variants.
But everywhere the common result has been that there is a striking disparity between incumbent and opposition power—a disparity that sus-
tains authoritarian rule. The remaining chapters in this book address the
contemporary state of political play in the Middle East. Together, the
authors vividly illustrate and dissect the entrenched, formidable position
of authoritarian incumbents relative to their would-be challengers.

As several authors note, two key material factors help produce this
power disparity. Middle East states of course benefit from substantial
rentier income. Revenues derived from hydrocarbon exports and external assistance mean that the financial resources available to incumbents
far outdistance those in the hands of their challengers. In addition, states
came to play a substantial role in national economies, either by explicitly pursuing a state-socialist path to development (which has not yet
been totally relinquished) and/or by exercising often politically slanted
discretion over goods central to the livelihoods of entrepreneurs (import
licenses, subsidized credit, etc.). As a result, key segments of society
that might otherwise wish to challenge the authoritarian status quo hold
back out of concern for their financial well-being.

Against this important material backdrop, the authors in this book
explore the institutional characteristics of politics that help determine the
distribution of power across key actors in the region. In so doing, they
offer a kind of "anatomy" of Middle East authoritarianism. To begin
with, coercive apparatuses in the region remain robust, their leaders and
foot soldiers willing and able to crush manifest expressions of dissent in
society. In Chapter 2, Eva Bellin explores this variable at a cross-
regional level, arguing that states' fiscal health, international support,

patrimonial security organizations, and low levels of popular mobilization work in concert to buttress this pivotal resource, which tilts the political playing field against the opposition. Of those four, the first two are particularly unique to the Middle East. In Chapter 3, Jason Brownlee probes regimes' coercive capability within the region, detailing incidences of the deployment of these apparatuses against the opposition— with results that restabilized authoritarian regimes—in Syria, Tunisia, Iraq, and Libya.

Turning to institutions whose missions center around tasks other than the use of force, incumbents in the Middle East enjoy numerous other advantages. As noted in Chapter 1, by Marsha Pripstein Posusney, all preside over executive branches that tower over their legislative counterparts. While Michael Herb (Chapter 8) focuses on the monarchies, the elements he points to as standing in the way of transitions from constitutional monarchy to parliamentarism are indicative of the contours of executive-parliamentary imbalances that favor incumbents while handicapping the opposition regionwide. Depending on the case, these include constitutions that greatly constrict parliaments' powers and chief executives who ignore the provisos of reasonably democratic constitutions. In many instances, both behaviors are enabled in part by electorates who aren't unanimously or vociferously demanding parliamentarism.

Those anti-regime opposition activists who *are* demanding parliamentarism run into at least three major obstacles when it comes to the rules that govern which individuals and groups can access even imperfect parliaments. First, many incumbent regimes steal elections by perpetrating electoral fraud, intimidating voters, and more. Second, incumbents have manipulated electoral rules purposefully and often in ways that tend to reinforce rather than undermine the status quo. Third, many authoritarians have cleverly divided their opponents by permitting only a subset of opposition groups to compete for parliamentary seats. Ellen Lust-Okar explains in Chapter 7 how this strategy has shielded Morocco's monarch from ongoing mass demonstrations in the face of a protracted economic crisis. Included oppositionists are reluctant to persist in mobilizing the masses for fear of jeopardizing the regime's preferential treatment of them and out of concern that such mobilization could be hijacked by excluded oppositionists. The same dynamic also arguably characterizes politics in Egypt and Tunisia.

Another problem plaguing anti-regime activists is that, in contrast to the time period I investigate in Chapter 6, in the contemporary period secular opposition parties in the Middle East are weak. Vickie Langohr (Chapter 9) attributes their organizational weakness to a number of factors: electoral fraud; generalized political repression; the opposition's paucity of financial resources and limited access to the public via radio, television, and public gatherings; incomplete parliamentarization; and the prevalence of independent candidacies. Posusney notes that in the face of the electoral rule dynamics described above, opposition parties are politically weak because they have few effective strategies by which to weaken authoritarian regimes. Electoral boycotts, coalitions, and campaigns to alter electoral rules are among them, but ideological differences, diverging size and goals among parties, and imperfect internal cohesion within them tend to hamper the achievement of these ends. At the same time, while civil society is expanding, Langohr argues that its members' dependence on foreign funds, weak domestic grassroots support, single-issue focus, and lack of internal democracy mean that they cannot stand in for powerful opposition parties and successfully push democratization processes forward.

Lessons from Iran

The Iranian experience is particularly suggestive for this book because it offers two very different cases of incumbent-opposition confrontation. The circumstances surrounding the fall of Mohammad Reza Pahlavi's dictatorship in the late 1970s resonate strongly with the analysis summarized above. The shah had crafted an undivided environment that excluded all opposition groups from meaningful participation in the political system. Consistent with Lust-Okar's findings, though the shah's opponents ranged from leftist secularists to conservative Shiite clerical activists, they joined forces against him and were responsible for producing widespread and increasingly massive public protests against his regime.

As Brownlee and Bellin's chapters would predict, the response of the shah's coercive apparatus was a crucial determinant of outcomes. Although the United States had long backed the shah and his reigns of power, beginning in 1976 President Jimmy Carter distanced the United States from its longtime regional client. Now insecure about the intentions of his superpower benefactor, the shah vacillated in the face of his opponents. Opposition forces viewed the Carter administration's stance as an invitation to protest, demanding political liberalization. In the end, the shah's army refused to continue violently repressing Iranian demonstrators, and the regime crumbled. While many in the Iranian opposition hoped to establish democracy in the wake of the shah's fall, the strongest, most well-organized element in the opposition were Islamists grouped around Ayatollah Ruhollah Khomeini. In the chaos of revolution, they would eventually rise to dominance and implement their preference for an undemocratic system of governance overseen by a segment of the clerical class.

The second instance of incumbent-opposition confrontation the Iranian case offers us is of course the present circumstance of the Islamic Republic. Arang Keshavarzian (Chapter 4) demonstrates that although Iran's regime is exceptional (even for a seemingly exceptional region), institutional analysis of incumbent-opposition relations is productive, yielding key insights about why the regime survives despite a multitude of realities that *should* be inauspicious for its prospects. Although the institutional dynamics of the Iranian state and regime differ somewhat from those of the wider Middle East, their effects are quite similar in that they tilt the political playing field in favor of incumbents.

The regime retains sufficient coercive capabilities because it presides over a multistranded security apparatus; those strands controlled by hard-liners help them to defend their position. For other state functions as well, multiple, parallel decisionmaking institutions with overlapping authorities and competing interests exist. A relatively wide collection of elites thus has access to state power and the attendant ability to distribute patronage. Yet state fragmentation means that not only are these elites isolated from one another in rival bureaucratic bodies, their clienteles (and thus society at large) are isolated and atomized as well. So while there has been popular mobilization against the regime, it has occurred in pockets and has not been sufficiently sustained or cross-class in nature to raise the costs of repression to a level incumbent hard-liners are uncomfortable with. Fragmentation also means the opposition can't guarantee to hard-liner incumbents that the former have control over radical elements and that democratization therefore won't ruin incumbents. Keshavarzian concludes that the lack of a significant, party-based organization among the opposition has been pivotal to the longevity of the status quo.

The Eight-Hundred-Pound Gorilla: Putting Islam in Perspective

As noted in Chapter 1, the most prominent cultural hypothesis regarding the Middle East's resistance to democratization identifies Islam's alleged incompatibility with democracy as the culprit. All of the works presented here—including Keshavarzian's chapter on the Islamic Republic of Iran—emphasize institutional variables and in so doing downplay Islam as a causal factor underlying Middle East authoritarianism.

At the same time, it is generally the case that the Islamist oppositions to authoritarian regimes in the Middle East are (or were, in Iran) the most potent, vocal, and organized, while secular parties are weaker—that is, less broadly supported and less rooted in society. So it is important here to underline what the analyses in this book have to say with regard to the question, What about Islam?

First, *Authoritarianism in the Middle East* cautions against assuming that Islam is inevitably central to political life in the Middle East. In Chapter 6, I show that in the immediate postindependence era, politicized Islam was essentially a nonstarter. In those countries where a single preponderant party secured independence and rapidly constructed authoritarian rule—while Islam had been used in the rhetorics of nationalist mobilization—the regimes that resulted were largely secular. In the polarized, mobilizationally asymmetrical multiparty cases, while Islamist parties were on the scene, the most contentious issues of the day were socioeconomic and geopolitical. In Turkey, the party system managed over time to remove Islam from the political agenda, where it stayed for several decades. One lesson, therefore, is that the salience of Islam as a political discourse and resource is a variable, not a constant.

Second, the chapters assembled here demonstrate that Islam indeed is an important (though not determinative) variable in the puzzle of regional authoritarianism. Importantly, however, politicized Islam is eminently amenable to social scientific analysis; it is not a unique, sui generis, and therefore exceptional phenomenon. As Brownlee notes, Islam's impact on the longevity of authoritarian regimes in the region is mediated through other processes—many of which are analyzed in this book. Brownlee argues that Western powers have not pressured incumbents in the region to democratize because in most cases their most formidable opponents are Islamist and anti-West in complexion. The assumption is that these would triumph in free elections, with deleterious consequences for Western interests. As Bellin also notes, this factor helps explain why those Middle East regimes that depend on Western financial and political support have been unfettered by external constraints as they have unleashed their coercive machines to quell domestic unrest.

The impact of political Islam is also seen in intraopposition relations. Lust-Okar notes that in Morocco the opposition groups that incumbents have excluded from the electoral game are primarily religious-based parties. The same holds true in Egypt and Tunisia, whose regimes have not accorded Islamist groups the same access to parliamentary politics enjoyed by secular oppositionists. The comparatively radical sociopolitical agenda of Islamist opposition groups serves to moderate the behavior of included groups. The latter appear to be incentivized *not* to mobilize the masses or take any other steps that could destabilize the system for fear that doing so might create an opening for an increase in Islamists' influence. More generally, the presence of Islamists helps explain why cooperation across opposition organizations is in short supply. Returning to Posusney's findings, Islamist groups' political aspirations are a key element of why parties' ideological differences and diverging short- and long-term goals prevent them from successfully teaming up to fell authoritarian regimes.

These observations oblige a discussion of the relationship between Islam and regime preferences in the region. It has already been noted that anti–West Islamist activism has encouraged external actors to prefer the authoritarian status quo in the region. Where do domestic constituencies stand?

The chapters by Bellin and Herb highlight the crucial fact that, to an important extent, there is simply not a lot of organized popular enthusiasm for democratic reform and the development of parliamentarism in the region. Islam is central to this phenomenon, but not because Muslims must always be averse to democratic norms and practices due to the substance, structure, and history of their faith tradition. Instead, it is so because, at this specific world-historical juncture, the strongest challengers to incumbents in some countries are Islamist groups whose leaders have chosen to interpret their duties as Muslims in a manner that demands an intimate, authoritarian marriage between religious law and the public sphere. As Bellin and Lust-Okar point out, this in turn renders those outside these Islamist circles reluctant to move politics to the point of truly free, competitive elections for parliaments that actually rule. Here again the worry is that Islamists would do well in such elections, exploiting them for the purpose of translating their political visions into reality.

Note that, in this dynamic, only certain Islamic groups truly do not *prefer* democracy. Islamists in some countries appear actually to be advancing democracy's cause. In Iran the reformist forces that advocate republicanism are Islamists, and Turkey's ruling Justice and Development Party—one with notable Islamist roots—has presided over a number of democratizing reforms. Elsewhere, more extreme Islamists paralyze many would-be opponents to authoritarian rule who might well advocate democratic rules in a more auspicious setting but who are not willing to push for such rules in the present context. Importantly, the shadow of Islamist groups is not the only factor that makes many in the Middle East at best ambivalent about democracy. As discussed earlier, material realities weigh heavily as well and a similar dynamic is at work. Authoritarian incumbents' intervention in economic life enervates the opposition because the former can punish critics in ways that include undermining their livelihoods. For the substantial segment of society whose financial well-being depends in part on staying in the state's good graces, then, opposition is hard to countenance at this juncture.

What Is to Be Done?

The analyses in this book offer a number of glimmers of hope for democratizing change. Herb shows that many of the region's monarchies of late have had to either entertain the idea of establishing parliaments (Dubai), create them for the first time (Saudi, Qatar), or reopen them (Jordan, Kuwait, Bahrain). More and more countries have held multiparty legislative elections in recent years, and Posusney points out that holding contested elections foregrounds the principle that citizens have a right to self-selected political representation. Domestic electoral monitoring activities are another rising trend that appears to be having some positive impacts. Posusney predicts such activities will increase, and the result should be that blatant electoral fraud will be harder to pull off as time goes on.

At the same time, the primary thrust of the analyses indicates that much, much more needs to be done to move Middle Eastern states toward democratization. Opposition parties must broaden their popular and financial bases, and incumbents must be prevailed upon to level the political playing field. Four key factors stand in the way of achieving these ends: (1) international (read: Western) support for regional regimes' coercive apparatuses and thus for these authoritarian regimes in general; (2) the flow of both hydrocarbon- and aid-based rents; (3) significant levels of state intervention in economic life; and (4) the presence of powerful, often antidemocratic, Islamist groups on the opposition landscape, along with the fears they engender. If democratization is to occur in the region, some if not all of these factors will need to recede.

Beginning with economic considerations, hydrocarbon export-based rentier income will continue to accrue to those regimes that possess such resources for the foreseeable future. This does not then represent a variable that can be "tweaked" by decisionmakers hoping to influence regime trajectories in the region. The same cannot be said about levels of state intervention in economic life. Many Middle East regimes are receiving IMF and World Bank assistance as they restructure their economies to jump start growth rates that had languished as a result of statist development policies. International financial institutions (IFIs) therefore have leverage over regional regimes: they *are* pressuring their clients to further privatize their economies and they *could* insist that they do so in a more transparent and politically neutral fashion.

Yet it may be the case that, while states' intervention in economies damps down opposition activity, advocating increased IFI pressure on Middle East regimes to privatize further will work at cross-purposes to democracy. In the near term, such reforms exacerbate already worrisome levels of poverty and unemployment, radicalizing populations and creating political instability that is not necessarily conducive to democratizing political reform. Liberalizing reforms also often reduce the power and influence of labor unions, historically a key collective actor that has pushed democratization processes forward. Moreover, as states retreat from their prior roles as employers, laid-off workers facing the loss of salary and benefits may turn to Islamist organizations for support. Thus, it may be the better part of wisdom not to push privatization too rapidly or too radically. Indeed, with these concerns in mind the IFIs have recently begun supporting the provision of severance packages and other transitional welfare schemes for laid-off workers in the region (Posusney 2003).

That said, the IFIs could do more to ensure that the reforms regimes *are* able to carry out are implemented in ways that are transparent and politically neutral. Tunisia, for example, dismantled dozens of agricultural cooperatives in the 1990s but did so in a fashion that purposely benefited large landholders almost exclusively—a strategy the government explicitly used to shore up the regime and thus that does not bode well for democratization. Despite the fact that Tunisian policy flies in the face of World Bank–endorsed "best practices" regarding the importance of small- and medium-sized farms for development, it has not insisted the regime act differently and has instead treated Tunisia as a diligent, "model" reformer (King 2003: 123–124). Still, in the end it is probably not realistic to expect IFIs to intervene to challenge the microdetails of the implementation of economic reform: such expressly political tinkering is really not the charge of IFIs, nor would the task of identifying where reforms were needed be a straightforward one for outsiders.

When we turn to more political considerations, we encounter those actors who *could* take different decisions to facilitate democratization. Those with the most latitude for behavioral change are Western and especially U.S. policymakers who historically have financed and otherwise backed regional dictators and their security forces. The Bush administration has broken new ground by arguing that backing autocracy in the Middle East for stability's sake is not in the United States' interests. It then brought down the Iraqi regime, partially with the rationale that a democratic Iraq could have important demonstration effects, helping change the tenor of politics throughout the region.

At the time of this writing, despite a democratic election that was in many ways extraordinary, serious security deficiencies and deep ethnic distrust suggest that for Iraq to successfully sustain democratic rule will be a tall order. Regionwide, the jury remains out as to whether the war will have made democratization a more proximate—or remote—prospect. Civil society has become emboldened in some areas, most notably in the Palestinian territories, Lebanon, and Egypt, and the Bush administration is claiming some credit for this regional ripple effect. However, daunting obstacles to continued democratization remain in all three political are-nas. Throughout the region, the sage and sustained application of external pressures and supports would be required over a considerable period of time if any momentum toward political opening is to be maintained.

Elsewhere, the war may have reduced democratization's prospects. Popular cynicism regarding U.S. motives for war, together with anger both at civilian loss of life and at the Abu Ghraib prison abuses, will likely combine to further weaken those regimes whose citizens already disapproved of their leaders' ties to the West before the Iraq War. Though incumbents must be weakened for democratization to take hold in the Middle East, these same factors that undermine incumbents also invigorate extremist Islamist groups for whom anti-Western rhetoric is central. They also discredit the more moderate, secular groups that seek to replicate Western institutions in the Middle East.

Still, if they are truly serious about regime change, the United States and other Western powers could proceed by using what political and eco-nomic leverage on regional regimes they retain to pressure the latter to liberalize in ways that the analyses here suggest would strengthen the opposition. This includes reducing levels of generalized repression, not flouting constitutions, empowering parliaments, altering electoral rules, creating undivided inclusive opposition environments, and granting the opposition equal access to media outlets.

Regimes' opponents, too, could change their ways. Political parties seeking to challenge the authoritarian status quo must build up their organizational and financial bases. They must also overcome internal cohesion problems and ideological and other differences in order to join forces and present a more substantive, sustained challenge to incum-bents. One strategy would be to form electoral coalitions while evincing an increased willingness to mobilize on a mass basis, although coordi-nated electoral boycotts also are an option when the political deck appears to be stacked too strongly against them. A key lesson from this book is that, as long as they allow themselves to be divided, opposition groups cannot hope to triumph over incumbents.

The fact that powerful, popular Islamist groups are waiting in the wings reduces the likelihood that either of the above courses of action actually takes place. The United States fears that enabling oppositions will bring anti–Western Islamist groups to power, while secular-Islamist ideological divides stymie opposition cooperation in the region. What we confront then is the paradoxical situation that Islamists, by their very existence, help sustain the regimes they seek to topple. Looked at another way, the Middle East's authoritarians simultaneously must fear, and be grateful to, their Islamist opponents. The latter have helped dissuade key external and internal actors from pressing for serious changes in the political status quo, and the result has been enduring authoritarianism.

Democracy proponents can begin to square this circle first by emphasizing this point to Islamists and making the case that, if they are truly interested in felling rather than enabling incumbent regimes, they need to rethink their discourse, policy agenda, and methods (if violence is among them). Next, external actors must pressure regimes to allow all Islamists—except those who use violence—access to the electoral process. Such pressure potentially incurs only modest risk because the widespread assumption (informed largely by the Algerian experience) that Islamists would do "dangerously" well in competitive elections is not necessarily accurate. After all, competitive and/or semicompetitive elections in Indonesia, Pakistan, and Bangladesh have seen fundamentalist Islamist parties poll poorly (Stepan 2001). And as Langohr points out, independent candidates did as well or better than their Islamist counterparts in elections in Egypt, Yemen, and Jordan. At the same time, the potential rewards for including Islamists could be substantial. Lust-Okar's discussion of the Jordanian case demonstrates that in an inclusive undivided environment, opposition parties are able to work together despite ideological differences to mobilize people in support of reforms. In this way, the costs to regimes of repressing dissent can be raised. The hope is that secularists and Islamists in such an environment will find additional ways of working together and bridging gaps—possibly through the formation of fronts—to achieve their common, immediate goal of ending extant regimes.

This projected trajectory is not without perils, of course. An overriding question is, if secular-Islamist opposition partnerships did succeed in bringing down regimes, what is to prevent an Iranian-style outcome wherein Islamists dominate the aftermath and install new forms of dictatorship? The Iranian example hopefully can serve as an object lesson to the secular opposition, underscoring the need to strengthen their organizations and broaden their mass appeal. At the same time, this very legitimate fear calls attention to just how badly external and internal opponents of authoritarianism need one another. Secular oppositionists can only build themselves up if external actors can prevail upon regimes to create political environments more conducive to that goal. And external actors may pressure regimes to loosen their grips only if they believe that secular opponents can assume much of the mantle of the opposition, denying Islamists a monopoly on any aftermaths of regime change.

Conclusion

The challenges involved in altering the Middle East status quo are substantial. In the short run, significant, sustainable democratic breakthroughs do not appear to be on the horizon. Although we may see incremental steps toward political liberalization in some countries, there is little sign that incumbent authoritarian rulers are prepared to relinquish their hold on power. Thus, both indigenous groups and foreign powers who seek to further the cause of democracy in the region may need to rethink their present strategies.

Acronyms

CDAs	Community Development Associations
CDT	Confédération Démocratique du Travail (Democratic Labor Confederation)
CEE	Central and Eastern Europe
CF	Civic Forum
CHRLA	Center for Human Rights Legal Aid
CNLT	Counseil National pour les Libertés en Tunisie (National Council on Liberties in Tunisia)
CNRS	Centre National de la Recherche Scientifique (National Center for Scientific Research)
CPLP	Closed party-list proportional representation
DP	Democrat Party
DFLP	Democratic Front for the Liberation of Palestine
EIU	Economist Intelligence Unit
EOHR	Egyptian Organization for Human Rights
FBIS	Foreign Broadcast Information Service
FRP	Free Republican Party
GCC	Gulf Cooperation Council
GNP	Gross national product
GPC	General People's Congress
HRW	Human Rights Watch
IAF	Islamic Action Front
ICG	International Crisis Group
IFI	International Financial Institution
IISS	International Institute of Strategic Studies
IMF	International Monetary Fund
IRGC	Islamic Revolutionary Guard Corps
IRP	Islamic Republic Party

LADE	Lebanese Association for the Democracy of Elections
LCPS	Lebanese Center for Policy Studies
LTDH	Ligue Tunisienne des Droits de l'Homme
	(Tunisian League for the Defense of Human Rights)
MENA	Middle East and North Africa
MNP	Mouvement National Populaire
	(National Popular Movement)
MOSA	Ministry of Social Affairs
MP	Member of parliament
MRO	Majority runoff
MTI	Mouvement de la Tendance Islamique
	(Islamic Tendency Movement)
NATO	North Atlantic Treaty Organization
NCC	National Consultative Council
ND	Neo-Destour
NDP	National Democratic Party
NGOs	Nongovernmental organizations
NPUP	National Progressive Unionist Party
OADP	Organisation de l'Action Démocratique et Populaire
	(Organization for Democratic and Popular Action)
PA	Palestinian Authority
PBV	Party-block vote
PDI	Parti Démocratique et de l'Independence
	(Party of Democracy and Independence)
PDRY	People's Democratic Republic of Yemen
PFLP	Popular Front for the Liberation of Palestine
PLC	Palestine Legislative Council
PLO	Palestine Liberation Organization
PNA	Palestinian National Authority
PND	Parti National Démocrate (National Democratic Party)
PPS	Parti du Progrès et du Socialisme
	(Party of Progress and Socialism)
PR	Proportional representation
PRI	Partido Revolucionaro Institucional
	(Institutional Revolutionary Party)
PRP	Progressive Republican Party
RCD	Rassemblement Constitutionnel Démocratique
	(Constitutional Democratic Rally)
RNI	Rassemblement National des Indépendants
	(National Assembly of Independents)
RPP	Republican People's Party
SLP	Socialist Labor Party

SMDP	Single-member district plurality
SNTV	Single nontransferable vote
SoCs	Structures of contestation
UAE	United Arab Emirates
UC	Union Constitutionnelle (Constitutional Union)
UGTM	Union Générale des Travailleurs au Maroc (General Union of Workers in Morocco)
UK	United Kingdom
UMT	Union Marocaine du Travail (Moroccan Labor Union)
UNDP	United Nations Development Program
UNFP	Union Nationale des Forces Populaires (National Union of Popular Forces)
USAID	U.S. Agency for International Development
USFP	Union Socialiste des Forces Populaires (Socialist Union of Popular Forces)
WTA	Winner takes all
YSP	Yemen Socialist Party

Bibliography

Abdelhaq, Mohamed, and Jean-Bernard Heumann. 2000. "Opposition et elections en Tunisie." *Monde Arabe Maghreb Machrek* 168 (April–June): 29–40.

Abdullah, Ahmad. 2001. *The Future of Associational Activity in Egypt: Proceedings of a Workshop on the Law of Associations* (in Arabic), Cairo.

Abrahamian, Ervand. 1993. *Khomeinism: Essays on the Islamic Republic.* London: I. B. Tauris & Co. Ltd.

Abu Khalil, As'ad. 1997. "Change and Democratisation in the Arab World: The Role of Political Parties." *Third World Quarterly* 18, 1: 14–63.

———. 2001. "Lebanon One Year After the Israeli Withdrawal." *MERIP Press Information Note* 58 (May 29).

Adelkhah, Fariba. 2000. *Being Modern in Iran.* Jonathan Derrick, trans. New York: Columbia University Press.

Agnouche, Abdelatif. n.d. "La fiction de l'alternance politique au Maroc." Unpublished manuscript.

Agwani, M. S. 1969. *Communism in the Arab East.* Bombay: Asia Publishing House.

Ahmad, Eqbal. 1982. "Rentier State and Shia Islam in the Iranian Revolution: Comments on Skocpol." *Theory and Society* 11, 3: 293–300.

Ahmad, Feroz. 1993. *The Making of Modern Turkey.* London: Routledge.

Ahmad, Mumtaz. 1985. "Parliament, Parties, Polls and Islam: Issues in the Current Debate on Religion and Politics in Pakistan." *The American Journal of Islamic Social Sciences* 2 (July): 15–28.

Alexander, Christopher. 1997. "Back from the Democratic Brink: Authoritarianism and Civil Society in Tunisia." *Middle East Report* 205 (October–December): 34–38.

Alougili, Mazen Ahmad. 1992. *Comparative Study of Jordan's Foreign Policy Toward Neighboring Arab States from 1967–1988.* PhD thesis, Boston University.

Amaoui, Nubir. 1995. Interview. Secretary-general of CDT, member of USFP Central Committee. Casablanca, May 1995.

Amy, Douglas. 1993. *Real Choices, New Voices: The Case for Proportional Representation in America.* New York: Columbia University Press.

Anderson, Lisa. 1987. "The State in the Middle East and North Africa." *Comparative Politics* 20 (October): 1–18.

———. 1991. "Political Pacts, Liberalism, and Democracy: The Tunisian National Pact of 1988." *Government and Opposition* 26, 2 (Spring): 244–260.

———. 1995a. "Democracy in the Arab World: A Critique of the Political Culture Approach." In Rex Brynen, Bahgat Korany, and Paul Noble, eds., *Political Liberalization and Democratization in the Arab World: Volume 1, Theoretical Perspectives*. Boulder: Lynne Rienner, 77–92.

———. 1995b. "Qadhafi's Legacy: An Evaluation of a Political Experiment." In Dirk Vandewalle, ed., *Qadhafi's Libya, 1969–1994*. New York: St. Martin's, 223–237.

———. 1997. "Prospects for Liberalism in North Africa: Identities and Interests in Pre-Industrial Welfare States." In John P. Entelis, ed., *Islam, Democracy, and the State in North Africa*. Bloomington: Indiana University Press, 127–140.

———. 2001. "Arab Democracy: Dismal Prospects." *World Policy Journal* 18, 3: 53–60.

Anderson, Lisa, ed. 1999. *Transitions to Democracy*. New York: Columbia University Press.

Andoni, Lamis. 1989a. "10 Reported Dead in Riots in Jordan." *Washington Post*, April 21: A22.

———. 1989b. "Jordan's Riots Spread." *Washington Post*, April 22: A1, 20.

———. 1989c. "Signal King Hussein Can't Ignore." *Christian Science Monitor*, May 1: 4.

———. 1989d. "Jordan King Affirms Democratic Course Despite Islamic Gains." *Christian Science Monitor*, November 16: 4.

———. 1995. "Jordan: Democratization in Danger." *Middle East International* 515 (December 15): 16–17.

Angrist, Michele Penner. 2000. *Political Parties and Regime Formation in the Middle East*. PhD thesis, Princeton University.

Arjomand, Said Amir. 1988. *The Turban for the Crown*. New York: Oxford University Press.

Aruri, Naseer Hasan. 1972. *Jordan: A Study in Political Development (1921–1965)*. The Hague: Martinus Nijhoff.

Assidon, Sion. 1998. "How the Monarchy Engineered the 1997 Moroccan Elections." Paper presented at the conference on "Controlled Contestation and Opposition Strategies: Multi-Party Elections in the Arab World," Brown University, Providence, RI, October 2–3.

Auda, Gehad. 1991. "Egypt's Uneasy Party Politics." *Journal of Democracy* 2, 2 (Spring).

Baaklini, Abdo, Guilain Denoeux, and Robert Springborg. 1999. *Legislative Politics in the Arab World: The Resurgence of Democratic Institutions*. Boulder: Lynne Rienner.

Baktiari, Bahman. 1996. *Parliamentary Politics in Revolutionary Iran: The Institutionalization of Factional Politics*. Gainesville: University Press of Florida.

Banac, Ivo, ed. 1992. *Eastern Europe in Revolution*. Ithaca: Cornell University Press.

Barkey, Henri, ed. 1992. *The Politics of Economic Reform in the Middle East*. New York: St. Martin's.

Barman, Roderick J. 1999. *Citizen Emperor: Pedro II and the Making of Brazil,*

1825–91. Stanford: Stanford University Press.

Barraoui, Jamal. 1995. "Vent de fronde sur les partis politiques." *La vie économique* 21 (Juillet): 3–4.

Batatu, Hanna. 1978. *The Old Social Classes and the Revolutionary Movements of Iraq: A Study of Iraq's Old Landed and Commercial Classes and of Its Communists, Ba'thists, and Free Officers.* Princeton: Princeton University Press.

———. 1982. "Syria's Muslim Brethren." *MERIP Reports* 110 (November–December): 12–20.

Bayer, Thomas C. 1993. *Morocco: Direct Legislative Elections Monitoring/ Observation Report.* Washington, DC: International Foundation for Electoral Systems.

Beblawi, Hazem, and Giacomo Luciano, eds. 1987. *The Rentier State in the Arab World.* London: Croom Helm.

Be'eri, Eliezer. 1970. *Army Officers in Arab Politics and Society.* New York: Praeger.

Behnoud, Masoud. 2004. "Nim Rokh: Haftom, Emad al-Din Baghi," *BBC Persian*, March 30. Online at http://www.bbc.co.uk/persian/iran/story/2004/03/040330_1-mb-nimrokh-baghi.shtml.

Bellin, Eva. 1995. "Civil Society in Formation: Tunisia." In Augustus Richard Norton, ed., *Civil Society in the Middle East*, Vol. I. Leiden: E. J. Brill, 120–147.

———. 2000. "Contingent Democrats: Industrialists, Labor, and Democratization in Late-Developing Countries." *World Politics* 52 (January): 175–205.

———. 2002. *Stalled Democracy: Capital, Labor, and the Paradox of State-Sponsored Development.* Ithaca: Cornell University Press.

———. 2003. "Iraq Post-Saddam: Prospects for Democracy." *Harvard Magazine* (July/August).

Ben Ali, Driss. 1989. "Changement de pacte sociale et continuité de l'ordre au Maroc." *Annuaire de l'Afrique du Nord:* 51–72.

———. 1991. "Émergence de l'espace socio-politique et stratégie de l'état au Maroc." In Ali Sedjari, ed., *État, Espace et Pouvoir Locale.* Rabat: Les éditions guessous, 61–74.

Ben Mlih, Abdellah. 2001. "Le Champ Politique Marocain Entre Tentatives De Réformes Et Conservatisme." *Monde Arabe Maghreb Machrek.*

Ben Nafisa, Sarah, and Amani Qandil. 1994. *Voluntary Associations in Egypt* (in Arabic). Cairo: Center for Political and Strategic Studies.

Benazzou, Chaouki. 1986. *Panorama economique du Maroc 1969/1985.* Casablanca: Les Éditions Maghrebines.

Benazzou, Chaouki, and Tawfik Mouline. 1993. *Panorama économique du Maroc, 1985/1990.* Rabat: El Maarif Al Jadida.

Bendourou, Omar. 1996. "Power and Opposition in Morocco." *Journal of Democracy* 7, 3 (July): 108–122.

Berman, Sheri. 2003. "Islamism, Revolution, and Civil Society." *Perspectives on Politics* 1 (June): 257–272.

Bermeo, Nancy. 1997. "Myths of Moderation: Confrontation and Conflict During Democratic Transitions." *Comparative Politics* 29 (April): 305–322.

Berrada, Abdelkader, and M. Said Saadi. 1992. "Le grand capital privé marocain." In Jean-Claude Santucci, ed., *Le Maroc Actuel.* Paris: Centre National de la Recherche Scientifique (CNRS), 325–391.

Bienen, Henry, and Jeffrey Herbst. 1996. "The Relationship between Political and Economic Reform in Africa." *Comparative Politics* 29, 1 (October): 23–42.

Bill, James A. 1972. *The Politics of Iran: Groups, Classes, and Modernization.* Columbus, OH: Charles E. Merrill Publishing Co.

Bishri, Tariq al-. 1987. *Dirasaat Fi Al-Dimuqratiyah Al-Misriyah.* Cairo: Dar al-Shuruq.

Bligh, Alexander. 2002. "The Jordanian Army: Between Domestic and External Challenges." In Barry Rubin and Thomas Keaney, eds., *Armed Forces in the Middle East.* London: Frank Cass.

Booth, John A. 1998. "The Somoza Regime in Nicaragua." In H. E. Chehabi and J. Linz, eds., *Sultanistic Regimes.* Boulder: Lynne Rienner, 132–152.

Botman, Selma. 1991. *Egypt from Independence to Revolution, 1919–1952.* Syracuse: Syracuse University Press.

Boulby, Marion. 1989. "The Islamic Challenge: Tunisia Since Independence." *Third World Quarterly* 10 (April): 590–614.

Bourqia, Rahma, and Susan Miller, eds. 1999. *In the Shadow of the Sultan: Culture, Power and Politics in Morocco.* Cambridge, MA: Harvard University Press.

Bouzouba, Dr. 'Abd al-Majid. 1995. Interview. Adjoint Secretary-general and secretary of information of CDT, council member of USFP, Rabat, July 14.

Brand, Laurie. 1994. *Jordan's Inter-Arab Relations.* New York: Columbia University Press.

———. 1998. *Women, the State, and Political Liberalization: Middle Eastern and North African Experiences.* New York: Columbia University Press.

Bras, Jean-Philippe. 2000. "Elections et representation au Maghreb." *Monde Arabe Maghreb Machrek* 168 (April–June): 3–13.

Bratton, Michael. 1989. "Beyond the State: Civil Society and Associational Life in Africa." *World Politics* 41 (April): 407–430.

Bratton, Michael, and Nicholas van de Walle. 1997. *Democratic Experiments in Africa: Regime Transitions in Comparative Perspective.* Cambridge, UK: Cambridge University Press.

Brooks, Risa. 1998. *Political-Military Relations and the Stability of Arab Regimes.* Oxford: Oxford University Press for IISS.

Brown, Nathan J. 2002. *Constitutions in a Nonconstitutional World: Arab Basic Laws and the Prospects for Accountable Government.* Albany: State University of New York Press.

Browne, Edward G. 1910. *The Persian Revolution of 1905–1909.* Cambridge, UK: The University Press.

Brownlee, Jason. 2001. "The Double Edge of Electoral Authoritarianism: A Comparison of Egypt and Iran." Paper presented at the annual meeting of the American Political Science Association, San Francisco, September.

———. 2002a. "Low Tide After the Third Wave: Exploring Politics Under Authoritarianism." *Comparative Politics* 34, 4: 477–498.

———. 2002b. "And Yet They Persist: Explaining Survival and Transition in Neopatrimonial Regimes." *Studies in Comparative International Development* 37, 3 (Fall): 35–63.

Brumberg, Daniel. 1995. "Authoritarian Legacies and Reform Strategies in the Arab World." In Rex Brynen, Bahgat Korany, and Paul Noble, eds., *Political Liberalization and Democratization in the Arab World: Volume 1, Theoretical Perspectives.* Boulder: Lynne Rienner, 229–260.

———. 2001. *Reinventing Khomeini: The Struggle for Reform in Iran.* Chicago: University of Chicago Press.

————. 2002. "The Trap of Liberalized Autocracy." *Journal of Democracy* 13, 4: 56–68.

————. 2003. "Liberalization Versus Democracy: Understanding Arab Political Reform." Carnegie Endowment Working Paper 37. Washington, DC: Carnegie Endowment for International Peace.

Brynen, Rex. 1998. "The Politics of Monarchical Liberalism." In Bahgat Korany, Rex Brynen, and Paul Noble, eds., *Political Liberalization and Democratization in the Arab World: Volume II, Comparative Experiences*. Boulder: Lynne Rienner, 71–100.

————. 2000. *A Very Political Economy: Peacebuilding and Foreign Aid in the West Bank and Gaza*. Washington, DC: U.S. Institute for Peace.

Brynen, Rex, Bahgat Korany, and Paul Noble, eds. 1995. *Political Liberalization and Democratization in the Arab World: Volume 1, Theoretical Perspectives*. Boulder: Lynne Rienner.

Buchta, Wilfred. 2000. *Who Rules Iran? The Structure of Power in the Islamic Republic*. Washington, DC: Washington Institute for Near East Policy and the Konrad Adenauer Stiftung.

Buendia, Jorge. 1996. "Economic Reform, Public Opinion, and Presidential Approval in Mexico, 1988–1993." *Comparative Political Studies* 29, 5 (October): 566–591.

Bunce, Valerie. 2000. "Comparative Democratization: Big and Bounded Generalizations." *Comparative Political Studies* 33, 6/7 (August/September): 703–734.

Burnell, Peter. 1998. "Arrivals and Departures: A Preliminary Classification of Democratic Failures and Their Explanation." *Commonwealth and Comparative Politics* 36, 3: 1–29.

Burton, Michael, Richard Gunther, and John Higley. 1991. "Introduction: Elite Transformations and Democratic Regimes." In Higley and Gunther, eds., *Elites and Democratic Consolidation in Latin America and Southern Europe*. Cambridge, UK: Cambridge University Press, 1–37.

Campbell, John Kennedy, and Philip Sherrard. 1968. *Modern Greece*. New York: Praeger.

Carapico, Sheila. 1993. "Elections and Mass Politics in Yemen." *Middle East Report* 185 (November–December): 2–6.

————. 1998. *Civil Society in Yemen: The Political Economy of Activism in Modern Arabia*. Cambridge, UK: Cambridge University Press.

Carothers, Thomas. 1997. "Democracy Assistance: The Question of Strategy." *Democratization* 4, 3 (Autumn).

————. 2000. "The Clinton Record on Democracy Promotion." *Carnegie Working Paper* No. 16.

————. 2002. "The End of the Transition Paradigm." *Journal of Democracy* 13, 1: 5–21.

Carr, Raymond. 1982. *Spain, 1808–1975*. 2nd ed. Oxford: Clarendon.

Catusse, Myriam. 2001. "Business, Scandals and Glass Ballot Boxes in Casablanca: The Ambiguities of the 'Local Democracy' in the Era of 'Good Governance.'" Paper presented at the Second Mediterranean Social and Political Research Meeting, Mediterranean Programme, Robert Schuman Centre for Advanced Studies, European University Institute, Florence, March 21–25.

Çavdar, Tevfik. 1983. "Serbest Fırka." *Cumhuriyet Dönemi Turk Ansiklopedisi* 8.

Center for Human Rights Legal Aid. 1996. "Egyptian Politics: The Fiction of a Multiparty System." Cairo.

Center for Strategic Studies. 1993. *Public Opinion Survey on Democracy in Jordan, Preliminary Findings.* Amman: University of Jordan.

Chaudhry, Kiren Aziz. 1989. "The Price of Wealth: Business and State in Labor Remittance and Oil Economies." *International Organization* 43 (Winter): 101–145.

———. 1997. *The Price of Wealth: Economies and Institutions in the Middle East.* Ithaca: Cornell University Press.

Chazan, Naomi. 1992. "Africa's Democratic Challenge: Strengthening Civil Society and the State." *World Policy Journal* 9, 2 (Spring): 279–307.

Chehabi, Houchang E. 1991. "Religion and Politics in Iran: How Theocratic Is the Islamic Republic?" *Daedalus* 120 (Summer): 48–70.

———. 2001. "The Political Regime of the Islamic Republic of Iran in Comparative Perspective." *Government and Opposition* 36 (Winter): 48–70.

Chehabi, H. E., and Juan J. Linz. 1998a. "A Theory of Sultanism." In H. E. Chehabi and Juan J. Linz, eds., *Sultanistic Regimes.* Baltimore: Johns Hopkins University Press, 3–48.

Chehabi, H. E., and Juan J. Linz., eds. 1998b. *Sultanistic Regimes.* Baltimore: Johns Hopkins University Press.

Claisse, Alain. 1985. "Élections communales et législatives au Maroc." *Annuaire de l'Afrique du Nord:* 631–668.

Clément, Jean-Francois. 1993. "Les Révoltes Urbaines." In Jean-Claude Santucci, ed., *Le Maroc Actuel.* Paris: CNRS, 392–406.

Colhoun, Jack. 1992. "Washington Watch: How Bush Backed Iraq." *Middle East Report* 176 (May–June): 35–37.

Collier, David. 1999. "Building a Disciplined, Rigorous Center in Comparative Politics." *APSA Comparative Politics Section Newsletter* (Summer).

Collier, David, and Ruth Berins Collier. 1991. *Shaping the Political Arena.* Princeton: Princeton University Press.

Collier, David, and Steven Levitsky. 1997. "Democracy with Adjectives: Conceptual Innovation in Comparative Research." *World Politics* 49 (April): 430–452.

Collier, David, and James Mahoney. 1996. "Insights and Pitfalls: Selection Bias in Qualitative Research." *World Politics* 49, 1: 56–91.

Collier, Ruth Berins, and James Mahoney. 1997. "Adding Collective Actors to Collective Outcomes." *Comparative Politics* 29 (April): 285–303.

Cooper, Mark. 1982. *The Transformation of Egypt.* Baltimore: Johns Hopkins University Press.

Cox, Gary W. 1997. *Making Votes Count: Strategic Coordination in the World's Electoral Systems.* Cambridge, UK: Cambridge University Press.

Crampton, R. J. 1997. *A Concise History of Bulgaria.* Cambridge, UK: Cambridge University Press.

Crystal, Jill. 1994. "Authoritarianism and Its Adversaries in the Arab World." *World Politics* 46 (January): 262–289.

———. 1995. *Oil and Politics in the Gulf.* New York: Cambridge University Press.

Dahl, Robert. 1971. *Polyarchy: Participation and Opposition.* New Haven: Yale University Press.

Davis, Helen Miller. 1947. *Constitutions, Electoral Laws, Treaties of States in the Near and Middle East.* Durham: Duke University Press.

Dawisha, Adeed, and I. William Zartman, eds. 1988. *Beyond Coercion: The Durability of the Arab State.* London: Croom Helm.

Deeb, Mary-Jane, and Ellen Laipson. 1991. "Tunisian Foreign Policy: Continuity and Change Under Bourguiba and Ben Ali." In I. W. Zartman, ed., *Tunisia: The Political Economy of Reform.* Boulder: Lynne Rienner, 221–241.

Denoeux, Guilain, and Abdeslam Maghraoui. 1998. "King Hassan's Strategy of Political Dualism." *Middle East Policy* 5, 4: 104.

Derry, T. K. 1957. *A Short History of Norway.* London: G. Allen & Unwin.

Detalle, Renaud. 1993. "The Yemeni Elections Up Close." *Middle East Report* 185 (November–December): 8–12.

Diamond, Larry. 1993. *Political Culture and Democracy in Developing Countries.* Boulder: Lynne Rienner.

———. 1994. "Toward Democratic Consolidation." *Journal of Democracy* 5, 3 (July): 4–17.

———. 1996. "Is the Third Wave Over?" *Journal of Democracy* 7: 20–37.

———. 1999. *Developing Democracy: Towards Consolidation.* Baltimore: Johns Hopkins University Press.

———. 2002a. "What Political Science Owes the World." *PS Online,* March.

———. 2002b. "Thinking About Hybrid Regimes." *Journal of Democracy* 34, 2: 21–35.

Diamond, Larry, Juan Linz, and Seymour Martin Lipset. 1990. *Politics in Developing Countries: Comparing Experiences with Democracy.* Boulder: Lynne Rienner.

Diamond, Larry, Juan J. Linz, and Seymour Martin Lipset, eds. 1988. *Democracy in Developing Countries.* Boulder: Lynne Rienner.

Diamond, Larry, and M. E. Plattner, eds. 1995. *Economic Reform and Democracy.* Baltimore: Johns Hopkins University Press.

Dillman, Bradford. 2000. "Parliamentary Elections and the Prospects for Political Pluralism in North Africa." *Government and Opposition* (Spring): 211–236.

DiPalma, Guiseppe. 1990. *To Craft Democracy.* Berkeley: University of California Press.

Direction de la Statistique. 1990. *La Population Active Urbaine.* Rabat: Direction de la Statistique.

———. 1993. *La Population Active Urbaine.* Rabat: Direction de la Statistique.

Dobers, H., W. Goussous, and Y. Sara, eds. 1992. *Democracy and the Rule of Law in Jordan.* Amman: Jordanian Printing Press.

Dodd, C. H. 1991. "Atatürk and Political Parties." In Metin Heper and Jacob M. Landau, eds., *Political Parties and Democracy in Turkey.* London: I. B. Tauris.

Doran, Michael Scott. 2004. "The Saudi Paradox." *Foreign Affairs* 83, 1: 35–51.

Doumato, Eleanor, and Marsha Pripstein Posusney, eds. 2003. *Women and Globalization in the Arab Mille East: Gender, Economy, and Society.* Boulder: Lynne Rienner.

Downing, Brian M. 1992. *The Military Revolution and Political Change: Origins of Democracy and Autocracy in Early Modern Europe.* Princeton: Princeton University Press.

Downs, Anthony. 1957. *An Economic Theory of Democracy.* New York: Harper and Row.

Droz-Vincent, Philippe. 1999. "Le Militaire et le Politique en Egypte." *Monde Arabe Maghreb Machrek* 165 (July–September): 16–35.

Drysdale, Alasdair. 1982. "The Asad Regime and Its Troubles." *MERIP Reports* 110 (November–December): 3–11.

Duverger, Maurice. 1954. *Political Parties: Their Organization and Activity in the Modern State*. Barbara and Robert North, trans. London: Methuen & Co., Ltd.

Eckert, Carter et al. 1990. *Korea Old and New*. Cambridge, MA: Harvard University Press.

Eckstein, Susan, ed. 1989. *Power and Popular Protest: Latin American Social Movements*. Berkeley: University of California Press.

Economic Research Forum for the Arab Countries, Iran, and Turkey. 2002. *Economic Trends in the MENA Region, 2002*. Cairo: American University in Cairo Press.

Economist Intelligence Unit (EIU). 1994. *Country Report: Jordan*.

———. 2000a. *Country Profile: Iraq 1999–2000*.

———. 2000b. *Country Profile: Libya 1999–2000*.

———. 2000c. *Country Profile: Syria 1999–2000*.

Egypt Almanac 2003: The Encyclopedia of Modern Egypt. 2002. Cairo: Egyptofile.

Egyptian Organization for Human Rights. 1995. "Democracy in Danger: The Elections Nobody Won" (in Arabic). Cairo.

Ehsani, Kaveh. 1999. "Existing Political Vessels Cannot Contain the Reform Movement: A Conversation with Sa'id Hajjarian." *Middle East Report* 209 (Fall): 40–42.

———. 2004. "Round 12 for Iran's Reformists." *Middle East Report Online*, January 29, 2004. Online at http://www.merip.org/mero/mero012904.html.

Eickelman, Dale F. 1986. "Royal Authority and Religious Legitimacy: Morocco's Elections, 1960–1984." In Myron J. Aronoff, ed., *The Frailty of Authority*. New Brunswick: Transaction Books, 181–205.

———. 1987. "Changing Perceptions of State Authority: Morocco, Egypt and Oman." In Ghassan Salamé, ed., *The Foundations of the Arab State*. New York: Croom Helm, 177–204.

El Fathaly, Omar I., and Monte Palmer. 1995. "Institutional Development in Qadhafi's Libya." In Dirk Vandewalle, ed., *Qadhafi's Libya, 1969–1994*. New York: St. Martin's, 157–176.

El Malki, Habib. 1989. *Trente ans d'economie marocaine 1960–1990*. Paris: CNRS.

El Merghadi, Muhammad. 1995. Interview. Member of USFP. Fes, Morocco, May 16.

Engstrom, Richard L. 1992. "Modified Multi-Seat Election Systems as Remedies for Minority Vote Dilution." *Stetson Law Review* 21, 3 (Summer): 743–770.

Entelis, John. 2000. "Democracy Denied: America's Authoritarian Approach Towards the Maghreb." Paper presented at the 18th World Congress of the International Political Science Association, Quebec, Canada, August 1–5.

Ertman, Thomas. 1998. "Democracy and Dictatorship in Interwar Western Europe Revisited." *World Politics* 50, 3 (April): 475–505.

Essam el-Din, Gamal. 2000. "Rank-and-File Dissenters." *Al-Ahram Weekly* (November): 23–29.

Fatemi, Khosrow. 1982. "Leadership by Distrust: The Shah's Modus

Operandi." *Middle East Journal* 36 (Winter): 48–61.

Fathi, Schirin. 1994. *Jordan: An Invented Nation?* Hamburg: Deutsches Orient-Institute.

Feaver, Peter. 1999. "Civil-Military Relations." *Annual Review of Political Science* 2: 211–241.

Fischer, Michael J. 1980. *Iran: From Religious Dispute to Revolution.* Cambridge, MA: Harvard University Press.

Fish, M. Steven. 2002. "Islam and Authoritarianism." *World Politics* 55 (October): 4–37.

Fish, M. Steven, and Robin S. Brooks. 2004. "Does Diversity Hurt Democracy?" *Journal of Democracy* 15, 1: 154–166.

Fletcher, Lehman. 1996. *Egypt's Agriculture in a Reform Era.* Iowa City: Iowa State University Press.

Foley, Michael, and Bob Edwards. 1996. "The Paradox of Civil Society." *Journal of Democracy* 7, 3 (July): 38–52.

Foreign Broadcast Information Service (FBIS).

Freedom House. 1998. "The Most Repressive Regimes of 1998: Libya." Washington, DC: Freedom House. Online at http://www.freedomhouse.org/reports/worst98/libya.html.

Friedman, Thomas. 1989. *From Beirut to Jerusalem.* New York: Farrar, Straus & Giroux.

Gambill, Gary C., and Elie Abou Aoun. 2000. "Special Report: How Syria Orchestrates Lebanon's Elections." *Middle East Intelligence Bulletin* 2, 7 (August 5).

Garfinkel, Alan. 1981. *Forms of Explanation: Rethinking the Questions in Social Theory.* New Haven: Yale University Press.

Gasiorowski, Mark. 1992. "The Failure of Reform in Tunisia." *Journal of Democracy* 3, 4 (October): 85–97.

Gause, F. Gregory III. 1995. "Regional Influences on Experiments in Political Liberalization in the Arab World." In Rex Brynen Bahgat Korany, and Paul Noble, eds., *Political Liberalization and Democratization: Volume I, Theoretical Perspectives.* Boulder: Lynne Rienner, 283–306.

Geddes, Barbara. 1990. "How the Cases You Choose Affect the Answers You Get: Selection Bias in Comparative Politics." *Political Analysis* 2: 131–150.

———. 1994. "Challenging the Conventional Wisdom." *Journal of Democracy* 5, 4 (October): 104–118.

———. 1999a. "Authoritarian Breakdown: Empirical Test of a Game Theoretic Argument." Paper presented at the Annual Meeting of the American Political Science Association, Atlanta, GA, August 29–September 1.

———. 1999b. "What Do We Know About Democratization After 20 Years?" *Annual Review of Political Science* 2: 115–144.

———. 2002. "The Great Transformation in the Study of Politics in Developing Countries." In Ira Katznelson and Helen V. Milner, eds., *Political Science: The State of the Discipline.* New York: W. W. Norton and Company, 343–346.

Geisser, Vincent. 2000. "Tunisie: des elections pour quoi faire? Enjeux et 'sens' du fait electoral de Bourguiba à Ben Ali." *Monde Arabe Maghreb Machrek* 168 (April–June): 14–28.

Gerber, Haim. 1987. *Social Origins of the Modern Middle East.* Boulder: Lynne Rienner.

Gerges, Fawaz A. 1999. *America and Political Islam: Clash of Cultures or Clash of Interests?* New York: Cambridge University Press.

Geyelin, Philip. 1989. "Glasnost' in Jordan." *Washington Post*, October 3: A25.

Ghanem, As'ad. 1996. "Founding Elections in a Transitional Period: The First Palestinian General Elections." *Middle East Journal* 50, 4 (Autumn): 513–528.

Giacomo, Luciani, ed. 1990. *The Arab State*. London: Routledge.

Glosemeyer, Iris. 1993. "The First Yemeni Parliamentary Elections in 1993: Practicing Democracy." *Orient* 34, 3 (September): 439–451.

———. 1998. "Parliamentary Elections in Yemen 1997." In Sven Behrendt and Christian-Peter Hanelt, eds., *Elections in the Middle East and North Africa*. Munich/Getersloh: Bertelsmann Foundations, 35–43.

Goldberg, Ellis, Resat Kasaba, and Joel S. Migdal, eds. 1993. *Rules and Rights in the Middle East: Society, Law, and Democracy*. Seattle: University of Washington Press.

Grofman, Bernard, and Arend Lijphart, eds. 1986. *Electoral Laws and Their Political Consequences*. New York: Agathon.

Haggard, Stephan, and Robert R. Kaufman. 1995. *The Political Economy of Democratic Transitions*. Princeton: Princeton University Press.

Hajjarian, Saeed. 1380 [2002]. "Estratezhiha-ye Siyasi dar Iran-e Emrouz." *Aftab* 12 (Bahman [February]): 12–15.

Hamilton, Nora, and Eun Mee Kim. 1993. "Economic and Political Liberalization in South Korea and Mexico." *Third World Quarterly* 14.

Hammami, Rema. 1995. "Nongovernmental Organizations: The Professionalisation of Politics." *Race and Class* 37, 2.

———. 2000. "Palestinian Nongovernmental Organizations Since Oslo: From NGO Politics to Social Movements." *Middle East Report* 214 (Spring).

Hammoudi, Abdellah. 1997. *Master and Disciple: The Cultural Foundations of Moroccan Authoritarianism*. Chicago: The University of Chicago Press.

Handy, Howard, and staff team. 1998. "Egypt: Beyond Stabilization, Toward a Dynamic Market Economy." Washington, DC: International Monetary Fund.

Harbeson, John, Donald Rothchild, and Naomi Chazan, eds. 1994. *Civil Society and the State in Africa*. Boulder: Lynne Rienner.

Harbi, Dabbi al-Haylim al-. 2003. *Al-Nitham Al-Intikhabi Fi Al-Kuwayt*. Kuwait: al-Siyasi lil-nashr wa al-tawzi'.

Harik, Iliya. 1975. "Political Elite of Lebanon." In George Lenczowski, ed., *Political Elites in the Middle East*. Washington, DC: American Enterprise Institute.

———. 1994. "Rethinking Civil Society: Pluralism in the Arab World." *Journal of Democracy* 5, 3 (July): 43–56.

———. 1999. "The Election Law and the Art of Dealing in Miracles" (in Arabic). *Al-Hayat*, May 9.

Harik, Iliya, and D. J. Sullivan, eds. 1992. *Privatization and Liberalization in the Middle East*. Bloomington: Indiana University Press.

Harik, Judith Palmer. 1998. "Democracy (Again) Derailed: Lebanon's Ta'if Paradox." In Bahgat Korany, Rex Brynen, and Paul Noble, eds., *Political Liberalization and Democratization in the Arab World: Volume 2, Comparative Experiences*. Boulder: Lynne Rienner, 127–156.

Hasani, Abd al-Razzaq al-. 1957. *Tarikh Al-Iraq Al-Siyasi Al-Hadith*. 2nd ed. Vol. 3. Sidon, Lebanon: Matba'a al-'irfan.

Hawatmeh, George al-. 1998. "The Changing Role of the Press." In George

Hawatmeh, ed., *The Jordanian Experience Since 1989, The Role of the Press.* Amman: Markaz al-Urdun al-Jadid lil-Dirasat: Dar Sindbad lil-Nashr.

Hawthorne, Amy. 2001. "Do We Want Democracy in the Middle East?" *American Foreign Service Journal* (February). Online at http://www.afsa.org/fsj/feb01/hawthorne01.cfm.

Hendriks, Bertus. 1985. "Egypt's Elections, Mubarak's Bind." *MERIP Reports* 129 (January): 11–18.

Henry, Clement, and Robert Springborg. 2001. *Globalization and the Politics of Development in the Middle East.* New York: Cambridge University Press.

Heper, Metin. 2002. "The Consolidation of Democracy Versus Democratization in Turkey." In Barry Rubin and Metin Heper, eds., *Political Parties in Turkey.* London: Frank Cass, 142–146.

Herb, Michael. 1999. *All in the Family: Absolutism, Revolution, and Democracy in the Middle Eastern Monarchies.* Albany: State University of New York Press.

———. Forthcoming. "No Representation Without Taxation? Rents, Development, and Democracy." *Comparative Politics.*

Herbst, Jeffrey. 2001. "Political Liberalization in Africa After Ten Years." *Comparative Politics* 33 (April): 357–375.

Hermassi, Elbaki. 1991. "The Islamicist Movement and November 7." In I. W. Zartman, ed., *Tunisia: The Political Economy of Reform.* Boulder: Lynne Rienner, 193–204.

Herr, Richard. 1971. *Spain.* Englewood Cliffs, NJ: Prentice-Hall.

Hewitson, Mark. 2001. "The Kaiserreich in Question: Constitutional Crisis in Germany Before the First World War." *The Journal of Modern History* 73, 4: 725–780.

Heydemann, Steven. 1993. "Taxation Without Representation: Authoritarianism and Economic Liberalization in Syria." In Ellis Goldberg, Reşat Kasaba, and Joel Migdal, eds., *Rules and Rights in the Middle East: Society, Law, and Democracy.* Seattle: University of Washington Press, 69–102.

———. 1999. *Authoritarianism in Syria: Institutions and Social Conflict 1946–1970.* Ithaca: Cornell University Press.

Higley, John, and Richard Gunther, eds. 1991. *Elites and Democratic Consolidation in Latin America and Southern Europe.* Baltimore: Johns Hopkins University Press.

Hinnebusch, Raymond. 1985. *Egyptian Politics Under Sadat.* Cambridge, UK: Cambridge University Press.

———. 1990. *Authoritarian Power and State Formation in Ba'thist Syria.* Boulder: Westview.

Hislaire, René. 1945. "Political Parties." In Jan Albert Goris, ed., *Belgium.* Berkeley: University of California Press.

Hitchins, Keith. 1994. *Rumania, 1866–1947.* Oxford: Oxford University Press.

Hizb al-Istiqlal. 1995. *Hizb al-Istiqlal Bayna al-Mu'tamarayn (1985–1994).* Rabat: Al Sharakat al-Maghrabia.

Holmes, Geoffrey S., and D. Szechi. 1993. *The Age of Oligarchy: Pre-Industrial Britain, 1722–1783.* London: Longman.

Horowitz, Donald. 1993. "Democracy in Divided Societies." *Journal of Democracy* 4 (October): 18–38.

Hourani, Hani. 1989. *Tarikh Al-Hayat Al-Niyabiya Fi Al-Urdun 1929–1957.* Nicosia, Cyprus: Sharq.

———. 1998. "Al-ihzab al-siyasiya wal-dimuqratiya fil-Urdun [Political parties and Democracy in Jordan] 1989–1998." Paper presented at the conference on "Controlled Contestation and Opposition Strategies: Multi-Party Elections in the Arab World," Brown University, Providence, RI, October 2–3.

Howeidy, Amira. 2000. "A Risky Business." *Al-Ahram Weekly Online,* July 20–26.

———. 2001. "Reluctant Grassroots." *Al-Ahram Weekly Online,* June 21–27.

Huber, Evelyne, Dietrich Rueschemeyer, and John D. Stephens. 1993. "The Impact of Economic Development on Democracy." *Journal of Economic Perspectives* 7, 3 (Summer): 71–86.

Hull, Adrian P. 1999. "Comparative Political Science: An Inventory and Assessment Since the 1980s." *PS: Political Science and Politics* 32, 1 (March): 117–124.

Human Rights Watch (HRW). 1997. "Jordan: Clamping Down on Critics—Human Rights Violations in Advance of the Parliamentary Elections." *Human Rights Watch* 9, 12 (October).

———. 2002a. "Human Rights Watch World Report: Introduction." New York: Human Rights Watch.

———. 2002b. "Human Rights Watch World Report: Tunisia." New York: Human Rights Watch.

———. 2002c. "Opportunism in the Face of Tragedy: Repression in the Name of Anti-terrorism." New York: Human Rights Watch.

Huntington, Samuel. 1968. *Political Order in Changing Societies.* New Haven: Yale University Press.

———. 1991. *The Third Wave: Democratization in the Late Twentieth Century.* Norman: University of Oklahoma Press.

———. 1991–1992. "How Countries Democratize." *Political Science Quarterly* 106: 579–615.

Hsiao, Michael, and Hagen Koo. 1997. "The Middle Classes and Democratization." In Larry Diamond, Marc F. Plattner, Yun-han Chu, and Hung-mao Tien, eds., *Consolidating the Third Wave Democracies: Themes and Perspectives.* Baltimore: Johns Hopkins University Press, 312–333.

Ibrahim, Saad Eddin. 1995. "Liberalization and Democratization in the Arab World: An Overview." In Rex Brynen, Bahgat Korany, and Paul Noble, eds., *Political Liberalization and Democratization in the Arab World: Volume 1, Theoretical Perspectives.* Boulder: Lynne Rienner, 29–60.

International Crisis Group (ICG). 2003. *The Challenge of Political Reform: Jordanian Democratisation and Regional Instability.* Amman/Brussels: International Crisis Group.

International Institute of Strategic Studies (IISS). 2002. *The Military Balance 2001–2002.* London: Oxford University Press.

Issawi, Charles. 1956. "Economic and Social Foundations of Democracy in the Middle East." *International Affairs* (January): 27–42.

Jabbar, Faleh Abd al-. 1992. "Why the Uprisings Failed." *Middle East Report* 176 (May–June): 3–4.

Jaber, Kamel Abu. 1990. "The 1989 Jordanian Parliamentary Elections." *Orient* 31: 61–83.

Jaber, Kamel Abu, and Schirin H. Fathi. 1990. "The 1989 Jordanian Parliamentary Elections." *Orient* 31, 1: 67–86.

Janos, Andrew. 2000. *East Central Europe in the Modern World.* Stanford: Stanford University Press.

Jenks, William A. 1974. *The Austrian Electoral Reform of 1907.* New York: Octagon Books.

Jibril, Muhammad. 1981. "Les evenements et les problèmes de Fond." *Lamalif* 127 (July–August): 28–31.

Jones, W. Glyn. 1970. *Denmark*. New York: Praeger.

Jones-Luong, Pauline. 2002. *Institutional Change and Political Continuity in Post-Soviet Central Asia: Power, Perceptions, and Pacts*. Cambridge, UK: Cambridge University Press.

Jureidini, P. A., and R. D. McLaurin. 1984. *Jordan: The Impact of Social Change on the Role of the Tribes*. New York: Praeger.

Kabariti, Abdul Karim. 1995. "Opening Remarks." At Seminar on Democracy and the Rule of Law, Amman, Jordan, November 19.

Kabasakal, Mehmet. 1991. *Türkiye'de Siyasal Parti Örgütlenmesi 1908–1960*. İstanbul: Tekin Yayınevi.

Kalyvas, Stathis N. 2000. "Commitment Problems in Emerging Democracies: The Case of Religious Parties." *Comparative Politics* 32 (July): 379–398.

Kamal, Karima. 1999. "Festival of the Nongovernmental Organizations" (in Arabic). *Sabah al Kheir,* May 13.

Kamal, Sana. 1996. "Bread Subsidy to Go." *Middle East International,* August 2: 11.

Kamrava, Mehran. 2000. "Military Professionalization and Civil-Military Relations in the Middle East." *Political Science Quarterly* 115 (Spring): 67–92.

Kamrava, Mehran, and Houchang Hassan-Yari. 2004. "Suspended Equilibrium in Iran's Political System." *Muslim World* 94 (October): 347–371.

Karam, Mohamed. 1998. "Al-Intikhabat fil-Maghreb" [Elections in Morocco]. Paper presented at the conference on "Controlled Contestation and Opposition Strategies: Multi-Party Elections in the Arab World," Brown University, Providence, RI, October 2–3.

Karatnycky, Adrian. 2002. "The 2001 Freedom House Survey: Muslim Countries and the Democracy Gap." *Journal of Democracy* 13, 1 (January): 99–112.

Karl, Terry Lynn. 1997. *The Paradox of Plenty: Oil Booms and Petro-States*. Berkeley: University of California Press.

Karl, Terry Lynn, and Philippe C. Schmitter. 1991. "Modes of Transition in Latin America, Southern and Eastern Europe." *International Social Science Journal* 43, 2 (May): 269–284.

Kasfir, Nelson. 1998. "Civil Society, the State, and Democracy in Africa." In Nelson Kasfir, ed., *Civil Society and Democracy in Africa: Critical Perspectives*. London: Frank Cass.

Kasza, Greg. 2001. "Perestroika: For an Ecumenical Science of Politics." *PS: Political Science and Politics* 34, 3 (September): 597–599.

Katznelson, Ira. 1986. "Working-Class Formation: Constructing Cases and Comparisons." In Ira Katznelson and Aristide R. Zolberg, eds., *Working-Class Formation: Nineteenth-Century Patterns in Western Europe and the United States*. Princeton: Princeton University Press.

———. 2003. *Desolation and Enlightenment: Political Knowledge After Total War, Totalitarianism, and the Holocaust*. New York: Columbia University Press.

Kawar, Samira. 1985. "Hussein Curbs Fundamentalists." *Washington Post.* December 27: A21.

Kazemipur, Abdolmohammad, and Ali Rezaei. 2003. "Religious Life Under Theocracy: The Case of Iran." *Journal of the Scientific Study of Religion* 42 (September): 347–361.

Keck, Margaret, and Kathryn Sikkink. 1998. *Activists Beyond Borders: Advocacy Networks in International Politics*. Ithaca: Cornell University Press.

Kedourie, Elie. 1994. *Democracy and Arab Political Culture*. London: Frank Cass.

Keyder, Çağlar. 1987. *State and Class in Turkey: A Study in Capitalist Development*. New York: Verso.

Khafaji, Isam al-. 1992. "State Terror and the Degradation of Politics." *Middle East Report* 176 (May–June): 16.

Khalid, Kamal. 1989. *The Struggle Against Tailoring Laws: Three Years Defending the Constitution* (in Arabic). Cairo: Dar al-I'tisam.

———. 1998. Comments presented at the conference on "Controlled Contestation and Opposition Strategies: Mulit-party Elections in the Arab World," Brown University, Providence, RI, October 2–3.

Khalil, Shubaki. 1995. "Brotherhood Leader Affirms Commitment to Non-Violent Approach." *Jordan Times*, October 12–13: A1.

Khazen, Farid el. 1994. "Lebanon's First Postwar Parliamentary Elections, 1993." *Middle East Policy* 3, 1: 120–136.

Khouri, A. W. 1981. "The National Consultative Council." *International Journal of Middle East Studies* 13, 4: 435–447.

Khouri, Rami. 1984. "Jordan's Parliament Approves Elections." *Washington Post*, January 10: A10.

Khouri, Riad al-. 1998. "The 1997 Parliamentary Elections in Jordan." In Sven Behrendt and Christian-Peter Hanelt, eds., *Elections in the Middle East and North Africa*. Munich: Gutersloh/Bertelsmann Foundation, 27–33.

Khrouz, Driss. 1988. *L'Economie marocaine: Les raisons de la crise*. Casablanca: Les Editions maghrebines.

Khuri, Fuad I. 1980. *Tribe and State in Bahrain: The Transformation of Social and Political Authority in an Arab State*. Chicago: University of Chicago Press.

Kienle, Eberhard. 1998. "More Than a Response to Islamism: The Political Deliberalization of Egypt in the 1990s." *Middle East Journal* 52, 2 (Spring): 219–235.

———. 2001. *A Grand Delusion: Democracy and Economic Reform in Egypt*. London: I. B. Tauris.

Kienle, Eberhard, ed. 1994. *Contemporary Syria: Liberalization Between Cold War and Cold Peace*. London: British Academic Press.

Kilani, Sa'eda. 1995a. Interview. Journalist for *Jordan Times*. December 1.

———. 1995b. "Shbeilat Arrested on Charges of Slandering the King, Faces Trial." *Jordan Times*, December 10: 3

King, Gary, Robert O. Keohane, and Sidney Verba. 1994. *Designing Social Inquiry: Scientific Inference in Qualitative Research*. Princeton: Princeton University Press.

King Husayn. 1985. "Letter to Prime Minister Zayd al-Rifa'i." *Jordan Times* November 11: 1.

King, Stephen J. 2003. *Liberalization against Democracy: The Local Politics of Economic Reform in Tunisia*. Bloomington and Indianapolis: Indiana University Press.

Kinzo, Maria D'Alva. 1988. *Legal Opposition Politics under Authoritarian Rule in Brazil*. New York: St. Martin's.

Kohli, Atul., ed. 2001. *The Success of India's Democracy*. New York: Cambridge University Press.

Korany, Bahgat, Rex Brynen, and Paul Noble, eds. 1998. *Political Liberaliza-tion and Democratization in the Arab World: Volume II, Comparative Experiences*. Boulder: Lynne Rienner.

Kossmann, E. H. 1978. *The Low Countries, 1780–1940*. Oxford: Oxford Uni-versity Press.

Kramer, Gudrun. 1992. "Liberalization and Democracy in the Arab World." *Middle East Report* 174 (January/February): 22–25.

———. 1997. "Islamist Notions of Democracy." In Joel Beinin and Joe Stork, eds., *Political Islam*. Berkeley: University of California Press, 71–82.

Kramer, Martin. 1993. "Islam vs. Democracy." *Commentary* 95 (January): 35–42.

Kubba, Laith. 2000. "Arabs and Democracy: The Awakening of Civil Society." *Journal of Democracy* 11, 3 (July): 84–90.

Kurzman, Charles. 1996. "Structural Opportunity and Perceived Opportunity in Social Movement Theory: The Iranian Revolution 1979." *American Soci-ological Review* 61, 1 (February): 153–170.

Lamchichi, Abderrahim. 1989. *Islam et contestation au Maghreb*. Paris: L'Harmattan.

Langohr, Vickie. 2000. "Cracks in Egypt's Electoral Engineering: The 2000 Vote." *MERIP Press Information Note* 39, November 7.

———. 2001. "Democracy in Egypt? A Discussion of the Recent Elections." Talk given at the University of Pennsylvania Middle East Center, January 18.

———. 2002. "An Exit from Arab Autocracy." *Journal of Democracy* 13, 3 (July): 116–122.

Larbi, Hanane, and Rachid Sbihi. 1986. *Économie marocaine: Une radioscope*. Rabat: Al Maarif Al Jadida.

Lardeyret, Guy. 1991. "Debate: Proportional Representation." *Journal of De-mocracy* 2, 3 (Summer): 30–48.

Lawson, Fred. 1982. "Social Bases of the Hamah Revolt." *MERIP Reports* 110 (November–December): 24–28.

Lebanese Center for Policy Studies (LCPS). 1996. "The Parliament of Yes-Men? Lebanon's Supreme Soviet." *The Lebanon Report* 3 (Fall).

Lerner, Daniel. 1958. *The Passing of Traditional Society*. Glencoe, IL: The Free Press.

Leveau, Rémy. 1981. "Islam et contrôle politique au Maroc." In Ernest Gellner and Jean-Claude Vatin, eds., *Islam et politique au Maghreb*. Paris: CNRS, 271– 279.

Levitsky, Steven, and Lucan A. Way. 2002. "Elections Without Democracy: The Rise of Competitive Authoritarianism." *Journal of Democracy* 13, 2: 51–65.

Leymarie, Serge, and Jean Tripier. 1992. *Maroc: Le prochain dragon?* Paris: Éditions EDDIF.

Lijnat al-Tansiq al-Watani wal-Dawli. 1993. *Nubir Amaoui, Rajal wa Qadiah*. Casablanca: Matba'a Dar al-Nashir al-Maghrabi.

Lijphart, Arend, and Carlos H. Waisman, eds. 1996. *Institutional Design in New Democracies: Eastern Europe and Latin America*. Boulder: Westview.

Ling, Dwight L. 1967. *Tunisia from Protectorate to Republic*. Bloomington: Indiana University Press.

Linz, Juan J. 1975. "Totalitarian and Authoritarian Regimes." In Fred Green-stein and Nelson Polsby, eds., *Handbook of Political Science: Vol. 3, Macropolitical Theory*. Reading, MA: Addison-Wesley, 175–373.

———. 1978a. "Non-Competitive Elections in Europe." In Guy Hermet,

Rishard Rose, and Alain Rouquie, eds., *Elections Without Choice*. New York: John Wiley and Sons, 36–65.

———. 1978b. *The Breakdown of Democratic Regimes: Crisis, Breakdown, and Reequilibration*. Baltimore: Johns Hopkins University Press.

Linz, Juan J., and Alfred Stepan. 1996. *Problems of Democratic Transition and Consolidation*. Baltimore: Johns Hopkins University Press.

Lipset, Seymour M. 1960. *Political Man: The Social Bases of Politics*. Garden City, NY: Doubleday.

Lipset, Seymour M., and Stein Rokkan, eds. 1967. *Party Systems and Voter Alignments: Cross-National Perspectives*. New York: The Free Press.

Livermore, H. V. 1976. *A New History of Portugal*. 2nd ed. Cambridge, UK: Cambridge University Press.

Louër, Laurence. 2004. "Bahrain's Fragile Political Reforms." *Arab Reform Bulletin* 2, 1.

Lucas, Russell. 2005. *Institutions and the Politics of Survival in Jordan: Domestic Responses to External Challenges: 1988–2001*. Albany: State University of New York Press.

Luciani, Giacomo. 1990. "Allocation vs. Production States: A Theoretical Framework." In Giacomo Luciani, ed., *The Arab State*. Berkeley: University of California Press, 65–84.

———. 1995. "The Oil Rent, the Fiscal Crisis of the State, and Democratization." In Ghassan Salamé, ed., *Democracy Without Democrats? The Renewal of Politics in the Middle East*. London: I. B. Tauris, 130–155.

Luckham, Robin. 1994. "The Military, Militarization, and Democratization in Africa." *African Studies Review* 37 (September): 13–75.

———. 1995. "Dilemmas of Military Disengagement and Democratization in Africa." *IDS Bulletin* 26: 49–61.

Lustick, Ian. 2000. "The Quality of Theory and the Comparative Disadvantage of Area Studies." *Middle East Studies Association Bulletin* 34, 2: 192.

Lust-Okar, Ellen. 2001. "The Decline of Jordanian Political Parties: Myth or Reality?" *International Journal of Middle East Studies* 33, 4.

———. 2004. "Divided They Rule: The Management and Manipulation of Political Opposition." *Comparative Politics* 36, 2 (January): 159–179.

———. 2005. *Structuring Conflict in the Arab World: Incumbents, Opponents, and Institutions*. Cambridge, UK: Cambridge University Press.

Lust-Okar, Ellen, and Amaney Ahmad Jamal. 2002. "Rulers and Rules: Reassessing the Influence of Regime Type on Electoral Law Formation." *Comparative Political Studies* 35, 3: 337–365.

Mack Smith, Denis. 1997. *Modern Italy: A Political History*. Ann Arbor: University of Michigan Press.

Madi, Munib, and Sulayman Musa. 1988 [1959]. *Tarikh Al-Urdun Fi Al-Qarn Al-'Ishrin*. 2nd ed. Amman: Maktabat al-muhtasib.

Maghraoui, Abdeslam. 2001a. "Monarchy and Political Reform in Morocco." *Journal of Democracy* 12, 1: 73–86.

———. 2001b. "Political Authority in Crisis: Mohammed VI's Morocco." *Middle East Report* 218 (Spring): 12–17.

Mahdavy, H. 1970. "The Pattern and Problems of Economic Development in Rentier States: The Case of Iran." In M. A. Cook, ed., *Studies in the Economic History of the Middle East*. London: Oxford University Press, 428–467.

Mahdi, Ali Akbar. 1999. "The Student Movement in the Islamic Republic of

Iran." *Journal of Iranian Research and Analysis* 15 (November): 1–29.

Mahoney, James, and Richard Snyder. 1999. "Rethinking Agency and Structure in the Study of Regime Change." *Studies in Comparative International Development* 34, 2 (Summer): 3–32.

Mainwaring, Scott. 1993. "Presidentialism, Multipartyism, and Democracy: The Difficult Combination." *Comparative Political Studies* 26, 2 (July): 198–228.

Mainwaring, Scott, and Timothy R. Scully, eds. 1995. *Building Democratic Institutions: Party Systems in Latin America.* Stanford: Stanford University Press.

Majid, Majdi. 1987. *Les Luttes de classes au Maroc depuis l'indépendance.* Rotterdam: Editions Hiwar.

Makiya, Kanan. 1993. *Cruelty and Silence: War, Tyranny, Uprising, and the Arab World.* New York: Norton.

Makram-Ebeid, Mona. 1996. "Egypt's 1995 Elections: One Step Forward, Two Steps Back?" *Middle East Policy* 4, 3 (March): 120–121.

Malki, Abdullah. 1992. "Returnees—How Much of a Burden?" *Jordan Times,* July 22: 1.

Mansour, Abdellatif. 1995. "Le coup de force de Muhammad el Yazghi." *Maroc hebdo,* July 21–27: 24–25.

Manzetti, Luigi. 1993. *Institutions, Parties, and Coalitions in Argentine Politics.* Pittsburgh: University of Pittsburgh Press.

Marks, Jon. 1993. *Maghreb: MEED Quarterly Report* (November): 24–25.

Martinez, Sara Kate. 2000. "Evolution of an Electoral System: The Case of Mexico." Paper presented at the annual conference of the American Political Science Association, Washington, DC, August 31–September 3.

Massad, Joseph. 2001. *Colonial Effects: The Making of National Identity in Jordan.* New York: Columbia University Press.

McCord, Norman. 1991. *British History, 1815–1906.* Oxford: Oxford University Press.

Mednicoff, David. 1994. "Morocco." In Frank Tachau, ed., *Political Parties in the Middle East and North Africa.* Westport, CT: Greenwood, 383–397.

Michaud, Gerard. 1982. "The Importance of Bodyguards." *MERIP Reports* 110 (November–December): 29–33.

Middlebrook, Kevin. 1985. "Political Liberalization in an Authoritarian Regime: The Case of Mexico." Center for U.S.-Mexican Studies *Research Report Series* 41. University of California at San Diego.

Middle East Report. 2003. "Our Letter to Khatami Was a Farewell: An Interview with Saeed Razavi-Faqih." *Middle East Report.* Online at http://www.merip.org/mero/ mero071503.html.

Milton-Edwards, Beverly. 1991. "A Temporary Alliance with the Crown: The Islamic Response in Jordan." In James Piscatori, ed., *Islamic Fundamentalism and the Gulf Crisis.* Chicago: American Academy of Arts and Sciences, 88–108.

Mitchell, Richard P. 1993. *The Society of the Muslim Brothers.* New York: Oxford University Press.

Mitchell, Timothy. 1999. "Dreamland: The Neoliberalism of Your Desires." *Middle East Report* (Spring).

Moffett, George III. 1988. "King Hussein Cornered." *Christian Science Monitor,* May 13: 9.

———. 1989. "Muslim Radicals Set Back Equality." *Christian Science Monitor,* November 2: 4.

————. 1993. "Jordan: Impetus for Change Grows." *Christian Science Monitor,* June 15: 3.

Moore, Barrington, Jr. 1966. *Social Origins of Dictatorship and Democracy: Lord and Peasant in the Making of the Modern World.* Boston: Beacon.

Moore, Clement H. 1965. *Tunisia Since Independence.* Berkeley: University of California Press.

————. 1966. "Political Parties in Independent North Africa." In Leon Carl Brown, ed., *State and Society in Independent North Africa.* Washington, DC: Middle East Institute.

————. 1970. "Tunisia: The Prospects for Institutionalization." In Samuel Huntington and Clement H. Moore, eds., *Authoritarian Politics in Modern Society: The Dynamics of One-Party Systems.* New York: Basic Books, 311–336.

————. 1993. "Political Parties." In I. William Zartman and William Mark Habeeb, eds., *Polity and Society in Contemporary North Africa.* Boulder: Westview, 42–67.

Morrisson, Christian. 1991. *Equity and Adjustment in Morocco.* Washington, DC: Organization for Economic Cooperation and Development.

Mortaji, Hojjat. 1378. *Jenah-haye Siyasi dar Iran-e Emrooz.* Tehran: Naqsh va Negar.

Moslem, Mehdi. 2002. *Factional Politics in Post-Khomeini Iran.* Syracuse: Syracuse University Press.

Mossadeq, Rkia El-. 1987. "Political Parties and Power-Sharing." In I. William Zartman, ed., *The Political Economy of Morocco.* New York: Praeger, 59–83.

Mottahedeh, Roy, P. 1985. *The Mantle of the Prophet: Religion and Politics in Iran.* New York: Pantheon.

Mudayris, Falah Abdallah al-. 1999. *Jama'at Al-Ikhwan Al-Muslimin Fi Al-Kuwayt.* Kuwait: Dar qurtas.

————. 2002. *Al-Haraka Al-Dusturiya Fi Al-Kuwayt.* Kuwait: Dar qurtas.

Mufti, Malik. 1999. "Elite Bargains and the Onset of Political Liberalization in Jordan." *Comparative Political Studies* 32 (February): 100–129.

Mughni, Haya al-. 2001. *Women in Kuwait: The Politics of Gender.* 2nd ed. London: Saqi.

Munson, Henry Jr. 1993. *Religion and Power in Morocco.* New Haven: Yale University Press.

————. 1998. "International Election Monitoring: A Critique Based on One Monitor's Experience in Morocco." *Middle East Report* 209 (Winter): 37–39.

————. 1999. "The Elections of 1993 and Democratization in Morocco." In Rahma Bourqia and Susan Miller, eds., *In the Shadow of the Sultan: Culture, Power, and Politics in Morocco.* Cambridge, MA: Harvard University Press, 259–281.

Murphy, Emma. 1999. *Economic and Political Change in Tunisia.* New York: St. Martin's.

Musa, Husayn. 1987. *Al-Bahrayn: Al-Nidal Al-Watani Wa Al-Dimuqrati 1920–1981.* N.p.: Al-haqiqa.

Mustafa, Hala. 1997. "Mu'ashrat wa nata'ij intikhabat 1995" [Indicators and Results of the 1995 Elections]. In Hala Mustafa, ed., *Al-Intikhabat al-*

Barlamaniya fi Misr 1995 [The 1995 Parliamentary Elections in Egypt]. Cairo: Al-Ahram Center for Political and Strategic Studies, 37–51.

Mutawi, S. A. 1987. *Jordan in the 1967 War.* New York: Cambridge University Press.

Naaman, Issam. 1998. "Dur Nizam al-intikhabi al-ikthari fi tadwim al-hakam al-ta'ifi" [The Role of the Plurality Election System in the Perpetuation of Communal Rule]. Paper presented at the conference on "Controlled Contestation and Opposition Strategies: Multi-Party Elections in the Arab World," Brown University, Providence, RI, October 2–3.

Najjar, Fauzi. 1989. "Elections and Democracy in Egypt." *American-Arab Affairs* (Summer).

Najjar, Ghanim al-. 2000. *Madkhal Lil-Tatawwur Al-Siyasi Fi Al-Kuwayt.* 3rd ed. Kuwait: Dar qurtas.

Nakash, Yitzhak. 1994. *The Shi'is of Iraq.* Princeton: Princeton University Press.

Nakhleh, Emile A. 1980. "Political Participation and the Constitutional Experiments in the Gulf: Bahrain and Qatar." In Tim Niblock, ed., *Social and Economic Development in the Arab Gulf.* London: Croom Helm, 161–176.

National Democratic Institute and the Carter Center. 1997. *The January 20, 1996 Palestinian Elections.* Washington, DC: National Democratic Institute.

Nelson, Harold D., series ed. 1985. *Morocco: A Country Study.* Washington, DC: American University Foreign Area Studies.

Nelson, Joan. 1995. "Linkages Between Politics and Economics." In Larry Diamond and Marc Plattner, eds., *Economic Reform and Democracy.* Baltimore: Johns Hopkins University Press, 45–58.

Newton, Gerald. 1978. *The Netherlands: A Historical and Cultural Survey, 1795–1977.* Boulder: Westview.

Nixon Center. 2002. "The Persian Gulf: Opportunities and Problems." Program Brief 8, no. 3 (March 14). Washington, DC: Nixon Center. Online at http://www.nixoncenter.org/Program%20Briefs/vol8no3gulf.htm.

Norton, Augustus R., ed. 1995, 1996. *Civil Society in the Middle East.* Vols. I and II. Leiden: E. J. Brill.

O'Donnell, Guillermo, and Phillippe Schmitter. 1986. *Transitions from Authoritarian Rule: Tentative Conclusions About Uncertain Democracies.* Baltimore: Johns Hopkins University Press.

O'Donnell, Guillermo, Phillippe Schmitter, and Laurence Whitehead, eds. 1986. *Transitions from Authoritarian Rule: Comparative Perspectives.* Baltimore: Johns Hopkins University Press.

Omar, Rageh. 1997. "A Changed Landscape." *Middle East International,* December 5: 12–13.

Ordeshook, Peter C., and Olga V. Shvetsova. 1994. "Ethnic Heterogeneity, District Magnitude, and the Number of Parties." *American Journal of Political Science* 38, 1 (February): 100–123.

Ottaway, Marina. 2003. *Democracy Challenged: The Rise of Semi-Authoritarianism.* Washington, DC: Carnegie Endowment for International Peace.

Ottaway, Marina, Thomas Carothers, Amy Hawthorne, and Daniel Brumberg. 2002. "Democratic Mirage in the Middle East." *Carnegie Endowment for International Peace Policy Brief* (October).

Page, John. 1998. "From Boom to Bust and Back? The Crisis of Growth in the Middle East and North Africa." In Nemat Shafik, ed., *Prospects for Middle*

Eastern and North African Economies: From Boom to Bust and Back? New York: St. Martin's.

Paul, Jim. 1984. "States of Emergency: The Riots in Tunisia and Morocco." *MERIP Reports* 127 (October): 3–6.

Payaslıoğlu, Arif T. 1964. "Political Leadership and Political Parties: Turkey." In Robert E. Ward and Dankwart A. Rustow, eds., *Political Modernization in Japan and Turkey.* Princeton: Princeton University Press.

Payne, Rhys. 1993. "Economic Crisis and Policy Reform." In I. William Zartman and William Mark Habeeb, eds., *Polity and Society in Contemporary North Africa.* Boulder: Westview, 139–167.

Penner, Michele. 1999. "Parties, Parliament, and Political Dissent in Tunisia." *Journal of North African Studies* 4, 4 (Winter): 89–104.

Perthes, Volker. 1994. "States of Economic and Political Liberalization." In Eberhard Kienle, ed., *Contemporary Syria: Liberalization Between Cold War and Cold Peace.* London: British Academic Press, 44–71.

———. 1995. *The Political Economy of Syria under Asad.* London: I. B. Tauris.

Peterson, J. E. 1988. *The Arab Gulf States: Steps Toward Political Participation.* New York: Praeger and the Center for Strategic and International Studies.

Pfeifer, Karen. 1999. "How Tunisia, Morocco, Jordan, and Even Egypt Became IMF 'Success Stories' in the 1990s." *Middle East Report* 210 (Spring): 23–27.

Piro, Timothy. 1992. "Parliament, Politics, and Pluralism in Jordan." *Middle East Insight* (July–October): 39–44.

Piscatori, James, ed. 1991. *Islamic Fundamentalism and the Gulf Crisis.* Chicago: American Academy of Arts and Sciences.

Pitner, Julia. 2000. "NGO's Dilemmas." *Middle East Report* 214 (Spring): 34–37.

Post, Erika. 1987. "Egypt's Elections." *Middle East Report* 147 (July–August): 17–22.

Posusney, Marsha Pripstein. 1998. "Behind the Ballot Box: Electoral Engineering in the Arab World." *Middle East Report* 209 (Winter): 12–15.

———. 1999. "Egyptian Privatization: New Challenges for the Left." *Middle East Report* 210 (Spring): 38–40.

———. 2003. "Globalization and Labor Protection in Oil-Poor Arab Countries: Racing to the Bottom?" *Global Social Policy* 3 (December): 267–297.

Prather, George Martin. 1978. *Movement, Structure, and Linkage: The Rise of the Turkish Democrat Party.* PhD. thesis, University of California at Los Angeles.

Pratt, Nicola. 2000. "Egypt Harasses Human Rights Activists." *Middle East Research and Information Project Press Information Note* 25, August 17.

Przeworski, Adam. 1988. "Democracy as a Contingent Outcome of Conflicts." In Jon Elster and Rune Slagstad, eds., *Constitutionalism and Democracy.* Cambridge, UK: Cambridge University Press, 59–80.

———. 1991. *Democracy and the Market: Political and Economic Reforms in Eastern Europe and Latin America.* New York: Cambridge University Press.

Przeworski, Adam, and John Sprague. 1986. *Paper Stones: A History of Electoral Socialism.* Chicago: University of Chicago Press.

Przeworski, Adam, Michael E. Alvarez, Jose Antonio Cheibub, and Fernando Limongo. 2000. *Democracy and Development: Political Institutions and*

Well-Being in the World, 1950–1990. Cambridge, UK: Cambridge University Press.

Pye, Lucian. 1985. *Asian Power and Politics*. New York: Cambridge University Press.

Qaddafi, Muammar. 1980. *The Green Book*. Tripoli: The Green Book Center.

Quinlivan, James. 1999. "Coup-Proofing: Its Practice and Consequences in the Middle East." *International Security* 24 (Fall): 131–165.

Radcliffe, Robert. 1990. "Fulbright Student Letter, Fez, Morocco; December 20, 1990." Unpublished manuscript.

Razjou, Koushan. 1382 (2003). "Gozar be Mardomsalari: Misaq, Eslah ya Enqelab." *Aftab* 31 (Azar): 16–27.

Reeve, Andrew, and Alan Ware. 1991. *Electoral Systems: A Comparative and Theoretical Approach*. London: Routledge.

Reidel, Tim H. 1994. "The 1993 Parliamentary Elections in Jordan." *Orient* 35 (1994).

Remmer, Karen. 1989. *Military Rule in Latin America*. Boston: Unwin Human.

Republic of Yemen. 1992. *The Republic of Yemen Election Law*. Information Committee of the Elections Supreme Committee. Translated September 21.

Reynolds, Andrew. 1999. "Patterns of Democratization and Institutional Design in Southern and West Africa." Paper presented at the annual meeting of the American Political Science Association, Atlanta, September 3.

Reynolds, Andrew, and Jorgan Elkit. 1997. "Jordan: Electoral System Design in the Arab World." In Andrew Reynolds and Ben Reilly, eds., *The International IDEA Handbook of Electoral System Design*. Stockholm: International Institute for Democracy and Electoral Assistance, 53–54.

Reynolds, Andrew, and Ben Reilly, eds. 1997. *The International IDEA Handbook of Electoral System Design*. Stockholm: International Institute for Democracy and Electoral Assistance.

Richards, Alan. 2002. "On Transition from Authoritarian Rule and the Democratic Potential of Arab Regimes." *Economic Research Forum Newsletter* (Summer): Q12–13.

Rifaat, Rahma. n.d. "Law 153/1999 of Association and Its Executive Regulations." Cairo: Center for Trade Union and Worker Services.

Robinson, Glenn. 1997. "Can Islamists Be Democrats? The Case of Jordan." *Middle East Journal* 51, 3 (Summer): 373–387.

———. 1998. "Defensive Democratization in Jordan." *International Journal of Middle East Studies* 30, 3 (August): 387–410.

Ross, Michael, L. 2001. "Does Oil Hinder Democracy?" *World Politics* 53, 3: 325–361.

Rubin, Barry. 2002. "The Military in Contemporary Middle Eastern Politics." In Barry Rubin and Thomas Keaney, eds., *Armed Forces in the Middle East*. London: Frank Cass.

Rudebeck, Lars. 1967. *Party and People*. Stockholm: Almqvist & Wiksell.

Rueschemeyer, Dietrich, Evelyne Huber Stephens, and John D. Stephens. 1992. *Capitalist Development and Democracy*. Cambridge, UK: Polity.

Rustow, Dankwart A. 1960. "The Politics of the Near East." In Gabriel A. Almond and James Coleman, eds., *The Politics of Developing Areas*. Princeton: Princeton University Press.

———. 1970. "Transitions to Democracy: Toward a Dynamic Model." *Comparative Politics* 2 (April): 337–363.

Ryan, Curtis. 1998. "Peace, Bread, and Riots: Jordan and the International

Monetary Fund." *Middle East Policy* 6, 2 (October): 54–66.

Sadeg al-Ali, Nadje. 2000. *Secularism, Gender, and the State in the Middle East: The Egyptian Women's Movement.* Cambridge, UK: Cambridge University Press.

Sadowski, Yahya. 1993. "The New Orientalism and the Democracy Debate." *Middle East Report* 183, 40: 14–21.

Said, Edward. 1978. *Orientalism.* New York: Random House.

Salamé, Ghassan. 1994. "Introduction: Where Are the Democrats?" In Ghassan Salamé, ed., *Democracy Without Democrats: The Renewal of Politics in the Muslim World.* New York: I. B. Taurus, 1–22.

Salamé, Ghassan, ed. 1987. *The Foundations of the Arab State.* New York: Croom Helm.

Salem, Paul. 1997. "Skirting Democracy: Lebanon's 1996 Elections and Beyond." *Middle East Report* 203 (Spring): 26–29.

Sani, Giacomo, and Giovanni Sartori. 1983. "Polarization, Fragmentation and Competition in Western Democracies." In Hans Daalder and Peter Mair, eds., *Western European Party Systems: Continuity and Change.* London: Sage, 307–340.

Santucci, Jean-Claude. 1986. "Chroniques politiques Maroc." *Annuaire de l'Afrique du Nord*: 904–932.

Santucci, Jean-Claude, ed. 1992. *Le Maroc Actuel.* Paris: CNRS.

Saqqaf, Muhammad. 1998. "Al-Intikhabat al-Yemeniya: Sirab Dimuqrati" [The Yemenese Elections: A Democratic Phantom]. Paper presented at the conference on "Controlled Contestation and Opposition Strategies: Multi-Party Elections in the Arab World," Brown University, Providence, RI, October 2–3.

Sartori, Giovanni. 1976. *Parties and Party Systems: A Framework for Analysis.* Vol. 1. Cambridge, UK: Cambridge University Press.

Satloff, Robert B. 1986. *Troubles on the East Bank: Challenges to the Domestic Stability of Jordan.* New York: Praeger.

———. 1994. *From Abdullah to Hussein: Jordan in Transition.* New York: Oxford University Press.

Sayyid, Mustapha Kamel al-. 1991. "Slow Thaw in the Arab World." *World Policy Journal* 8 (Fall): 711–738.

———. 1995. "The Concept of Civil Society in the Arab World." In Rex Brynens, Bahgat Korany, and Paul Noble, eds. *Political Liberalization and Democratization in the Arab World: Volume 1, Theoretical Perspectives.* Boulder: Lynne Rienner, 131–148.

Scalapino, Robert A. 1953. *Democracy and the Party Movement in Prewar Japan.* Berkeley: University of California Press.

Schedler, Andreas. 2002. "The Menu of Manipulation." *Journal of Democracy* 13, 2 (April): 36–50.

Schirazi, Asghar. 1998. *The Constitution of Iran: Politics and the State in the Islamic Republic.* John O'Kane, trans. London: I. B. Tauris.

Schmitter, Philippe. 1997. "Civil Society East and West." In Larry Diamond, Marc Plattner, Yun-han Chu, and Hung-Mao Tien, eds., *Consolidating the Third Wave Democracies: Themes and Perspectives.* Baltimore: Johns Hopkins University Press.

Schwedler, Jillian. 2002. "Yemen's Aborted Opening." *Journal of Democracy* 13, 4 (October): 48–55.

Seale, Patrick. 1988. *Asad: The Struggle for the Middle East.* Berkeley: University of California Press.

Seddon, David. 1984. "Winter of Discontent: Economic Crisis in Tunisia and Morocco." *MERIP Reports* 127 (October): 7–16.

———. 1986. "Popular Protest and Political Opposition in Tunisia, Morocco, and Sudan 1984–1985." In Kenneth Brown, ed., *État, ville et mouvements sociaux au Maghreb et au Moyen-Orient.* Paris: CNRS, 179–197.

Sehimi, Mustapha. 1992. "Les élites ministérielles au Maroc: Constantes et variables." In Jean-Claude Santucci, ed., *Le Maroc Actuel.* Paris: CNRS.

Seton-Watson, Christopher. 1967. *Italy from Liberalism to Fascism, 1870–1925.* London: Methuen.

Sezgin, Ömür, and Gencay Şaylan. 1983. "Terakkiperver Cumhuriyet Fırkası." *Cumhuriyet Dönemi Turk Ansiklopedisi* 8.

Sfakianakis, John, and Robert Springborg. 2001. "The President, the Son, and Military Succession in Egypt." *Arab Studies Journal* (Fall): 73–88.

Shafik, Nemat, ed. 1998. *Prospects for Middle Eastern and North African Economies: From Boom to Bust?* New York: St. Martin's.

Shahin, Mariam. 1992. "De Facto Political Group Dissolves Itself." *Jordan Times,* June 17: 1,

———. 2000. "For Liberty, Prosperity, Fraternity?" *Middle East* 305 (October): 19–21.

Shambayati, Hootan. 1994. "The Rentier State, Interest Groups, and the Paradox of Autonomy: State and Business in Turkey and Iran." *Comparative Politics* 26 (April): 307–331.

Sharabi, Hisham. 1988. *Neopatriarchy: A Theory of Distorted Change in Arab Society.* New York: Oxford University Press.

Share, Donald, and Scott Mainwaring. 1986. "'Transitions Through Transaction': Democratization in Brazil and Spain." In W. Selcher, ed., *Political Liberalization in Brazil.* Boulder: Westview, 175–215.

Shikaki, Khalil. 1996. "The Palestinian Elections: An Assessment." *Journal of Palestine Studies* 25, 3 (Spring).

Shin, Doh Chull. 1994. "On the Third Wave of Democratization: A Synthesis and Evaluation of Recent Theory and Research." *World Politics* 47, 1 (October): 135–170.

Skidmore, Thomas. 1988. *The Politics of Military Rule in Brazil 1964–85.* New York: Oxford University Press.

Skocpol, Theda. 1979. *States and Social Revolutions.* Cambridge, UK: Cambridge University Press.

———. 1982. "Rentier State and Shi'a Islam in the Iranian Revolution." *Theory and Society* 11 (May): 265–283.

———. 1992. *Protecting Soldiers and Mothers: The Political Origins of Social Policy in the United States.* Cambridge, MA: Harvard University Press.

Smith, Rogers. 2002. "Putting the Substance Back Into Political Science." *Chronicle of Higher Education* (April 5).

Snyder, Richard. 1992. "Explaining Transitions from Neopatrimonial Dictatorships." *Comparative Politics* 24 (October): 379–399.

———. 1998. "Paths Out of Sultanistic Regimes: Combining Structural and Voluntarist Perspectives." In H. E. Chehabi and Juan J. Linz, eds., *Sultanistic Regimes.* Boulder: Lynne Rienner, 49–81.

Snyder, Richard, and James Mahoney. 1999. "The Missing Variable: Institutions and the Study of Regime Change." *Comparative Politics* 32, 1 (October): 103–122.

Sobelman, Daniel. 2001. "Gamal Mubarak, President of Egypt?" *Middle East Quarterly* (Spring): 31–40.

Soudan, Francois. 1995. "L'attente." *Jeune Afrique* 22 au 28 Juin: 16–17.

Steinmo, Sven, Kathleen Thelen, and Frank Longstreth, eds., 1992. *Structuring Politics: Historical Institutionalism in Comparative Analysis.* Cambridge, UK: Cambridge University Press.

Stepan, Alfred. 1988. *Rethinking Military Politics: Brazil and the Southern Cone.* Princeton: Princeton University Press.

———. 2001. "Religion, Democracy, and the 'Twin Tolerations.'" In Alfred Stepan, *Arguing Comparative Politics.* New York: Oxford University Press.

Stepan, Alfred, and Graeme B. Robertson. 2003. "An 'Arab' More Than a 'Muslim' Electoral Gap." *Journal of Democracy* 14 (3): 30–44.

Stokes, Susan C. 1996. "Economic Reform and Public Opinion in Peru, 1990–1995." *Comparative Political Studies* 29, 5 (October): 544–565.

Storing, James A. 1963. *Norwegian Democracy.* Boston: Houghton Mifflin.

Suval, Stanley. 1985. *Electoral Politics in Wilhelmine Germany.* Chapel Hill: University of North Carolina Press.

Sweet, Catherine. 2001. "Democratization Without Democracy: Political Openings and Closures in Modern Morocco." *Middle East Report* 218 (Spring).

Tadros, Mariz. 1999. "NGOs Campaign On." *Al-Ahram Weekly Online,* June 3–9.

Taji-Farouki, Suha. 1996. *A Fundamental Quest: Hizb al-Tahrir and the Search for the Islamic Caliphate.* London: Grey Seal.

Takeyh, Ray, and Gideon Rose. 1998. "Special Policy Forum Report: Qadhafi, Lockerbie, and Prospects for Libya." *Washington Institute Policywatch* 342 (October 1).

Talbi, Mohamed. 2000. "Arabs and Democracy: A Record of Failure." *Journal of Democracy* 11, 3 (July): 58–68.

Terrab, Mustapha. 1995. Interview. Adviser to King Hassan II. Rabat, July 12.

Terry, Janice J. 1982. *The Wafd 1919–1952.* London: Third World Centre for Research and Publishing.

Tessler, Mark A., John P. Entelis, and Gregory W. White. 1995a. "Kingdom of Morocco." In David E. Long and Bernard Reich, eds., *The Government and Politics of the Middle East and North Africa.* Boulder: Westview, 369–386.

———. 1995b. "Republic of Tunisia." In David E. Long and Bernard Reich, eds., *The Government and Politics of the Middle East and North Africa.* Boulder: Westview, 423–445.

Tétreault, Mary Ann. 2000. *Stories of Democracy: Politics and Society in Contemporary Kuwait.* New York: Columbia University Press.

———. 2001. "A State of Two Minds: State Cultures, Women, and Politics in Kuwait." *International Journal of Middle East Studies* 33, 2: 203–220.

Thelen, Kathleen, and Sven Steinmo. 1992. "Historical Institutionalism in Comparative Politics." In Sven Steinmo, Kathleen Thelen, and Frank Longstreth, eds., *Structuring Politics: Historical Institutionalism in Comparative Analysis.* Cambridge, UK: Cambridge University Press.

Thompson, Mark R. 2001. "To Shoot or Not to Shoot: Post-Totalitarianism in China and Eastern Europe." *Comparative Politics* 34 (October): 63–84.

Tilly, Charles. 1978. *From Mobilization to Revolution*. Reading, MA: Addison-Wesley, Chapter 3.

Tunaya, Tarık Z. 1952. *Türkiye'de Siyasi Partiler 1859–1952*. İstanbul: Doğan Kardeş Yayınları.

Tyler, Patrick. 1989a. "Jordan Grapples with Political, Economic Woes." *Washington Post,* March 14: A21.

———. 1989b. "Hussein Arrives in Jordan, Appeals for Calm," *Washington Post,* April 24: A 23.

United Nations Development Program (UNDP). 2001. *Arab Human Development Report*. New York: UNDP.

U.S. Department of State. 1996. Libya Report on Human Rights Practices for 1996. Online at http://www.state.gov/www/global/human_rights/1996_hrp_report/libya.html.

al-Urdun al-Jadid Research Center. 1995. *Post-Election Seminar: A Discussion of Jordan's 1993 Parliamentary Election*. Amman, Jordan: al-Urdun al-Jadid.

Usta, Veysel. 1994. "Trabzon'da Terakkiperver Fırka'nın Kuruluşu." *Tarih ve Toplum* 21 (June): 27–31.

Vandewalle, Dirk. 1998. *Libya Since Independence*. Ithaca: Cornell University Press.

Varzi, Roxanne. 2002. "Visionary Terrains: Youth, Identity and Space in Post–Revolutionary Iran." Paper presented at the 2002 Middle East Studies Association annual conference, Washington, DC.

Vatikiotis, P. J. 1978. *Nasser and His Generation*. New York: St. Martin's.

———. 1987. *Islam and the State*. New York: Croom Helm.

Vengroff, Richard, and Lucy Cheevey. 1997. "Senegal: The Evolution of a Quasi Democracy." In J. Clark and D. Gardinier, eds., *Political Reform in Francophone Africa*. Boulder: Westview, 204–222.

Vengroff, Richard, and Michael Magala. 2000. The Transformation of Senegal's Electorate: Institutional Reform, Political Culture, and Democratic Transition." Paper presented at the annual meeting of the American Political Science Association, Washington, DC, August 30–September 3.

Vengroff, Richard, and Shaheen Mozaffar. 2002. "A 'Whole System' Approach to the Study of Electoral Rules in Emerging Democracies: Senegal in Comparative Perspective." *Electoral Studies* 21, 4 (December): 601–616.

Verney, Douglas V. 1957. *Parliamentary Reform in Sweden, 1866–1921*. Oxford: Clarendon.

Vitalis, Robert. 1995. *When Capitalists Collide: Business Conflict and the End of Empire in Egypt*. Berkeley and Los Angeles: University of California Press.

Waldner, David. 1999. *State-Building and Late Development*. Ithaca: Cornell University Press.

Waltz, Susan. 1991. "Clientelism and Reform in Ben Ali's Tunisia." In I. W. Zartman, ed., *Tunisia: The Political Economy of Reform*. Boulder: Lynne Rienner, 29–44.

———. 1999. "Interpreting Political Reform in Morocco." In Rahma Bourqia and Susan Miller, eds., *In the Shadow of the Sultan*: *Culture, Power, and Politics in Morocco*. Cambridge, MA: Harvard University Press, 282–305.

Waterbury, John. 1970. *Commander of the Faithful*. London: Weidenfeld & Nicolson.

———. 1983. *The Egypt of Nasser and Sadat*. Princeton: Princeton University Press.

————. 1994. "Democracy Without Democrats? The Potential for Political Liberalization in the Middle East." In Ghassan Salamé, ed., *Democracy Without Democrats: The Renewal of Politics in the Muslim World*. New York: I. B. Taurus, 23–47.

————. 1997a. "Fortuitous By-Products." *Comparative Politics* 29 (April): 383–402.

————. 1997b. "From Social Contracts to Extraction Contracts: The Political Economy of Authoritarianism and Democracy." In John P. Entelis, ed., *Islam, Democracy, and the State in North Africa*. Bloomington: Indiana University Press, 141–176.

Wedeen, Lisa. 1999. *Ambiguities of Domination: Politics, Rhetoric, and Symbols in Contemporary Syria*. Chicago: University of Chicago Press.

Wederman, Ben. 1993. "Democracy in Jordan" *Middle East Insight* (November–December).

Weiker, Walter F. 1973. *Political Tutelage and Democracy in Turkey: The Free Party and Its Aftermath*. Leiden: E. J. Brill.

Welch, Claude. 1995. *Protecting Human Rights in Africa: Strategies and Roles of Nongovernmental Organizations*. Philadelphia: University of Pennsylvania Press.

Welch, David. 2002. "American Policy in the Middle East." Speech for the English Public Lecture Series. Cairo: American University in Cairo, January 28.

White, Gregory. 1997. "The Advent of Electoral Democracy in Morocco? The Referendum of 1996." *Middle East Journal* 51, 3 (Summer): 389–404.

Whitehead, Lawrence. 1986. "International Aspects of Democratization." In Guillermo O'Donnell, Philippe Schmitter, and Lawrence Whitehead, eds., *Transitions from Authoritarian Rule: Comparative Perspectives*. Baltimore: Johns Hopkins University Press, 3–47.

Wiarda, Howard J. 1974. "Social Change and Political Development in Latin America: Summary." In Howard Wiarda, ed. *Politics and Social Change in Latin America*. Amherst: University of Massachusetts Press.

Wickham, Carrie Rosefsky. 2004. "The Path to Moderation: Strategy and Learning in the Formation of Egypt's Wasat Party." *Comparative Politics* 36, 2 (January): 205–228.

Widner, Jennifer, ed. 1994. *Economic Change and Political Liberalization in Sub-Saharan Africa*. Baltimore: Johns Hopkins University Press.

Wiktorowicz, Quintan. 1999. "The Limits of Democracy in the Middle East: The Case of Jordan." *The Middle East Journal* 53, 4 (Autumn): 606–620.

————. 2000. "Civil Society as Social Control: State Power in Jordan." *Comparative Politics* 33 (October): 43–61.

Williamson, John, ed. 1994. *The Political Economy of Policy Reform*. Washington, DC: Institute for International Economics.

Wilson, Peter, and Douglas F. Graham. 1994. *Saudi Arabia: The Coming Storm*. New York: M. E. Sharpe.

World Bank. 1995. *Bureaucrats in Business*. New York: Oxford University Press.

————. 2002. *World Development Report*. Washington, DC: World Bank.

Wright, Zakariya. 1999. "Chasing Democracy in Tunisia." Online at http://www.iviews.com.

Yassini, Ayman al-. 1985. *Religion and State in the Kingdom of Saudi Arabia*. Boulder: Westview.

Yata, 'Ali. 1992. "Le PPS, la question nationale et le mouvement national et progressiste." *Economie et socialisme* 11 (January): 87–114.

Yeşil, Ahmet. 1992. *Türkiye Cumhuriyeti'nde İlk Teşkilatlı Muhalefet Hareketi.* PhD thesis, Hacettepe University, Ankara.

Yılmaz, Hakan. 1996. *The International Context of Regime Change: Turkey, 1923–1960.* PhD thesis, Columbia University.

Younger, Sam. 1985. "Morocco and Western Sahara." *Africa Review*: 205–211.

Zartman, I. William. 1988. "Opposition as Support of the State." In Adeed Dawisha and I. William Zartman, eds., *Beyond Coercion: The Durability of the Arab State.* London: Croom Helm, 61–87.

Zartman, I. William, ed. 1973. *Man, State, and Society in the Contemporary Maghrib.* New York: Praeger.

Zartman, I. William, and William Mark Habeeb, eds. 1993. *Polity and Society in Contemporary North Africa.* Boulder: Westview.

Zayd, Sharif. 1995. "Government Concern Is to Safeguard 'Responsible' Press." *Jordan Times,* December 11: 1.

Zisser, Eyal. 2002. "The Syrian Army on the Domestic and External Fronts." In Barry Rubin and Thomas Keaney, eds., *Armed Forces in the Middle East.* London: Frank Cass.

Zouby, Salim al-. 1992. "Discussion to the Report of the Committee or Formulation of Conclusions, by Dr. Ahmad al-Momany, Dr. Mahmoud Kilani." In H. Dobers, W. Goussous, and Y. Sara, eds., *Democracy and the Rule of Law in Jordan.* Amman: Jordanian Printing Press, 92–121.

Zürcher, Erik Jan. 1991. *Political Opposition in the Early Turkish Republic: The Progressive Republican Party, 1924–1925.* Leiden: E. J. Brill.

The Contributors

Michele Penner Angrist is an assistant professor of political science at Union College. Her first book, *Party Building in the Modern Middle East: The Origins of Competitive and Coercive Rule,* is forthcoming from University of Washington Press. Her work on political development and the Middle East has also appeared in *Comparative Politics, Comparative Studies in Society and History,* and *Journal of North African Studies.*

Eva Bellin is an associate professor of political science at Hunter College and the author of *Stalled Democracy: Capital, Labor, and the Paradox of State-Sponsored Development.* She has published articles in *World Politics, Comparative Politics,* and *World Development* and is currently working on a project exploring the relationship between political and economic reform in the region.

Jason Brownlee is an assistant professor of political science at the University of Texas at Austin. He has undertaken original fieldwork in Egypt, Iran, Malaysia, and the Philippines. He has published articles in *Comparative Politics, Studies in Comparative International Development,* and *Journal of Democracy.*

Michael Herb is an assistant professor of political science at Georgia State University and the author of *All in the Family: Absolutism, Revolution, and Democracy in the Middle Eastern Monarchies.* He has articles forthcoming in *Studies in Comparative International Development* and *Middle East Journal.*

Arang Keshavarzian is an assistant professor of political science at Concordia University in Montreal, Canada. He has published articles on state-clergy relations in Iran and on the political economy of the Tehran bazaar in *Politics and Society, Journal of Church and State, ISIM Newsletter,* and *Goft-o-Gu.*

Vickie Langohr is an associate professor of political science at Holy Cross College. She has published articles in *Comparative Studies in Society and History, International Journal of Middle East Studies, Journal of Democracy,* and *Comparative Studies of South Asia, Africa, and the Middle East,* and is currently working on a book on religious nationalist movements in Egypt, India, and Indonesia.

Ellen Lust-Okar is an assistant professor of political science at Yale University. She is the author of *Structuring Contestation in the Middle East: Incumbents, Opponents, and Institutions,* and is currently working on a second book, *Linking Domestic and International Conflict: The Case of Middle East Rivalries,* with Paul Huth. She has published articles on government-opposition relations in Arab countries in *Comparative Politics, Comparative Political Studies, Politics and Society, International Journal of Middle East Studies,* and *Middle Eastern Studies.*

Marsha Pripstein Posusney is a professor of political science at Bryant University and adjunct professor of international relations (research) at the Watson Institute for International Studies, Brown University. She recently coedited *Women and Globalization in the Arab Middle East: Gender, Economy, and Society.* Her first book, *Labor and the State in Egypt: Workers, Unions, and Economic Restructuring,* was cowinner of the 1998 Middle East Studies Association's Albert Hourani Prize for outstanding original scholarly work on the Middle East. She has published articles in *World Politics, Studies in Comparative International Development, Comparative Politics, Middle East Report,* and *Global Social Policy.*

Index

About the Book

Why do authoritarian regimes prevail in the Middle East while success-ful democratic transitions are occurring elsewhere in the developing world? *Authoritarianism in the Middle East* addresses this question, focusing on the role of political institutions and the strategic choices made by both rulers and opposition challengers.

The authors eschew cultural explanations, highlighting instead the importance of robust coercive apparatuses in the region and the context of incumbent-opposition struggles. Their work sheds light on pivotal political dynamics throughout the Middle East, revealing the numerous ways in which the balance of power continues to favor the status quo.

Marsha Pripstein Posusney is professor of political science at Bryant University and adjunct professor of international relations at the Watson Institute for International Studies, Brown University. Her publications include *Labor and the State in Egypt,* winner of the Hourani prize, and *Women and Globalization in the Arab Middle East* (coedited with Eleanor Doumato). **Michele Penner Angrist** is assistant professor of political science at Union College. Her first book, *Party Building in the Modern Middle East: The Origins of Competitive and Coercive Rule,* is forthcoming from University of Washington Press.